944580

Success in
MARKETING

D0581013

Success Studybooks

Success in
MARKETING

Rosemarie Stefanou

John Murray

First published 1993
by John Murray (Publishers) Ltd
50 Albemarle Street, London W1X 4BD

Reprinted 1996

Typeset in 9/11pt and 8/10pt Compugraphic English Times by Colset Private Ltd
Printed and bound in Great Britain by
Biddles Ltd, Guildford and King's Lynn

ISBN 0–7195–4989–2

Contents

Foreword

Success in Marketing is designed to cover the marketing component of A level Business Studies and BTEC National Courses. It should also prove useful for students following higher level courses and those pursuing professional qualifications such as the Certificate of the Chartered Institute of Marketing.

Inevitably, any book bears the stamp of its author's approach to the subject and this one is no exception. My primary aim has been to make the subject come alive for students and to give them a real 'feel' for what marketing is all about. To this end, the key facts, theories and concepts are backed up by lively case studies which have been used as illustrative examples to accompany the text. These, together with the many shorter references to companies, products and people who have achieved success (or notoriety) in the world of marketing, provide topical examples with which every student can readily identify.

There are numerous quotes, not just from marketing 'gurus', but also from people working in various areas of marketing. The book also deals with recent developments and their implications for marketers such as the rise of the grey market, the growth of database marketing and so on.

The text assumes no prior knowledge of marketing. Specific terminology is explained in context and there is a glossary at the end of the book for reference. The book has been designed with the needs of students in mind and essential facts are summarized in point form or in tables wherever possible in order to make the information more accessible and to aid examination revision.

The overall structure of the book mirrors that of the sequence of tasks in the marketing process itself. After a brief introduction on the role of marketing, the first half of the book describes the procedures that need to be covered before a marketing strategy can be devised. There are sections on analysing buyer behaviour, understanding the market environment, conducting marketing research and identifying the most potentially profitable target group by means of market segmentation. The unit on preparing a marketing plan leads into the second half of the book which deals in detail with the four key elements of product, price, promotion and place.

Acknowledgements

I am particularly grateful to Cynthia Gordon of Mercury Communications and Richard Vincent of Nationwide Building Society for their many helpful suggestions and constructive criticism of the manuscript and to Margaret White for her care and patience in typing each successive draft. I should also like to thank my husband for his support and encouragement while I was working on this book.

Thanks are also due to the companies who provided me with much useful information: Abbott Mead Vickers, Amstrad, Bartle Bogle Hegarty, British Telecom, James R Adams and Associates, Levi Strauss, SmithKline Beecham, Sony, United Biscuits and 3M.

The author and publishers would also like to thank the following organizations for their kind permission to reproduce photographs and articles: 3M (fig. 2.4); United Biscuits Plc (fig. 4.1); James R Adams and Associates (fig. 4.2); SmithKline Beecham (fig. 5.3); Sony Corporation (fig. 7.1); Amstrad Plc (fig. 8.1); Bartle Bogle Hegarty (fig. 10.3); Abbott Mead Vickers (fig. 10.4); Pedigree Chum: *Offensive Marketing,* Hugh Davidson, Penguin Books; Agatha Christie books: *The Mystery of the Declining Sales*, Sue Williams, *Survey magazine*, Summer 1989; Coca-Cola: *The New Marketing*, Richard W Brookes, Gower Publishing Group; Saab: *Targeting Customers*, Jane Bird, *Management Today*, November 1991; Tobacco advertising: *No Smoke Without Brand Fire*, Alan Mitchell, *Marketing*, February 1991; Sony Walkman: *Walkman's Global Stride*, Nigel Cope, *Business magazine*, March 1990; PG Tips: *Thirty-five Years of Monkey Business*, Emily Bell, *Observer*, November 1990; Dickie Dirts: *The Shrunken Dreams of Nigel Wright*, Sally Hamilton, *Business magazine*, March 1990; CDs: *Money for Nothing as CDs go on Spinning out the Profits*, Adam Raphael, *Observer*, February 1990; Filofax: *Organized but not Personally*, The Economist, November 1988.

The role of marketing

From the moment we switch on the radio in the morning to the time when we set the alarm clock at night we are in constant contact with products and services that have been made available to us through the activities of marketers. The firms who have been most successful in gaining widespread customer acceptance for their products and services are invariably those who have accorded marketing a central role in their operations.

1.1 The marketing effort

In reality of course, all organizations market themselves, if only through the kinds of products and services they offer and the standards of their customer service. Firms do not, therefore, have any choice about whether or not to carry out marketing. The only real choice is between whether the marketing is done haphazardly or whether it is done systematically, through co-ordinating every aspect of the **marketing effort**.

Marketing is not just a fancy word for selling or advertising. Whilst both of these activities are obviously important elements, they are actually only facets of a much broader process. The total marketing effort also involves assessing customer needs and carrying out market research, together with the development of the product and its pricing, promotion and distribution. For the marketing effort to be successful, all of these factors need to be planned and co-ordinated as a whole.

The key task for any business is to get its marketing right, but this also means the company must be good at everything else from research and development to manufacturing and from quality control to financial control. In other words, marketing should not be regarded as an activity which functions in isolation from other areas. Instead, it should be seen as a way of doing business – a guiding philosophy which permeates the entire company. Underpinning this philosophy should be the recognition that the marketing department does not have exclusive responsibility for marketing any more than the finance department has sole responsibility for cost control and profitability.

1.2 A strong customer focus

The success of any marketing initiative depends ultimately on how well the products and services which are offered by firms satisfy the needs of the customers they serve. This process of matching the resources and capabilities of firms to the needs and requirements of customers constitutes the essence of all marketing. Though usually associated with **fast-moving consumer goods** (FMCG) companies, the marketing process is equally applicable to manufacturing and service industries as well as to non-profit-making organizations such as hospitals, museums, universities, charities, government departments and so on.

It goes without saying that a strong customer focus is the major distinguishing characteristic of all organizations who have adopted an overall marketing philosophy. According to marketing expert Ted Levitt, firms operating from such a perspective view 'the entire business process as consisting of a tightly integrated effort to discover, create, arouse and satisfy customer needs'.

Management writer Peter Drucker goes further in maintaining that 'There is only one valid definition of business purpose: to create a customer' – the implication being that businesses survive only as long as they have customers. It is not surprising, therefore, that Drucker views marketing as the 'central dimension' of business. His message makes it clear that the first priority for managers is to concentrate on satisfying the needs of their customers.

However, it is equally clear that firms cannot expect to survive and prosper in the long term unless they can make a profit from satisfying the needs of their customers. This fundamental qualification is recognized in the definition devised by the Chartered Institute of Marketing (CIM) which states that 'Marketing is the management process responsible for identifying, anticipating and satisfying customer requirements profitably.' The CIM definition also acknowledges the importance of a flexible approach, i.e. not just identifying existing needs but anticipating future ones – a skill which has become ever more essential for survival in the rapidly changing business climate of today. Ultimately, of course, the firms who succeed in satisfying customer requirements profitably are in the process also likely to fulfil their own goals.

IBM is often hailed as the classic example of a company whose commercial success can be directly attributed to a strong customer orientation. As Peter Drucker has pointed out, 'IBM does not owe its meteoric rise to technological innovation or product leadership. It was a Johnny-come-lately when it entered the computer field, without technical expertise or scientific knowledge. But while the technological leaders in the early computer days were product-focused and technology-focused, the people who ran IBM asked: "Who are the customers? What is value for them? How do they buy? And what do they need?" As a result, IBM took over the market.'

Most observers concede that this market leadership stems from a genuine commitment to customer service – a tradition which can be traced back to the legendary founder of IBM, Thomas J. Watson Senior. The incident described by Peters and Waterman in their book *In Search of Excellence* revealed what happened on one occasion when a meeting of sales managers was called to assess some customer problems.

'On the front table there were eight or ten piles of papers, identifying the source of problems: "manufacturing problems", "engineering problems" and the like. After much discussion, Mr Watson, a big man, walked slowly to the front of the room and, with a flash of his hand, swept the table clean and sent papers flying all over the room. He said, "There aren't any categories of problems here. There's just one problem. Some of us aren't paying enough attention to our customers." He then turned crisply on his heel and walked out, leaving twenty people wondering whether or not they still had jobs.'

Watson's insistence on customer satisfaction as the key to commercial success is just as applicable today, if not more so, with firms facing greater competitive pressures than ever before. In fact, it is hard to believe that there was ever a time when firms did not have to worry about satisfying the needs of their customers.

1.3 A marketing orientation

Yet this was precisely the situation that existed during the early days of industrialization. At that time, manufacturing output could not keep pace with demand and industries therefore operated in a **seller's market**. This resulted in a **production orientation**, where firms concentrated on producing what they had the resources to make, believing that by improving production efficiency they could lower prices and thus increase sales.

In some cases, this concern with efficient mass production was carried to extremes, like when Ford USA calculated in the 1950s that it had accumulated in its warehouses a supply of spare parts for older models which was enough to last for 1000 years!

From the consumer's point of view, a production orientation meant very little choice and producers could therefore expect to sell whatever they made. The general disregard for consumer preferences was typified by the famous comment made by Henry Ford, 'They can have any colour they like: as long as it's black' – an off-hand attitude which reflected the lack of competition at that time. Ford had a 50 per cent share of the American car market in the 1920s.

Today, new and innovative products can expect to enjoy a seller's market for a limited period after they are first launched – at least until competitors are able to enter the market and increase supply. However, the pace of technological change today is such that even highly innovative products are quickly superseded by more advanced models.

Clearly, then, a production orientation was no longer appropriate. Once productivity improved to the point where supply outstripped demand, industries began to operate in a **buyer's market**. Since the Second World War, firms have adopted a **marketing orientation**, in order to survive fiercely competitive trading conditions. Consumers can now choose what they want to buy from the immense variety of products and services on offer. Producers cannot, therefore, count on selling whatever they make and have to concentrate instead on making what the market wants.

Writing in 1776, Adam Smith argued in *The Wealth of Nations* that, 'If a man maketh a better mousetrap, then even though he liveth in a wood, the world will beat a path to his door.' Obviously, Adam Smith could not have envisaged then the intense competition that was eventually to turn the rules of the game upside-down. Certainly today, firms can no longer presume, as in the early days of industrialization, that people will buy whatever they happen to make – even if they do have a vastly superior product.

As Robert Heller points out in his book, *The Supermarketers*, 'It's quite misguided to pursue the technology-push policy – a delusion with much industrial blood on its hands. The myth goes that if you make a better mousetrap the world will beat a path to your door. It is venerable to the point of decrepitude and has been disproved again and again, never more comprehensively than by the total defeat of competitors who had genuinely stolen technological marches on IBM in mainframe computers. . . Despite all such evidence, many allegedly marketing orientated companies still operate on the mousetrap principle: improve the product, they think, and technology push will create the sales.'

In practice, commercial success hinges on much more than having a good product. It means finding out what consumers need or want and then deciding whether the product can actually be sold at a profit. This involves:

- conducting market research;
- identifying the groups of consumers who are to be targeted;
- assessing consumer reaction to the product specification and packaging;
- working out a suitable price in line with production costs and what the market will bear;
- designing advertising and promotional tactics appropriate to the target group;
- organizing the retailers, wholesalers and methods of physical transport that are to be used to distribute the product.

In short, commercial success depends essentially on good marketing. It follows from this that firms who do not accord marketing a central role in their operations have effectively made a decision not to be in business in ten or fifteen years. But what of those who have made marketing a priority? The research carried out by Peters and Waterman in America (and confirmed by other writers) revealed that the key factor distinguishing 'excellent' companies from those with a more ordinary performance was the way they treated their customers. As Peters and Waterman emphasize, 'the excellent companies *really are* close to their customers. Other companies talk about it: the excellent companies do it.'

Buyer behaviour

2.1 The importance of understanding customer needs

Marketing starts with finding out what motivates customers to buy a particular product or service. As Peter Drucker has pointed out, 'The aim of marketing is to make selling superfluous.' In other words, businesses should know and understand the customer so well that the product or service sells itself. This applies whether their products are aimed at **consumer markets** or at **organizational markets**, which include manufacturing and service industries, as well as wholesalers and retailers, government organizations and non-profit-making organizations. Gaining an understanding of the buying decision-making process, whether it is for consumer buyers or organizational buyers, forms the essential groundwork of an effective marketing plan.

Are there any differences between the two types of buyers? The traditional wisdom has always been that organizational buyers make their decisions on entirely logical and rational grounds whereas consumer buyers are supposedly more easily influenced by irrational, emotional factors.

Clearly, differences do exist. Organizational buying decisions are generally based on a more systematic and objective analysis of products and suppliers. Decisions also tend to be made by groups of people rather than by individuals. However, recent research has revealed that organizational buyers, who are after all human, can also make decisions on emotional grounds.

Marketers need to understand how buyers make their purchasing decisions for different kinds of products and services. The time and effort devoted to the process of gathering and evaluating information will obviously vary greatly according to the cost of the item and the frequency with which it is purchased. Buying decisions concerning inexpensive, regularly purchased items such as bars of chocolate or newspapers are generally habitual, involve very little conscious thought and are therefore called **low-involvement decisions**. In contrast, the purchase of expensive, infrequently purchased items such as cars, major electrical appliances or furniture requires a lengthy and detailed analysis of products and suppliers, which is why these are known as **high-involvement decisions**.

These are, of course, very broad generalizations. A millionaire might well buy a new car as casually as most people would buy a magazine! Other factors may cut across this neat division. Some people buy the same make of car every time they buy a new car, in which case they will not go through the kind of complex decision-making process usually associated with such major purchases.

It is important, at this point, to distinguish between customers and consumers, as the customers who actually make purchases may not necessarily be the **end consumers**. For example, a housewife who buys food in a supermarket is the customer even though it is her family who are the ultimate end consumers. Products must therefore appeal to the customers who purchase them. This point is made by James Myers in his book *Marketing*, when he describes how Budweiser began, at one point, to lose market share to other premium-priced beers. 'Research studies showed that Budweiser had a much more masculine image than any of the other popular beers at that time. This was very appropriate as long as most beer was sold through liquor stores, where men made most of the purchases. But when beer began selling through supermarkets (in the late 1950s), it was bought mainly by women. They rejected Budweiser in favour of beers with designs and advertising that were more appealing to them. These findings forced Budweiser to make two major changes:

'1. a substantial re-design of the can label;
'2. a major change in advertising strategy, to include women in most advertisements (women had not appeared in any Budweiser advertisements for a period of about ten years prior to that time).

'After these changes, Budweiser sales immediately increased to their former level.'

Apart from appealing to the needs of the customers themselves, marketers strive also to address the needs of end consumers as they will often exert a powerful influence on the purchasing decision. It is no accident that a flood of advertisements for toys appears on television just before Christmas each year!

The success of the Mighty White loaf demonstrates why it is important for marketers to take into account the needs of end consumers. Mighty White catered for the fact that whilst parents wanted their children to eat healthy brown bread, the children themselves preferred the taste and appearance of stodgy white bread.

Marketers need also to be aware that many products and services ranging from cars and annual holidays through to general grocery items are consumed by entire households, rather than by individuals, the implication being that in many cases advertising needs to be directed at families as a whole.

Once the needs of customers and consumers have been identified, marketers can match the benefits of their products and services to those needs. Advertising can then be used to promote a particular benefit. For example, a computer manufacturer may stress that its models have the advantage of being easy to operate compared to those of competitors.

The penalty for introducing products which have been developed without reference to consumer needs can be high. The Sinclair C5 is a classic example of a product which, although it was extremely innovative, failed within a very short time of being launched. This was largely because the market need for an electronic vehicle with a limited carrying capacity and performance was never properly established.

A full-scale market research campaign was out of the question because of the emphasis on secrecy. Instead, a small sample of 63 families was shown the vehicle and allowed to drive it around a large room. The C5 was launched on the basis of this limited research and of course the personal conviction of Sir Clive Sinclair. In October 1985 the *Financial Times* reported that the Receiver put the debts of Sinclair's C5 concern at £7.75 million. It is, however, interesting to speculate whether the C5 might have survived if it had been designed and marketed to meet a specific consumer need. Would it have been a success if it had been promoted as a golf trolley or invalid's wheelchair?

In contrast to the C5 fiasco, the dramatic transformation in the fortunes of Chum dog food after it was changed to Pedigree Chum illustrates what can be achieved if companies are successful in identifying and catering for a particular consumer need.

Case study *Pedigree Chum* **Formulated to meet the needs of dog owners** Chum dog food was introduced in the early 1960s by Petfoods Ltd to counter Spiller's Kennomeat, but was an undistinguished product. It achieved only moderate success and by 1963, when a new brand manager was appointed, the Chum share was declining.

The new employee, who had no prior experience of the pet-food market, picked up in conversation with one of the company vets that pedigree dogs had different nutritional requirements from other dogs. On checking available consumer research, he discovered that almost 50 per cent of owners claimed their dogs were pedigree and that this percentage was growing. Consequently, it was decided to reposition Chum as 'the food specially formulated for pedigree dogs'.

The Research and Development Department discovered that this claim could be validated legally by incorporating large doses of thiamine into the product, since pedigree dogs are more highly strung and sensitive than others. The product was improved in other ways – by stiffening up the consistency, putting in large pieces of liver and making it look more like a meat loaf. A quality package and new advertising were also developed to underline the new claim, and the brand's price was increased.

Gradually Pedigree Chum's market share stopped falling and began to climb. It gained brand leadership in the mid-1960s and by the mid-1980s had achieved sales in excess of £100 million a year.

The strength of the Pedigree Chum approach was that it appealed to the owners of pedigree dogs, who saw it as a tailor-made product, but also to pet owners who regarded their dogs as of pedigree quality or wished to give their mongrels the 'best' food there was. Its positioning enabled Pedigree Chum to establish itself as the quality product in the category. Eventually Petfoods Ltd followed psychological logic and changed its name to the present Pedigree Petfoods Ltd.

Source: *Offensive Marketing*, Hugh Davidson, Penguin Books.

2.2 Understanding buyer behaviour in consumer markets

In order to understand how consumers make their purchase decisions marketers need to be able to answer six key questions (Table 2.1).

Table 2.1 Understanding consumer buyer behaviour

Question	Implications for marketers
What do they buy? What benefits are the customers buying?	What types of products and models are bought? Which features are regarded as most/least important? Which competing products also answer the same need?
Who decides what to buy? Who are our real customers?	Who actually influences the purchase decision? What are the characteristics (age, sex, income, occupation, lifestyle) of these key influencers?
Why do they buy? Why do customers buy from our company rather than others?	What are the strengths and weaknesses of the product/brand in relation to those of competitors?
How do they buy? How do customers go about buying from our company?	How do they get to know about the products? How often do they buy? How much do they buy? How brand loyal are they?
Where do they buy? Where are the highest concentrations of buyers?	Which geographical regions account for most/least sales? Are most of the products sold through supermarkets or specialist stores?
When do they buy? When do most sales occur?	Which time of the day or week are most products bought? Is there any seasonal variation in sales?

(a) Recognition of a problem or need

To understand how and why consumers make their buying decisions we need to understand first what motivates consumers – the factors which channel and direct their behaviour towards fulfilling certain **needs** and **wants** – see fig. 2.1. Philip Kotler, in his book *Principles of Marketing*, defines needs as 'a state of felt deprivation in a person' while wants are 'needs as shaped by our culture and personality'. In other words, all people need to eat and drink but one person may want fish and chips and a beer while another might want caviar and champagne. Wants only become **demand** when people have the resources to acquire what they want. For example, many people might want a Porsche but only a few can afford to buy one, so the demand for Porsches is small.

Most needs are inborn **biogenic needs** such as the need for food and water and shelter from the elements. In addition, human beings experience other needs which go beyond inborn needs. These **psychogenic needs**, such as the need for job satisfaction or status, are acquired or learned as children grow up and become subject to various socializing influences from their family and friends, school, work, the media and so on.

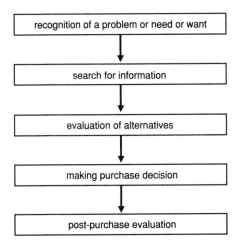

Fig. 2.1 Stages in the consumer buying decision process

(i) Maslow's hierarchy of needs   The most widely used theory of needs is that developed by American psychologist Abraham Maslow. He identifies five classes of needs which he ranks according to their degree of importance. These are shown in fig 2.2.

The model is based on the principle that lower level needs such as the need for food and safety will be satisfied first of all. A starving person will be pre-occupied with obtaining food as a priority. Higher level needs such as esteem or belonging will be considered unimportant. Then as each lower level need is satisfied, the need in the next level of the hierarchy becomes of over-riding

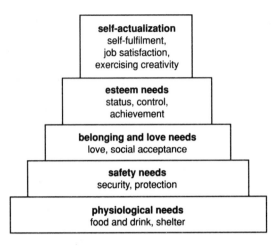

Fig. 2.2 Maslow's hierarchy of needs

importance. However, various needs do overlap and lower-level needs can become dominant again if circumstances change. For instance, if a person becomes homeless the need for shelter will become the priority. In reality, as the majority of people in advanced industrial nations are not pre-occupied with meeting basic needs for food and shelter, marketers seek increasingly to exploit higher level needs. Marketers of food products do not promote their products as a means of staving-off hunger; instead they use messages which appeal to our need for safety or status.

Marketers now recognize that individuals vary in the emphasis they place on satisfying particular needs, which in turn is reflected in the kind of lifestyle they choose to adopt. Within a particular market, consumers can be divided into distinct groups on the basis of the lifestyle choices they have made. This is discussed in more detail in Unit 5.

Consumer needs can be very complex. For example, there is no practical reason why men should put on a tie to go to work, yet the need for social acceptance leads millions of men to wear a purely decorative piece of cloth round their necks every day of their working lives. Nevertheless, whether a need is biogenic, such as the need to eat and drink, or psychogenic, such as the need to conform socially, consumers will not act to satisfy their needs unless a stimulus motivates them to do so.

The decision to purchase a new jacket for instance, can be triggered by an internal stimulus such as feeling cold, or it can be triggered by an external stimulus such as the onset of cold weather or the sight of a display of jackets in a shop window. Marketers obviously have no control over internal stimuli though they can use external stimuli such as advertising to prompt consumers into taking action to satisfy their needs or wants. We can probably all think of times when we have bought a product because the price was reduced, the packaging looked attractive or because we had seen it advertised on television and thought it was worth trying.

As most existing consumer needs are already being catered for in our affluent society the challenge now facing marketers is to go one stage further by stimulating subconscious needs. Much effort goes into creating innovative products designed to exploit **latent needs** which are not expressed consciously until the new product or service actually becomes available. How many of you knew you wanted a personal stereo until Sony actually brought out their Walkman?

In his book *The Design Dimension* Christopher Lorenz describes Sony's approach to the launch of new products. When Sony unveiled their new portable black-and-white TV set with an 8-inch screen in the USA, during the 1960s, it was an immediate success. Yet only weeks earlier, General Electric had completed a major piece of market research on the potential of small, portable TVs whose findings included conclusions like 'people do not place a high value on portability of the television set'.

Rather than asking consumers to predict their feelings towards an unfamiliar product, Sony had instead observed the growing number of sets sold and the increasing number of TV channels and realized that these two factors would create a demand for a second set in many homes. Lorenz went on to say that, 'In effect, the company had looked beyond consumers' expressed needs to their underlying behaviour patterns and had led the market by stimulating a new want. It has since done precisely the same with the video cassette recorder, Walkman personal stereo and the Watchman flat-tube TV.'

Clearly, companies with a successful record of product innovation are those who consistently manage to introduce products which satisfy the existing or latent needs of a target market. Most importantly, successful companies are those whose marketing effort is geared to stressing the benefits of their products. As marketing guru Ted Levitt has pointed out, customers do not buy drills – they buy holes. In other words, customers do not simply buy products or services – they buy solutions to their problems. This was summed up by the founder of a major cosmetics company who is reputed to have said, 'In the factory we make cosmetics, in the market we sell hope!'

It is for this reason that markets should always be divided up on the basis of what customers want or need, rather than on the basis of what they buy. This is an important distinction. If a firm thinks that it is just in the business of making slide rules, it can easily go out of business because it has not realized that what consumers actually want is a product which carries out calculations quickly. They do not want a slide rule as such, so if a better product becomes available like a calculator, people will stop buying slide rules.

Once an individual is aware of a **felt need** or problem (e.g. what can I wear to the party next Saturday?), they will be motivated towards satisfying that need. The felt need then becomes a much stronger **drive**.

(b) Search for information

The next stage of the buying decision-making process is where consumers search for a way of satisfying that need. For many of our simple, everyday needs the problem can be solved quickly. The information search process is almost automatic for frequently purchased items which are inexpensive, low-risk purchases like a bar of chocolate or a newspaper, whereas costly, high-risk purchases such as that of a new television or house generally involve a thorough and detailed investigation over a lengthy period of time. The extent of the information search is also related to the importance of the purchase in terms of the individual's own budget and lifestyle.

The process usually begins with consumers making an internal search of their own memory, which relates firstly to how the problem was solved in the past. (Where did I buy the outfit that I wore to the last party?) In fact, if consumers are happy with a previous purchasing decision, they will not bother to go through any further stages and will simply repeat the purchase. Consumers who are satisfied with a purchase, in terms of its price, quality, reliability, after-sales service and so on, are likely to buy the same brand again. This process is shown in fig. 2.3. Marketers strive to increase the level of positive reinforcement and thus expand the core of customers who exhibit **brand loyalty**. Consumers may also decide to carry out an external search for information if the buying decision concerns an expensive item or one which is not regularly bought. The external sources used include getting advice from informal sources such as friends and relatives as well as independent sources such as specialist magazines like *Which*? It can also extend to consulting commercial sources such as manufacturers' sales literature.

(c) Evaluation of alternatives

Having assembled enough information to make a particular purchase decision, consumers will by now be faced with a number of possible courses of action. They will need to weigh up the advantages and disadvantages of competing brands or options and decide which one best satisfies their particular need. (Should I buy an outfit from Top Shop or Next? Should I buy a pair of trousers or a dress?) Consumers then narrow down the buying decision to a set of choices. For example, they may eliminate some brands which are too expensive and others which do not have the required product features.

When evaluating the attributes of each brand, consumers are influenced by their existing attitudes, beliefs and perceptions, as well as by any previous experiences of the brand – whether good or bad. If marketers can discover which attributes are most important to consumers they can emphasize those product features in their advertising.

(d) Making purchase decision

Once the various alternatives open to them have been evaluated, consumers should, in theory, be ready to make a purchase decision. In practice, however, research has shown that consumers who have reached the 'intention to purchase' stage do not necessarily go on to make an actual purchase, particularly if there is a long delay before the purchase is finally made.

So why do people change their minds even when they have every intention of buying? Several unforeseen factors can intervene at this stage. For example,

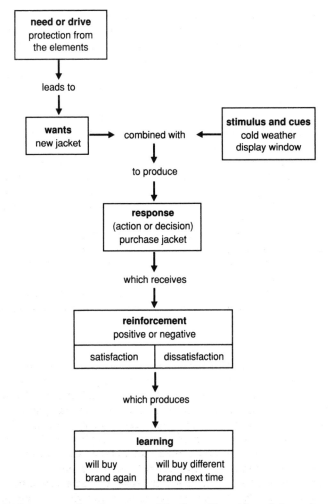

Fig. 2.3 The consumer learning process. Stimuli combine with needs to produce action (a purchase). Satisfaction or dissatisfaction with the purchase produces learning which influences future purchases
Source: *Marketing*, Peter D. Bennett, McGraw Hill.

family pressure may force someone who had decided on an expensive purchase to re-think. Unexpected expenses which crop up, such as higher mortgage payments due to a rise in interest rates or a repair bill for a leaking roof can also result in a planned purchase being shelved. Alternatively, the preferred brand may turn out to be too expensive or the shop may not have the right size or colour in stock. Aside from such unforeseen factors, purchasing decisions may, in any event, be influenced by a number of **intervening variables** such as a person's moods, habits, aspirations and so on.

The level of **perceived risk** associated with the purchase is another important factor. An expensive purchase such as buying a house will obviously carry a high degree of risk. Perceived risk may be physical (Is the wiring in the house safe?), financial (Will I be able to keep up with the mortgage payments?), or social (Will people think I'm showing off if I buy a bigger house?). In order to reduce the level of risk experienced by consumers when they purchase major items such as cars, electrical goods and furniture, firms tend to offer 'money back if not satisfied' deals, five-year guarantees, free trial periods and so on. The success of Marks and Spencer's 'no quibble' refund policy provides strong evidence that reducing the level of risk associated with a purchase can pay off handsomely in terms of increased sales.

(e) Post-purchase evaluation

It might be assumed that the consumer decision making process ends, as far as the marketer is concerned, once an actual purchase has been made. In reality, however, consumers will generally continue evaluating major purchases for some time afterwards. They will experience some degree of satisfaction or dissatisfaction once they have used the product or service a few times. If the purchase lives up to all or most of their expectations consumers are likely to buy that product again. Most importantly, they are likely to recommend the product to family and friends. The positive feelings may then encourage them to buy other products made by the firm. By the same token, negative feelings of dissatisfaction can have equally far-reaching effects. It goes without saying that a satisfied customer is a marketer's best friend.

Wise marketers also recognize that consumers almost always tend to have second thoughts after important purchases. The US psychologist Leon Festinger has called these uncertainties produced by doubt about the wisdom of an important decision **cognitive dissonance**. This occurs because consumers begin to realize that some of the products they discounted have desirable features whilst the product they did choose also has a few undesirable features. Consumers will attempt to reduce this discomfort or dissonance by playing down the negative features of the purchase and emphasizing the positive benefits. This need to justify a purchase decision is called **post-rationalization**. It is for this reason that much advertising is aimed at encouraging consumers to feel satisfied with their purchase. For instance, BMW advertising re-assures its customers that they have made the right choice by buying the 'ultimate driving machine'.

The ideal situation for marketers is when consumers are satisfied with their choice, to the point where in subsequent purchases they pass through the stages in the buying decision process almost automatically, without any conscious thought. Creating a pool of customers who make habitual **repeat purchases** in this way is the goal of all marketers, particularly as it then becomes considerably more difficult for marketers of alternative products to make consumers 'unlearn' their entrenched shopping habits.

2.3 The changing emphasis in satisfying consumer needs

If marketers are to be successful in catering for consumer needs they must first understand the underlying motivations which drive consumers into satisfying those needs by making a purchase. This sounds very straightforward. In reality, however, people often have very complex reasons for making purchases. More often than not they are motivated by subconscious needs and wants which are difficult to identify through market research. Would you want to admit to an interviewer that the real reason you bought a particular make of trainers was to impress your friends?

In any case, marketers recognize that consumer needs are changing constantly, which means they have to ensure that their efforts are not geared to catering for yesterday's needs and wants. Increasingly, marketers are also faced with the fact that it is no longer enough simply to satisfy the basic needs and wants of consumers.

In a recent article in *Marketing* magazine Robert Heller has put forward the view that businesses are experiencing a fundamental shift in their whole outlook. Companies are no longer dealing with the marketing of needs, instead they are increasingly concerned with the marketing of desire. So what does this mean? As Heller explains, 'If you go back to the 1950s, consumers simply took what they got. If you wanted anything different, you couldn't get it. The number of brands around was tiny, there were shortages of supply, people were simply not used to choice, and the atmosphere was much cosier for companies. There was less to spend too. That's all changed. Now people buy from desire, not need. Even in the most basic foodstuffs there is an endless variety in what you can eat and drink.'

It follows from this that marketers must now aim not just to meet consumer needs but to exceed them. As ever, it appears that the Japanese are setting the standards to beat. According to Simon Caulkin in a recent article in *Management Today*, 'Already the Japanese are beginning to talk of "taken for granted" quality and product features and are moving on to compete by "surprising" and "delighting" customers.' In other words, the standards for world-class competition are constantly expanding.

Most importantly, the challenge for marketers is to look beyond the satisfaction of existing consumer needs to the identification of new consumer needs. Marketing needs, therefore, to be pro-active. As Robert Heller argues, 'If you wait and see what the consumer wants you will wait for ever.' The focus is now shifting towards developing innovative products which stimulate new consumer needs. The successful introduction of Post-it notes provides a prime example of this trend.

> **Case study** *Post-it notes* **The case of a product looking for a need** In 1970, Dr Spencer Silver, working in 3M's Central Research Laboratory in the USA, was looking for a way to make stronger adhesives. He tried a different procedure and came up with an unexpected result – a low tack adhesive that would stick

but could be pulled off easily. Silver sent out samples to other technical departments within 3M, but the product did not seem to have any immediate practical applications so it was put 'on the shelf'. Several years later, another 3M scientist, Art Fry, had the idea of using Silver's barely sticky adhesive along the edge of his church hymn book to mark the pages.

In this way the familiar yellow Post-it notes were born. Today, Post-it notes are indispensable in homes and offices around the world. Yet the journey from that early book-mark to a successful world-beating product has not been smooth or easy. In fact, there were times when the product looked like being a complete flop.

Fry started work on developing a note-pad with peelable pages in the 15 per cent of research and development time that 3M allows its scientists for pursuing projects of their own choosing. As a first step there were many technical problems to be solved before the product could be shown to anyone. For instance, the adhesive did not stay put and had to be chemically bonded to the paper. The adhesive also had to be so thin that the sticky part of the paper was no thicker than the rest even when it was made into a pad.

It was only once the first good-quality prototypes were ready that the product could be manufactured and marketed on a large scale. However, the marketing people were sceptical. After all, the world had got along perfectly well without sticky notes up to now. Then there was the fact that the notes cost around seven to ten times more than ordinary jotting pads.

Results from the initial market research survey were not hopeful either. Customers had always managed without sticky notes so they did not see any need for such a product. This is, in fact, what often happens with products which do not resemble what is currently available. People find it difficult to imagine that they would have any use for a product which is radically different to anything else on the market. If people are quite happy with using ordinary jotting pads, they do not see why they should want to buy sticky note-pads.

In the face of these negative research results, Art Fry reasoned that the only way people would discover how to use the notes was for them to be given trial samples. In the event, when samples were distributed within 3M actual usage rates were much higher than expected, even though external market research results continued to show low consumer interest.

Nevertheless, encouraged by the level of internal usage 3M began test marketing in four US cities, backed up with an advertising campaign but no trial samples. Sales were very disappointing and the marketing people were ready to kill the project. This would have been the end of Post-it notes but for the determination of Art Fry who persuaded two of his managers to get on a plane and go and talk to some of the customers. The managers were amazed by what they heard. Some of the users even started pleading with them not to remove the product from the market because they were dependent upon it! On the basis of this feedback, a new marketing programme was set up in Boise, Idaho. It came to be known as 'The Boise Blitz'. Promotional materials were revised, extra sales people brought in and an army of people hired to distribute samples.

The results were sensational. In the office supply business an 'intent-to-reorder' rate of 40 to 50 per cent is considered exceptional. In Boise, a 90 per cent 'intent-to-reorder' rate was achieved in the space of a few weeks. The few remaining sceptics were silenced. In 1979, 3M began selling Post-it notes in the western states, intending to have an orderly **roll-out** as the product was launched across the USA. Instead, distributors with multiple outlets started leaking the product into other parts of the country. From then on, it was a scramble just to stay ahead of the back-log of orders. By 1981, Post-it notes were on sale throughout the world.

The removable notes are now one of the top-selling office supply products in the USA, Europe and Japan. They have become one of 3M's most successful products – no mean feat in a company that manufactures over 60 000 products! The sales success has spawned a host of **product variants**, though the original yellow

Fig. 2.4 Post-it note variants

notes still remain the most popular line. Growth looks set to continue. In an age of automated offices with word processors, fax machines, photocopiers and the like, the simple Post-it note provides a form of communication which is direct, informal, and highly effective.

The Post-it note provides a classic example of a product which has succeeded by stimulating new consumer needs. The fact that it failed to reveal its true potential in market research tests is not really surprising. Innovative products invariably research badly because they have no immediate relevance to existing consumer needs. In this case, the use of trial samples proved to be the key factor in gaining consumer acceptance. The lesson is clear. Marketers should not be afraid to look beyond existing consumer needs in order to find or stimulate new and different needs.

2.4 Analysing buyer behaviour in organizational markets

A significant area of marketing is directed not at consumers but at other firms and organizations. This includes manufacturing firms who need to buy materials and components to use as part of their production processes. In addition, all organizations need to buy goods and services of some kind in order to run their businesses. Selling to **organizational markets** therefore involves selling to manufacturing and service industries as well as wholesalers and retailers, government departments and non-profit-making organizations such as hospitals, museums, universities, etc. (Table 2.2).

Organizational markets differ from consumer markets in terms of their characteristics (e.g. fewer customers who place larger orders), buying motivations (e.g. reliability of supplier), and in the stages of the decision making process (e.g. long negotiation period with suppliers). The decision making process itself also tends to be a more formal and lengthy procedure involving a number of people, where products and suppliers are systematically evaluated in an objective and analytical way. As a result, decisions are generally made on rational grounds, unlike most consumer buying decisions.

This does not mean, however, that the marketing effort is ineffective and unnecessary in organizational markets. In reality, the same principles apply. Marketers need to be aware that organizations, like consumers, have differing needs and requirements. If their marketing effort is to be successful, it must meet and satisfy those needs.

2.5 Organizational buying motivations

The underlying motivations for organizational buying decisions differ from consumer buying decisions in many ways. In general, decisions made by organizational buyers tend to be based on careful consideration of factors such as price and product characteristics, the quality of service offered and the

Table 2.2 The types of products and services bought by organizational markets

Types of products and services	Description	Examples
raw materials	Unprocessed materials used in the manufacture of products.	Coal, iron ore, metals, timber, wheat, wool, livestock.
components and materials	Processed materials and manufactured parts included in the finished products.	Glass, plastics, nylon, gearboxes, cement, bricks, sugar, flour, nuts and bolts.
capital plant and equipment	Large items of plant and equipment needed to make products or provide services.	Factory and office buildings, large production machinery, main-frame computers, delivery vans
accessory equipment	Small equipment needed to make products and provide services.	Screwdrivers, saws, small power tools, desks and filing cabinets.
operating supplies	Supplies used up but not included in the product that is made or service that is provided.	Lubricating machine oil, petrol for cars and vans, cleaning materials, office stationery, paper cups, light bulbs.
professional and commercial services	Support services needed to run the organization.	Legal and accountancy services, banking, insurance, advertising, marketing research, catering, contract cleaning, maintenance services.

reliability of suppliers. Other factors, such as the prospect of reciprocal buying and the extent of derived demand may also be influential.

Nevertheless, recent research has shown that some organizational buyers will buy from suppliers with whom they have a good relationship, even if those suppliers charge higher than normal prices or offer a poor service. This sounds highly unlikely, but bearing in mind that organizational buyers are human and therefore fallible, it is perhaps not so surprising that irrational motivating factors can at times influence organizational buying decisions in much the same way as consumer buying decisions.

(a) Reliability of supplier
The reliability of the supplier, especially in relation to the accuracy of orders and timing of deliveries has always been of importance to organizational buyers, but has become even more critical with the increasing use of **just-in-time (JIT)** methods of stock control. In order to reduce the amount of capital tied up in holding large amounts of stock and to save on warehousing space, many manufacturing firms are adopting JIT systems, which involve components being delivered to the assembly line only when needed. If such systems are to operate successfully it is obviously essential that the right parts are delivered at the right time. Related to this is the need for components to arrive free of defects, which is why many organizational buyers now insist that their suppliers conform to stringent **quality assurance** standards.

(b) Quality of service offered
The quality of the after-sales service is far more important to organizational buyers than to consumer buyers, essentially because they need to be sure that when equipment breaks down, suppliers can carry out repairs as quickly as possible. If production equipment is out of action for long periods, they stand to lose a great deal of money while machines and workers are standing idle, not to mention the danger of orders being cancelled if delivery dates are missed.

(c) Reciprocal buying
A common practice amongst organizational buyers is **reciprocal buying**, which is based on the principle of 'If you buy from me, I'll buy from you.' An example might be when a photocopier manufacturer chooses to buy the computers it needs from a company that uses its photocopiers.

(d) Derived demand
Organizational buyers are aware that demand for their own products is influenced by consumer demand for other products. This is known as **derived demand**. For example, a manufacturer of gearboxes will analyse carefully trends in the sales of new cars. Organizational marketers need to take into account the level of derived demand when deciding on the amounts of materials they need to buy for their own requirements.

2.6 Factors that distinguish organizational markets from consumer markets

It is important to understand the ways in which organizational markets are different from consumer markets as these will have a great influence on the planning of an appropriate marketing strategy.

(a) Fewer but larger customers

Firms selling to consumer markets generally have many thousands or even millions of potential customers, whereas firms selling to organizational markets tend to deal with a handful of firms or even perhaps with a single firm or organization who will account for a large proportion of their sales. For many aircraft manufacturers, their sole customer is their own national Government, some medical suppliers sell only to the National Health Service, and some food manufacturers may have the bulk of their production taken by one of the major retailers such as Marks and Spencer, Sainsbury or Tesco.

The obvious disadvantage of this situation is that firms selling to organizational markets are vulnerable in that their fortunes are tied to those of a few large customers. However, they do have the considerable advantage of being able to direct their marketing effort to the needs of those particular customers rather than at the market in general, which is a much more efficient use of resources. For example, sales representatives in firms serving organizational markets, unlike those in consumer markets, do not need to waste time visiting a cross-section of customers, some of whom may not actually place an order.

(b) Geographical concentration

Organizational markets are often concentrated in particular geographical locations, whereas consumer markets tend to be more widely dispersed. Firms supplying particular organizational markets also tend, therefore, to locate within or near the markets they serve. For example, manufacturers of automobile components are located within the West Midlands region where a high concentration of car manufacturers is found.

If their customers are clustered in a particular area, it makes sense for organizational marketers to locate their manufacturing facilities as well as their sales and administration functions within the same area.

(c) Professional buyers

Firms selling to organizational markets have to deal with professionally-trained buyers who are generally experts with a specialist knowledge of their field.

(d) Vertical and horizontal markets

Organizational markets can be classified either vertically or horizontally. **Vertical organizational markets** are those where products and services are sold to companies who are all within the same industry such as computer firms, oil companies, textile firms and so on. A firm manufacturing oil drilling equipment will supply only to oil companies. **Horizontal organizational markets**, in contrast, cut across several types of industries. The markets for office equipment, production line machinery and catering services, for instance, cut across a wide range of industries.

Marketers who supply vertical markets can build up a specialist knowledge of the field in which they operate. As they generally deal only with a few major customers they can ensure that their marketing effort is tailored to meeting the specific needs of those customers.

(e) Emphasis on personal selling

Personal selling methods are used commonly to promote products in organizational markets in preference to advertising, largely because organizational marketers tend to deal with a few buyers who place large orders, as opposed to consumer marketers who need to reach large numbers of buyers.

The main advantage of personal selling methods is that sales representatives can gear their sales presentations directly to the needs of particular organizational buyers. They can also obtain customer feedback instantly, which enables them to modify quickly their products or services where necessary.

(f) Direct channels of distribution

In most organizational markets, the chain of distribution separating the producer and consumer is quite short and direct, unlike consumer markets where there may be many levels of wholesalers and retailers between the producer and consumer. Channels of distribution are discussed in more detail in Unit 11.

(g) Greater degree of negotiation

A far greater degree of negotiation takes place between buyers and sellers in organizational markets than in consumer markets. The negotiations can concern any aspect of the purchase, though discussions usually centre on the price and product specification.

Bidding, which is where buyers compare different bids that suppliers have submitted, is also far more common in organizational markets than in consumer markets. If the firm is looking to buy a new piece of production equipment, install a new word-processing system or employ a new firm to clean the office, buyers will obtain bids from at least three or four suppliers. In **open bidding**, suppliers may be told what their competitors have bid, whilst in **closed bidding**, suppliers are not allowed to know what their competitors have bid until after the order has been awarded.

(h) Numbers of people involved in the purchase decision

In most organizational markets, purchase decisions will be made by a group of people rather than by individuals, particularly when the purchase involves expensive items of capital equipment. The people who participate in the buying decision are known as the **decision making unit (DMU)**, which may sometimes be a formal committee but is in most cases an informal collection of people who become involved at different stages of the buying process.

The numbers of people involved will vary according to the size of the organization and the importance of the purchase decision, though at the very least, the DMU will usually comprise the purchasing manager and a specialist from the department that is to use the purchase. If a new word-processing system is to be installed, for example, the office manager might be involved in the choice of system. The finance director as well as senior management may be consulted if the purchase is costly.

However, whatever the size and make-up of the DMU, individuals within the group will at different stages in the buying process assume different roles.

2.7 Roles assumed by people within the decision making unit

In any organizational purchase decision, people within the DMU are likely to assume one or more of the following roles.

(i) Initiators   The people who first suggest that the purchase be made in response to a need they have identified. Initiators can be employees, managers, outside consultants and so on.

(ii) Users   The people who will actually be using the product or service such as the secretaries who would use a new word-processing system. The extent to which users can influence the purchase decision depends on the company's attitudes towards involving employees in decision making.

(iii) Influencers   The people with technical or specialist knowledge who can influence whether a purchase actually goes ahead or is dropped. They can influence a purchase decision at an early stage by stating that the product specification must conform to a certain standard and also at a later stage when potential purchases are being evaluated. Influencers can be design engineers, production line managers, maintenance supervisors, outside consultants and so on. The finance department can often sway the final decision if they feel that a purchase is either affordable or too expensive.

(iv) Deciders   The people who have authority to select suppliers and approve a purchase decision for major items of capital expenditure. In some cases the deciders may be a formal buying committee or even senior management, whilst in other companies it is the users who act as deciders.

(v) Buyers   The people who carry out the administrative procedures for purchase and delivery. Buyers are not necessarily deciders or even influencers, they simply make the practical arrangements. However, buyers may function as deciders for some routine purchases of minor items such as office stationery.

(vi) Gatekeepers   The people who control the flow of information from outside to members of the DMU and also to prospective suppliers. Purchasing managers who may decide which people sales representatives visit are one example. Receptionists who direct incoming calls can function as gatekeepers and so can secretaries. The person responsible for distributing incoming mail such as sales literature and trade journals can also be influential.

(a) Targeting the right people

The fact that buying decisions are influenced by people who function in these different roles has far-reaching implications for marketers in firms supplying organizational markets. Clearly, marketers need to categorize the people they are dealing with in order to direct their marketing effort at the right people. There is not much point in targeting buyers, for instance, yet this is precisely what happens in many cases. Research has revealed that many firms concentrate their sales and promotional effort on the buyers who merely place orders rather than on those who decide what to order.

Marketers need to ensure that the key influencers of purchase decisions are kept informed of all the sales literature on their products. Most importantly, suppliers need to target the crucial deciders, though deciders can often prove difficult to identify as they are not always visibly involved in purchase decisions. It goes without saying that marketers need to maintain good relationships with the gatekeepers who control the flow of information to people within the DMU.

2.8 The organizational buying decision process

Like consumer buying decisions, organizational buying decisions involve a number of well-defined stages. However, the organizational decision-making process tends to be carried out in a much more formal and analytical way, with alternative products and suppliers being methodically researched and objectively evaluated. As a result, organizational buyers can take months or even years to reach a decision, particularly when the purchase represents a major investment (see fig. 2.5).

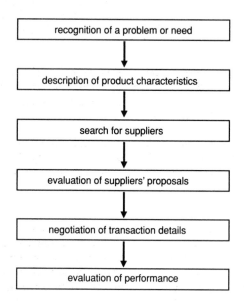

Fig. 2.5 Stages in the organizational buying decision process

(i) Recognition of a problem or need   This can be triggered by internal stimuli such as dissatisfaction with a previous purchase, the discovery that a machine is beyond repair, or by external stimuli such as the introduction of a technologically superior product.

(ii) Description of product characteristics   Once a need or problem has been recognized, the next stage is to identify and describe the characteristics of the product that will best satisfy that need or problem. The features that are required and performance standards that will have to be met are discussed by the specialist members of the DMU such as designers, engineers and production managers. A detailed product specification is then drawn up.

(iii) Search for suppliers   Next, a search is carried out to identify potential suppliers of this product and a shortlist of those that are most suitable is drawn up. The extent of the search process is related to the cost of the product and the degree of risk attached to the purchase. Buyers will in most cases prefer to avoid the uncertainty of dealing with small suppliers by opting for the safe option of a reputable 'big-name' – an attitude summed up by the adage 'Nobody ever got fired for buying IBM.'

(iv) Evaluation of suppliers' proposals   Suppliers are invited to submit their bids or quotations, which are then evaluated. The proposals are compared in terms of product price and performance, quality of service offered, reputation of supplier and so on. Buyers may, at this stage, negotiate with suppliers over prices and terms.

(v) Negotiation of transaction details   Even when a supplier has been chosen, the process does not end there. Arrangements over payment and credit terms, delivery dates, packing methods and maintenance contracts all have to be settled before the order can be placed finally.

(vi) Evaluation of performance   The quality and performance of the product is usually evaluated, as well as the reliability of the supplier. If buyers are satisfied with the product it will be re-ordered, but if not, the entire buying process may be re-opened.

(a) Timing
Marketers need to be aware of how the buying decision process works in organizations so that they can concentrate their marketing effort on the crucial stages. For instance, the distribution of sales literature and visits by sales representatives is likely to be most effective if timed to coincide with the key information search stage when suppliers can promote the benefits of their product over those of competitors.

2.9 Types of organizational buying situations
There are three types of buying situations found in large organizations.

(a) New task

This is where the organizational DMU is making a completely new purchase. As there are no precedents for the purchase it is invariably a time-consuming and complex procedure involving all stages of the buying process, which will usually require a large DMU made up of people drawn from all parts of the organization. The DMU will, in addition to consulting the likely users, also seek advice from a variety of technical experts as well as financial and legal experts. It is a situation commonly associated with the purchase of major items of capital expenditure, where the final buying decision will almost certainly need to be sanctioned by senior management.

The challenge for marketers in firms supplying organizational markets is to ensure that customers are provided with all the product information they need to make an informed choice. Most importantly, the DMU needs to be reassured about the quality of the product and reliability of the suppliers themselves. Suppliers who are successful in reducing the degree of uncertainty experienced by buyers of major items are likely to stand a much better chance of getting the order.

(b) The straight re-buy

This is the buying situation at the opposite end of the scale. It is essentially where buyers reorder stock items that are regularly used up on a routine basis. As the items have been purchased many times before, buyers have already been through the stages where they have researched the market, evaluated suppliers and so on.

Once purchase arrangements are in place with an existing tried and trusted supplier, unless the company is dissatisfied with the product or the supplier, buyers will not think it necessary to look for alternatives and will simply reorder the same items. Much reordering of stock items is done nowadays automatically by computer, which is obviously an ideal arrangement as far as suppliers are concerned because repeat sales are guaranteed. It does, however, make it very difficult for new suppliers to get their products accepted, unless these are substantially cheaper or significantly better in some respect. It takes some very strong stimulus or 'precipitating circumstance' for buyers to switch to a new supplier.

(c) The modified re-buy

A number of factors can transform what would otherwise have been a straight re-buy into a modified re-buy. Dissatisfaction with an existing product or supplier or technological changes which result in a better product becoming available are the most common catalysts for change.

In a modified re-buy the organizational buyer has some experience of the market having previously bought a similar type of product, so all that is needed is a fairly limited information search of competing products and alternative suppliers.

The marketing environment

3.1 Operating in a wider framework

Having identified the needs which consumers have, firms then need to co-ordinate their marketing efforts towards satisfying those needs – a process which seems, on the face of it, to be deceptively straightforward. In reality, of course, this process of matching products and services to the relevant consumer needs does not take place in a vacuum and is as a result fraught with difficulties. Inevitably, both customer needs and the ability of firms to market goods and services to meet those needs are influenced by a range of outside factors.

Marketers can modify product specifications, raise or lower prices, develop new advertising campaigns and choose different retailers and wholesalers to distribute their products. Whilst they have direct control over such internal aspects, marketers have virtually no control over the external elements of the environment, such as political, economic, technological and socio-cultural factors. Firms can influence these external factors to a certain extent. For example, they can attempt to alter Government policy by lobbying Parliament through organizations like the TUC or CBI. In general, however, firms recognize that they need to operate within the wider framework of an external **marketing environment** over which they have very little control.

It is essential, therefore, for marketers to keep abreast of changing trends in the external environment. Monitoring trends enables firms to anticipate and forecast changes which are likely to affect their activities. They can then devise contingency plans to deal with new situations arising from demographic factors such as the rise of the 55+ age group, technological factors such as the impact of the silicon chip, socio-cultural factors such as the increasing proportion of married women in the workforce or economic factors such as high interest rates.

Almost the only certainty firms can count on today is that the pace of change is accelerating, which means that firms need to be flexible enough to respond quickly to a constant stream of new challenges. At best, firms that do not adapt to change are likely to miss potentially valuable marketing opportunities. At worst, they run the risk of being overtaken by competitors and of being forced out of the market.

3.2 The demographic environment

Marketers need to understand the demographic environment, including such characteristics as the size, age structure and geographical distribution of the population. Demographic trends are carefully analysed in order to forecast changes in consumer behaviour. It is important for marketers to know how many people the market contains and whether the population is growing, stable or declining, what proportion of the population is young or old and which geographical areas are likely to contain the most buyers.

(i) Population size and growth   The size of the total population of a country reflects the relationship between the **birth rate** (the number of live births per 1000 of the population in a given year) and the **death rate** (the number of deaths per 1000 of the population in a given year).

The birth rate in Britain has declined steadily since the peak 'baby boom' years following the Second World War. A number of factors have contributed towards the falling birth rate – changing social attitudes towards large families (linked to rising standards of living), the widespread availability of contraception and legalization of abortion, together with the increasing proportion of married women following a career.

In common with many other advanced industrial nations, the birth rate in Britain has now stabilized at the replacement level, where the number of births only slightly exceeds the number of deaths. Eventually, Britain may follow the pattern of countries like Germany, where the population has actually started to decline as the birth rate has dropped below the death rate.

The Bruntland Report by the World Commission on Environment and Development estimates that the population of the world is expected to increase from the present figure of around five billion to between ten and fourteen billion by the year 2050. Most of this growth will continue to take place in the developing nations who are currently experiencing the high growth rates that were found in the developed nations when they were first industrializing. However, the rate of increase is much faster, partly due to improved standards of health care and partly due to the advances made in medical technology.

The multi-national corporations have not been slow to respond to the opportunities presented by these contrasting trends in population growth. Many have turned their attention away from stagnant western markets towards the as yet largely untapped markets of the third world.

(ii) Geographical distribution   An understanding of the geographical distribution of the population is vital for marketing planning. Once the areas of highest population density are known, marketers can then establish where the greatest concentrations of buyers are likely to be found. In Britain, these areas tend to be found south and east of a line extending between the River Tees and

River Exe, including the South East and West Midlands regions. High population densities also exist around the major conurbations such as London, Birmingham, Manchester, Liverpool, Glasgow, etc. The lowest densities are found in the peripheral regions such as the highlands and islands of Scotland, the interior of Wales, the Lake District and the South West peninsula.

(iii) Age structure Most consumer goods and services tend to be aimed at the needs of a particular age group rather than at the population as a whole. Firms tend to concentrate their efforts on the age group that is most likely to buy their products and services. For instance, shops selling trendy but affordable clothes cater for the teenage market whilst sheltered housing developments are obviously geared to the needs of the elderly.

Marketers need therefore to be aware of population trends affecting the proportion of people in various age groups. In most advanced industrial nations falling birth rates have caused a corresponding decline in the numbers of young people. At the same time there has been a marked increase in the proportion of older people in the population, reflecting the advances that have been made in medical techniques and in standards of health care, hygiene and diet.

The rise of the so-called 'grey' consumer group (most of whom are younger (55 +), fitter and more affluent than previous generations of retired people) is forcing marketers to re-evaluate their conceptions of 'the elderly'. This active and youthful 'fiftysomething' group with their high discretionary incomes represents enormous potential for marketers, particularly in the areas of home improvements, travel and financial services.

3.3 The rise of the 'grey' market

Slavishly courting the youth market and obsessed with the need to keep in touch with the 'kids on the street', the advertising industry has, until recently, been slow to respond to the opportunities presented by the growth of the over fifties market. However, spurred on by media predictions that the over fifties are poised to become the age group with the greatest disposable income, marketers are now scrambling to exploit the potential of the so-called 'grey market'.

The demographic figures explain this heightened interest. In 1991, the over fifties accounted for about a third of the UK population. Within this group, the number of 50–60 year olds is set to increase by a startling 20 per cent during the course of the decade. Most importantly, recent research has shown that a significant proportion are likely to be wealthier than ever before in their lives.

Many over fifties own their own homes outright or are close to paying off their mortgage, which coupled with the fact that children have generally grown up and left home leaves them with relatively low outgoings. On top of this they have often inherited property from deceased parents. The trend towards earlier retirement means that a high proportion are also likely to have an income from occupational pension schemes in addition to the state pension. Not surprisingly, the over fifties account for 70 per cent of the nation's savings. It is this powerful combination of low outgoings and substantial resources, leading to a high discretionary income, which marketers are beginning to realize constitutes a profitable and as yet largely untapped goldmine.

As a result, the focus of attention has shifted towards this group, particularly as the recent recession highlighted the fact that the purchasing power of the over fifties was largely unaffected by high interest rates, unlike the traditionally high-spending 25-44 year olds who were badly hit by soaring mortgage payments.

So which sectors of the market offer the greatest potential for targeting this lucrative group? Marketers have identified several key growth areas including travel and leisure activities, home improvements, consumer durables, cars and health care. The travel industry has been quicker than most to spot the potential of the 'grey' market. The Saga Group, for instance, has built a successful business by identifying facilities that were under-utilized out of season and offering them at good-value prices for retired people. Other successful examples include *Choice* magazine in the world of magazine publishing and National Savings in the area of financial services.

How, then, should advertisers attempt to reach this older age group? The campaign in 1989 for a Guardian Royal Exchange scheme is one example which did not receive a good press within the industry, largely because the 'trendy' old-age pensioner on his skateboard came to be seen in a rather negative light as a figure of fun. In contrast, the campaign for Commercial Union life insurance, which emphasizes the need to plan for old age, reinforces a positive image in its portrayal of a retired couple enjoying a cruise together on the fruits of an insurance policy.

As Liz Levy points out in an article in *Marketing* magazine in March 1989, 'Certainly there is the danger of patronizing or mishandling the target audience. A cautionary tale comes from the toiletries world. When Johnson and Johnson launched its Affinity shampoo in the US at the over fifties market, it alienated its target audience by over-emphasizing age. When the emphasis shifted to "hair that time has changed", results picked up. So targeting the over fifties purely on the basis of their advanced years is not necessarily a recipe for success. A major pitfall is that older people don't necessarily view, or want to view, themselves as old.'

This is a timely reminder when you consider that people like Mick Jagger, Peter Shilton, Anita Roddick and Cher are just some of those who will make up the 'grey' market in the nineties – hardly the stereotype of the frail, white-haired pensioner – and the last thing they would want is to be treated as 'old'.

In addition to avoiding inappropriate stereotypes, advertisers may also need to make other sweeping changes. Evidence suggests that older age groups tend to 'know the value of money' and are therefore more discerning buyers. It follows from this that they are more suspicious of advertising 'hype' and less susceptible to aspirational lifestyle advertisements which are totally unrealistic. They are also more risk-averse. In short, older consumers are not so easily parted from their money. On top of this they are also more demanding in other respects – expecting old-fashioned standards of quality and service for one thing.

Selling to the 'grey' market is clearly not going to be easy. Nevertheless, given that one pound in three is now spent by someone over 50 years old, it has obviously got to be worth the effort. It remains to be seen whether marketers can rise to the challenge of catering for the needs of this demanding group.

3.4 The socio-cultural environment

We are all products of the culture in which we live. **Material culture** consists of all the things people like to buy, use and do – buying T-shirts and jeans, three-piece suites, hi-fi systems, watching television, going to a football match, eating roast beef and Yorkshire pudding on Sunday and so on. **Non-material culture** encompasses the more abstract shared rules and guidelines which influence what is generally regarded as acceptable or desirable behaviour in a society. These include:

- **values** refraining from killing, stealing, committing adultery, etc.;
- **beliefs** getting a good education, getting married, having children, etc.;
- **customs** giving presents at Christmas, sending postcards on holiday, wearing a suit and tie to work, etc.

The fundamental values and beliefs which govern people's attitudes and actions are reinforced by the important institutions of society such as the family, school, government and the church. Rules which regulate standards of behaviour in relation to crimes like murder, fraud, burglary, rape and so on are regarded as so important that they must be enforced by official laws.

Cultural traditions are transmitted from generation to generation during the process of **socialization**. Children learn the physical, intellectual and social skills which they need as members of society from their family, **peer group** (friends and contemporaries of a similar age) and school, not to mention the invidious influence of the mass media, and television in particular.

Marketers are aware that cultural traditions shape the tastes and preferences which influence what types of goods and services consumers choose to buy. For example, the consumption of alcohol, which is a socially-acceptable, if not integral, part of most Western cultures is strictly taboo within Muslim societies.

Even within a particular society, cultural traditions can change. It is important, therefore, for marketers to monitor changing cultural and social trends as these can affect how firms divide up their markets and position products. Such changes can, of course, present new marketing opportunities. The growth of health-food shops, low calorie meals, DIY chains and environmentally-friendly products have all been introduced in response to changing patterns of behaviour. They are designed to exploit the greater consumer concern with issues such as health and fitness, dieting, home improvement and environmental protection.

Marketers recognize that they should also take into account the needs of the various **subcultures** which exist within every society. These are the groups of people whose cultural values (and hence buying habits) differ in some important respects from the dominant culture. Sub-cultures can develop based on one or more factors: age (e.g. teenagers), social class (e.g. working class), geographical region (e.g. Northerners), ethnic group (e.g. Asians) and religion (e.g. Jewish).

As individuals, we are all influenced by other people when deciding how we should behave, where we should work and spend our leisure time, what we should wear on various occasions, how we should treat others and so on. The people we look to for guidance on these matters provide a reference point against which we can measure our own standards of behaviour. The small, informal **reference groups** with which we associate such as family and peer group are likely to have a greater influence than wider reference groups such as school, employer and trade union. Individuals may consider as reference groups the top management team of the company they work for, members of the golf club they belong to, or simply a set of people they admire.

Evidence suggests that consumers tend to buy the same kinds of products and services as the members of the reference groups with which they identify. The implication is that marketers should use advertisements which stress the social acceptability of their products through portraying them being used by groups of people. The way in which Coca-Cola and Pepsi are promoted provides a classic example. Both companies have for many years made use of this approach in their advertisements which primarily target young people. Similarly, companies launching a new product will often first target the opinion leaders who influence others to buy.

(a) The influence of family

Marketers are particularly interested in monitoring the family as a reference group. For one thing, families exert a crucial influence on the later buying behaviour of individuals through the socialization process which takes place in the early formative years. The family is also an important consumption unit. Many purchasing decisions relating to cars, furniture, annual holidays and so on are made by entire households rather than by individual consumers.

It is essential, therefore, to understand the socio-cultural changes taking place in traditional family roles. Marketers recognize that the stereotype 'average' family with 'Dad' at work, 'Mum' a full-time housewife and 2.4 children is fast becoming a rare commodity – representing only about 4 per cent of all families today. Rising divorce rates mean that there are now many more single-parent families. In addition, the proportion of single-person (either unmarried or divorced) households is increasing dramatically. There are also many married couples with no children. The resulting increase in the number of households has created a greater demand for goods like vacuum cleaners and washing machines which are needed in every home. Manufacturers are responding to this trend towards a greater number of small households by introducing more convenience foods and smaller packages for food and other groceries.

Marketers are also aware that people today do not necessarily conform to the traditional pattern of getting married in their early twenties and having a family soon after. The stage reached in the **family life cycle** is in many ways a more accurate predictor of buying behaviour (see page 74). For example, purchases of beds, washing machines, tables and chairs, etc. are likely to be made soon after marriage regardless of whether the couple are in their twenties or forties. Similarly, purchases of cots, prams, toys and so on are likely to be made when the first baby arrives, at whatever age that occurs.

(b) The impact of changing male and female roles

The role of women has changed dramatically during this century and particularly in the last few decades. Women now represent 42 per cent of the UK workforce. The forecast that the number of young people entering employment will fall by 27 per cent between 1985 and 1995 has received widespread press coverage. However, what is less commonly recognized is that as the number of 18 year olds declines, by the year 1995, 83 per cent of new entrants and re-entrants to the workforce will inevitably have to be female.

The increasing numbers of married women following careers has stimulated a demand for labour-saving appliances like dishwashers, convenience foods, childcare services and shops selling 'career wardrobe' tailored clothing. Other changes resulting from this trend include the fact that families can now afford to eat out far more regularly.

Women now have a much greater say in the way purchase decisions are made, which applies not just to women following a career but also to women who are full-time housewives. Evidence suggests that decisions traditionally made by men, such as what kind of car to buy, are increasingly being made by women.

A recent report conducted by advertising agency Lowe Howard Spink entitled *The Balance of Power*, which looked at the sweeping changes taking place in traditional male and female roles, argues that marketers run the risk of losing out if they continue to employ outdated images of family life in their advertisements. The research, which was carried out in the early part of 1991 and involved surveying a sample of 1000 men and women, claims that the so-called demise of 'the housewife' is at a more advanced stage than most companies realize.

According to the report, traditional roles are becoming increasingly blurred. Household chores are now often shared, with 64 per cent of men claiming to do the vacuuming as often as their wives, 88 per cent doing the washing-up as often and 79 per cent being as likely as their wives to do the main grocery shopping. At the same time, women have been taking on some of the classic male roles, with 45 per cent painting and decorating the home and 97 per cent looking after the household finances. About ten million couples are already thought to conform to this pattern of the 'self-regulating household'. These shifts in traditional male/female roles have meant that much of the imagery and stereotyping which has conventionally been used in advertising is no longer relevant. The research shows that around 50 per cent of married couples currently share household tasks. Given that an estimated 80 per cent of married women in Britain will be working by 1995, it seems likely that the trend towards sharing responsibility for household tasks is likely to continue.

Marketers who persist in using inappropriate stereotypes in their advertising appeals will inevitably alienate their target audiences. There is a growing dislike amongst both sexes for advertisements that portray men as incompetent around the home and women enthusing about the whiteness of their wash.

(c) The influence of social class

Market planners have long recognized that different **social class groups** exhibit very different spending patterns. At first sight, it might be thought that this is merely a reflection of their contrasting levels of income. In reality, though, the situation is far more complex. Whilst there is indeed a broad general correlation between the two factors (airline pilots and surgeons clearly do earn more than caretakers or gardeners), income levels are in fact no longer as closely related to social class as they once were. For example, many skilled working class people may earn considerably more than some 'white collar' office workers. In addition, working class households often have high aggregate incomes because there may be several wage earners within the family.

Yet interestingly enough, even when people from different social class groups have the same income, there is often a vast difference in the way the money is spent, reflecting their differing tastes and preferences, values and aspirations. The differences can be seen in relation to their contrasting attitudes towards savings, use of credit cards, private education, etc.

Taken in isolation, level of income is therefore a poor indicator of social class. Evidence suggests that occupation, which tends to be closely linked to level of education, is a far better determinant of social class.

3.5 The technological environment

In 1938, an amateur physicist living in New York called Chester Carlson developed a process which he called 'electro-photography'. Carlson approached more than 20 companies to try and get them to develop his product, including RCA, IBM and General Electric, but was turned down by every one. Eventually, a small company called Haloid agreed to develop his process commercially. Haloid, which later became Xerox, is now one of the largest corporations in the USA. The fact that Haloid spotted the market potential of photocopying when so many other firms had not underlines the key importance of keeping an open mind towards emerging technologies. The accelerated pace of technological progress in recent years has made this essential for survival, not just for growth. The impact on the Swiss watchmakers of digital technology is a case in point. Whilst the experience was painful for most (and terminal for some) a few firms did incorporate the new quartz digital technology and survived.

Monitoring, or better still forecasting, technological change is vital for all firms but particularly for those in the fast growing 'sunrise' industries such as the motor vehicle, electronics, aerospace, pharmaceuticals and consumer goods industries. These 'high-tech' industries offer the greatest profit potential and export potential, though by their very nature they also experience the fiercest competition. New products are quickly superseded as competitors scramble to bring out a technically more advanced version.

Firms need, therefore, to introduce a constant stream of new products in order to stay ahead of the competition. Few can aim to be as prolific as Hewlett Packard, who manage to generate ideas for eight new products a week! Not all of these ideas are implemented – nevertheless, this does represent a phenomenal rate of innovation. Sustaining a high degree of innovation does, of course, require a substantial commitment of funds for research and development (R & D).

Within the automobile industry, the R & D costs for a new car can amount to around £300 million. The bill for taking a new model from the initial design stage through to full production can be as much as £700 million. With outlays like these, manufacturers obviously have to produce in huge volumes in order to make a profit. According to Philips, the Dutch electronics group, many electronics products today must capture an 8 per cent share of the world market simply to break even on R & D costs. This is before other costs are recouped and before any profit is made.

The costs of developing innovative new products in high technology industries and of installing automation and robotics are so great that there is generally a long payback period before the investment can be expected to yield any returns. It follows from this that if firms wish to match the performance of aggressive overseas competitors, they may need to forgo short-term profits in order to make the necessary long-term investments.

Technological advances can give rise to new products and processes. Equally, they can promote the demise of others, witness the impact of electronic calculators on slide rules. Similarly, the introduction of word-processors was a hard blow for the manufacturers of typewriters.

Marketers need to take account of new technological advances as these can determine the following.

(i) The kinds of products and services that can be offered e.g. antibiotics, microwave ovens, compact disc players, fax machines, personal computers, satellite TV, digital audio tapes, payment by credit cards, ATM 'hole-in-the-wall' cash machines, electronic point of sale (EPOS) tills in supermarkets, etc.

(ii) The kinds of raw materials that are available e.g. artificial diamonds, ceramic parts for car engines, fibre-optic telephone cables, nylon/polyester textiles, new generations of plastics, graphite tennis rackets, aseptic packing for products like fruit juices which previously required refrigeration. In particular, the widespread use of the micro-processor chip, introduced as recently as 1970, has revolutionized the power of electronic devices by permitting ever greater degrees of sophistication and miniaturization.

(iii) The ways in which these items can be designed and produced The use of **computer-aided design (CAD)** techniques has lessened the time taken to design and engineer new products. The performance characteristics of a product, such as its resistance to stress, can be tested accurately whilst the product is still a 2D image on the screen. This effectively reduces the number of prototypes that have to be built. For instance, whereas in the past a company like Rolls Royce would have needed to build as many as 39 test engines when developing a new aero-engine, today 9 or 10 would be enough as much of the early testing is done by computer simulation. CAD thus reduces the **lead time**, i.e. the time taken to introduce a product onto the market. Most importantly, there is a greater likelihood that the product specification will be 'right first time' once manufacture begins.

The use of **robots** has revolutionized production lines in industries like car manufacturing because they ensure a level of consistent quality that even the most skilled and dedicated workers cannot achieve week after week. They also handle heavy, demanding and repetitive tasks which are generally disliked by workers.

A firm's output can be improved still further when production lines are computer controlled and a central computer controls not only the operation of the robots on the assembly line but also the delivery of components to the line and the automatic reordering of parts which have been used.

Firms need to be flexible enough to respond to each wave of technological progress. Ultimately, firms who are unwilling to adapt to the rapidly accelerating pace of change are likely to face an increasingly uncertain future.

3.6 The political environment

The political climate created by the Government of a country inevitably exerts a powerful influence on the conditions under which business firms have to operate. The stark contrast between capitalist and communist countries in the attitudes of their governments toward issues such as the private ownership of firms and personal profit-making is a case in point. Above all, it is essential that governments maintain a stable business climate. Politically unstable regimes, such as those in certain Middle Eastern countries, tend to suffer from a low level of long-term investment reflecting the lack of business confidence.

Firms flourish when governments create a favourable business climate by lowering inflation and interest rates, reducing the level of corporate taxation and so on. Conversely, if a recession occurs, high inflation and interest rates undermine business activity and cause many firms to fail.

Governments often protect home industries against foreign competition by setting **quotas,** which restrict the number of imported goods such as cars or videos that are allowed into the country. They can also impose **tariffs** or taxes on imported goods that serve to make the price of these goods uncompetitive relative to home-produced goods.

3.7 The legal environment

Businesses are subject to a huge variety of legislation which controls and regulates their activities. In order to plan their marketing strategies businesses therefore need to be aware of all the relevant legislation which restricts what they can and cannot do.

Today, businesses are regulated by legislation to an extent that would not have been thought possible in the early days of industrialization. Firms were allowed to do almost entirely what they pleased during the eighteenth and nineteenth centuries. During this period of **laissez-faire capitalism** many businesses pursued their own self-interest with a zeal which showed a complete lack of concern for the safety of their customers (or indeed their employees) and which ignored the damage they were causing to the environment.

However, businesses now have to operate in a very different climate – one which expects them not only to work within the framework of the law but also to behave in an ethical and socially responsible way.

Of the huge volume of legislation which exists, marketers are most concerned with three main groups of laws. These include laws designed to:

- maintain free competition between businesses so that no one company can dominate and control a market;
- protect the consumer against unsafe products and unfair trading practices;
- protect society as a whole by reducing pollution, preventing drink driving, controlling tobacco advertising and so on.

3.8 The economic environment

The economic environment of a particular country inevitably reflects the policies adopted by successive governments, and more recently the impact of wider global economic trends. Literally hundreds of variables can be used to monitor economic trends. However, the key factors which concern marketers most include: the wealth of the country, interest and inflation rates, the purchasing power of the people and the distribution of income within the population.

(i) The wealth of a country The wealth of a country is usually expressed in terms of its **Gross National Product (GNP)**. This is the total market value of all the goods and services produced within the economy, together with the country's overseas earnings, for any given year. GNP figures provide a general indication of the economic health of a country.

However, a total GNP figure may give a misleading impression of a country's wealth if taken in isolation. For instance, China has a high total GNP because it is such a large country, yet it is very poor. In contrast, the tiny United Arab Emirates has a low total GNP because it has a small population, though it is in fact one of the richest oil states. It is more meaningful, therefore, to use a 'per capita' figure which is where the total GNP of a country is divided by the

Table 3.1 Population and per capita GNP of some countries (1989)

Country	Population (*millions*)	GNP per capita (*US $*)	GNP per capita (*world rank*)
Switzerland	6.5	30 270	1
Japan	123.0	23 730	2
Finland	5.0	22 060	3
Norway	4.2	21 850	4
Sweden	8.5	21 710	5
United States	248.2	21 100	6
Germany, Federal Republic	61.3	20 750	7
Denmark	5.1	20 510	8
Canada	28.3	19 020	9
United Arab Emirates	1.5	18 430	10
France	56.1	17 830	11
Austria	7.6	17 360	12
Belgium	9.9	16 390	13
Kuwait	2.0	16 380	14
Netherlands	14.8	16 010	15
Italy	57.5	15 150	16
United Kingdom	57.3	14 570	17
Australia	16.8	14 440	18
New Zealand	3.3	11 800	19
Singapore	2.7	10 450	20

Source: *The World Bank Atlas*, 1990.

number of people in the population to give an average figure per head of the population (Table 3.1).

(ii) Purchasing power   Marketers are also interested in the purchasing power of customers in their target markets, since this affects the amount and types of goods and services that they can afford to buy. There are two measures of purchasing power. **Disposable income** is the amount of money remaining after deductions such as tax, national insurance and occupational pension schemes have been made. However, these are merely the basic deductions. Given that the majority of people also have to set aside money for their mortgage or rent, food, clothes, fares to work and so on, **discretionary income**, which is the money left after such necessities have been taken into account, is actually a more accurate indication of spending power. This is an important distinction. People with a high disposable income may well have a low discretionary income if their outgoings, such as mortgage payments, are very high. Equally, there may be people with a low disposable income who have a high discretionary income.

(iii) Distribution of income   Marketers are aware, however, that average GNP and personal income figures inevitably hide tremendous variations between individuals and households. A high average per capita income is meaningless if in reality the majority of the population is very poor yet the overall figure is distorted by the presence of an immensely wealthy ruling elite, as is the case with many of the oil-rich Middle Eastern countries.

Even in countries which do not have such a sharp division between rich and poor, factors such as educational level, occupational type, social class and racial group can all have a powerful influence on the distribution of income.

(iv) Inflation and interest rates   The level of inflation is also of crucial concern to marketers. When inflation is high the price of goods and services increases and the purchasing power of consumers declines correspondingly. Consumers will tend to postpone the purchase of any major items such as cars, furniture and household appliances, as well as holidays and other non-essential services. High interest rates have a similar effect on the willingness and ability of consumers to make purchases, particularly those involving a large financial commitment.

Given that consumer demand is so strongly affected by the ups and downs of the economy, it is obviously essential that marketers take into account the projections made by economists concerning future trends in inflation and interest rates.

Marketing research

4.1 Is marketing research important?

Marketers gather information to back up vital decisions, especially those where large sums of money are at stake, as in new product launches. They need to know when, where, how and why buyers make their purchases. They also need to know who their buyers are, what they think and feel, what opinions and attitudes they hold and how these motivate their purchasing behaviour.

Carrying out research is generally the first step in any properly planned marketing campaign. **Market research**, which involves the investigation of specific markets, is, in fact, only a small part of the much broader process of **marketing research**, which involves analysis of every aspect of the marketing sequence, covering consumers' needs, attitudes and buying behaviour as well as their reactions to the product itself and the way it is priced, promoted and distributed.

Marketing research can provide the answers to a huge variety of 'what if?' questions. What if we increase the price, change the packaging, introduce new advertising, change the product formulation? Most importantly, it can provide the answer to the bottom line question known in marketing as 'Do the dogs like the dog food?'

One US company devised a cake mix that was so simple all buyers had to do was add water. But when the product was launched, sales were disappointing. Research revealed that consumers felt as if they were cheating when they used the mix – they did not feel that they had actually baked the cake themselves. As a result, the company changed the formula so that a fresh egg now had to be added. The new cake mix was re-introduced and proved to be a resounding success!

Many firms benefit from marketing research which provides them with this kind of valuable insight into what are often quite small and seemingly insignificant aspects of their marketing operations. Thorough market research can make the difference between success and failure. This is why firms generally base their plans and decisions on detailed, accurate and up-to-date information which has been systematically and objectively gathered. Research cannot, of course, eliminate business risk but it can greatly reduce the guesswork element, which helps to reduce the possibility of an expensive mistake being made. Would the Sinclair C5 have been launched if extensive market research had been carried out beforehand?

It is, however, notoriously difficult to gauge the likely consumer reaction to highly innovative products which are unlike anything else on the market, as consumers tend to dislike products they cannot visualize. In fact, if companies always heeded research findings they would never launch radically different products at all. For instance, the Sony Walkman was launched despite research that warned it would be a complete flop. In the event, Sony decided to ignore the research and went on to reap the marketing coup of the decade. It goes to prove that decisions made on the strength of research recommendations should always be taken in the light of managers' experience and judgement and in terms of their 'feel' for the market.

Nevertheless, although there may be times, as with the launch of highly innovative products, when it makes sense to distrust research findings, in the majority of cases properly conducted research is a reliable predictor of market performance. The role played by thorough market research in the successful development of a product such as Hob-nobs illustrates this most clearly.

Case study *Hob-nobs* **How market research helped to create a successful new product** As a nation, we munch our way through over two million Hob-nob biscuits a day, creating in the process sales worth a hefty £35 million in 1989. Introduced by United Biscuits under the McVitie's label, Hob-nobs were designed to capitalize on the growing consumer trend towards healthy eating. Since being launched in 1984, they have taken the market by storm to become the most successful new biscuit brand for over 60 years. This is all the more remarkable for having taken place against the background of a mature and crowded market with almost 1000 biscuit lines already on offer. Yet despite this competition and the notoriously high failure rate of new products, the painstaking research involved in developing the product over a period of five years made the success of Hob-nobs almost inevitable.

In the early part of the 1980s, United Biscuits had identified from their research a marked swing in consumer preference towards products that were more natural and wholesome. By early 1983, they had come up with a number of products that might fill this need. **Qualitative research**, involving discussions conducted by trained interviewers with small groups of consumers, was then carried out to get some initial reactions. The response was not good. The biscuits were considered too small and insubstantial and the flavour too light and refined.

The company decided, therefore, that fresh research should be carried out to try and determine exactly what consumers wanted.

This time, a number of product concepts (ideas for products presented in the form of descriptive statements, pictures and so on) were tested with a different set of consumer groups. The sessions generated some useful ideas and helped to give them a better 'feel' for the market. Words like 'butter', 'honey', 'bits' and 'natural' cropped up often in the discussions. The consensus of opinion was that consumers wanted a product which was solid and robust, with a distinctive flavour and no 'frills'.

Based on this feedback, two new biscuits were produced, one based on butter and the other on oats. Once again, these were tested. The oat biscuit emerged as the clear winner when the results were analysed. Respondents liked the open, crunchy texture, the oat pieces and the overall cragginess, all of which combined to give the biscuits a definite home-made look. Most importantly, the biscuits were widely perceived as being 'better for you'. The next stage of the research involved home trials of the product, as a result of which the biscuits were adapted to create a more coarse and golden appearance.

Confident it now had a product that was going to capture a high enough sales volume to form a worthwhile prospect, the company started considering pack designs and names. A rough-spun hessian design was soon chosen for the packaging but it took about a year to find the right name. Literally hundreds of names were discarded before settling on Hob-nobs. This proved an excellent choice and tested well – the evocative blend of farmhouse kitchen hobs and melting knobs of butter conjuring up exactly the right images of home-baked country goodness.

By early 1984, the final piece of research could be done. A full scale **quantitative research** study of a large sample of consumers was carried out to provide hard statistical data on the likely market acceptance. This revealed that two-thirds of the sample liked the product 'very much'. The study also indicated a high 'intention to purchase' level.

These results confirmed the findings from the earlier qualitative work. Accordingly, Hob-nobs were launched later that year, though initially only in selected **test markets**, in order to assess the level of sales before the commitment of a full national launch. In the event, the rate of trial purchases in the test regions of Scotland and Lancashire was so encouraging, with over 60 per cent of shoppers who tried the product also making repeat purchases, that the company immediately went ahead with the **national roll-out**. Sales soared once Hob-nobs became available throughout the country – a tribute to the thorough research carried out behind the scenes at every stage of their development.

Fig. 4.1 Hob-nobs: product and pack design

4.2 Common uses of market research

Table 4.1 (overleaf) shows the areas of marketing research most frequently used by firms, based on a survey of the largest American corporations.

The table shows that firms use market research studies to guide decision making on a wide variety of marketing issues. Yet despite these differences in purpose most research projects are actually based on a very similar approach following an established sequence of stages. These stages are shown in fig. 4.3 on page 50.

4.3 Types of research

Having decided to go ahead with a market research study, the next step is to determine what type of research would be best. It is important, first of all, to make sure that the right issue is being investigated. For example, a problem of declining sales could be due to any number of reasons connected with the quality of the product itself, the price that is set, the places through which it is distributed, or the way in which it is promoted. Alternatively, the falling sales could simply be a result of competitors having lowered their prices.

(a) Qualitative research

It would obviously be a huge waste of time and money for the firm to embark on a research project looking into the effectiveness of their own advertising, for example, if the real problem lies elsewhere. This is why research campaigns generally start with a small scale **qualitative research** study, in order to establish the true nature of the problem or issue that needs to be explored by the later statistical study.

Table 4.1 Marketing research activities

Research activity

Sales and market research

- Measurement of market potential
- Market share analysis
- Determination of market characteristics
- Sales analysis

Business economics and corporate research

- Short-range forecasting
- Long-range forecasting
- Studies of business trends
- Pricing

Product research

- New product acceptance and potential
- Competitive product studies
- Testing of existing products
- Packaging research

Advertising research

- Motivation research
- Copy research
- Media research
- Studies of ad effectiveness

Source: *Survey of Marketing Research*, American Marketing Association Chicago, 1983.

There are two forms of qualitative research:

(i) Individual depth interview   These are detailed one-to-one interviews between the researcher and consumer or organizational buyer. They are used in situations where the subject matter is such that consumers are unlikely to express their true views in front of others or where in-depth probing is required to discover underlying motivations.

(ii) Group discussions   These are discussions involving a small group of six to eight people of similar backgrounds and interests brought together to discuss a particular product or issue. A researcher will moderate and guide the discussion to ensure that the relevant points are covered. Discussion groups are often watched through a one-way mirror by marketers from the firm which commissioned the research. **Focus groups** are smaller versions of group discussions where the number of participants is limited to three or four.

Qualitative research is aimed at getting consumers to reveal their true feelings which often lie buried in the subconscious of their minds. According to Eric Clark in his book *The Want Makers*, 'Groups are sometimes encouraged not only to talk, but to act, to play, even to paint or to model. They are urged to pretend to be salesmen or creators of adverts, or even to be the brand itself which has sprung into walking and talking life. They may be asked to finish stories that begin with openings such as "*x* (the brand) went to a party one day and . . .". Consumers may be asked to link brands or products with pieces of music or pretty pictures.'

These are called **projective techniques**, where the image or opinion that a consumer has of a product is 'projected' onto another object or situation. Respondents often find it much easier to express their opinions in these ways rather than by trying to explain what they think or feel in words.

Both types of qualitative research are conducted by trained interviewers who are skilled at probing consumers' thought processes. Opinions and attitudes are often revealed more freely in these loosely structured situations. These are then interpreted by the interviewers in their reports, which tend to include many direct quotes from comments made during the interviews or the group discussions.

Qualitative research is exploratory in nature. It provides useful pointers which help to identify and clarify the exact nature of the issue or problem that needs to be investigated. The insights gained also shape the design of the later quantitative study since it is important to know what type of questions to ask and how to ask them.

(b) Quantitative research

A full scale **quantitative research** study is based on a statistically valid sample of a target market. The results should predict how the entire market will behave (to within a small margin of error). Quantitative research is therefore confirmatory in nature, providing the hard statistical data that managers need to make sound commercial decisions. For this reason, quantitative research is often described as the 'counting noses' part of market research, in contrast to qualitative research which can be defined as the process of 'getting into people's heads' in order to discover their true attitudes and feelings.

> **Case study   The mystery of the declining sales**   When sales of Agatha Christie's books began to show a marked decline by the mid 1980s after many decades of booming sales, it was an unexpected turn of events for William Collins, the publishers who were responsible for handling the majority of her books. Could this be the result of a decline in the popularity of crime fiction as a whole or was it that Agatha Christie had begun to lose her appeal as a crime writer? Might some other factor be involved like the book covers not being sufficiently attractive or not enough money being spent on promotion? Perhaps it was simply that book sales were declining through a general lack of interest in reading due to increased levels of television viewing.

To provide answers to these questions Collins decided that a full-scale market research study was needed. This may well have been an obvious move for a company marketing fast-moving consumer goods which wanted to find out why sales of its breakfast cereals, shampoos or chocolate bars were falling, but it was a remarkably innovative step for any publishing firm to take.

In the event, the research agency commissioned by Collins in March 1985 to identify the exact nature of the problem and make recommendations as to how it could be solved proved an excellent choice. The 'Queen of Crime' herself would have approved of the thorough and probing research methods adopted by the London based agency James R. Adams and Associates in solving 'The Mystery of the Declining Sales'.

As with any research project, the first stage in the process once the objectives of the study had been defined was to carry out some initial desk research. To find out whether sales of paperbacks were suffering because reading itself was in decline, data from the Target Group Index (TGI), which monitors the buying behaviour of a sample of 24 000 consumers, was purchased and analysed. The analysis showed that the number of adults claiming to have bought a paperback in the previous year had declined by about 5 per cent between 1978 and 1984. Although this was not good news, it did not on its own account for the drop in sales of Christie books.

The TGI also enabled the agency to work out the typical profile of paperback buyers and especially of the 'heavy buyers' – those who had bought more than ten paperbacks a year. They found that the total market was biased towards the young, those in higher socio-economic groups and the better educated. However, the bias towards the higher socio-economic groups was balanced in absolute terms by the larger numbers of people in the lower socio-economic groups. It was also discovered that men were just as likely to be heavy buyers as women and in terms of geographical location the two most important television regions were London, which accounted for nearly 26 per cent of the market and Central, which accounted for nearly 18 per cent.

The analysis of TGI data provided much useful information. However, the real detective work started when the agency wanted to find out whether the entire crime category was becoming less popular and in particular whether Christie as an author was losing her appeal. Desk research from sources of secondary information such as the TGI cannot provide this kind of detailed and specific information. The next step was therefore to conduct field research in order to collect primary information first hand from consumers.

Researchers generally start by carrying out some small-scale qualitative research, usually by holding group discussions, before embarking on a full-scale quantitative research study. In this instance, four discussion groups were consulted. The respondents were all Christie readers and buyers of paperback books. The TGI profiles of paperback readers determined what types of people the agency needed to talk to and the composition of the groups in terms of age, sex and socio-economic grade was therefore closely matched to that of the 'typical' buyer. Two of the groups were held in London and two in the Central television region as these were the regions with the highest concentrations of paperback readers.

Researchers had to cover a lot of ground in the discussions, each of which lasted between one and a half to two hours. As often happens, the sessions yielded some unexpected findings, as well as hinting at a possible clue to the solution of the problem. But before drawing any firm conclusions, the agency advised a repeat study with four further groups who were not Christie readers (but were matched in terms of demographic profile and paperback buying behaviour) to see whether they responded in a similar way to Christie readers.

Both sets of discussions confirmed that there was a great deal of interest in crime fiction. Most importantly, they established that Christie was still viewed as the 'Queen of Crime'. The idea that she was in any way dated as an author received no support, even from non-readers. If anything, Christie's style was seen as unique in many ways. Her books encouraged involvement. Readers were always trying (and failing!) to guess the identity of the murderer. An interesting finding was that her books were always seen as having 'nice' murders, unlike those of other crime writers.

In fact, this last discovery actually proved the most important clue in the mystery. Reactions in the group discussions to the current range of book covers revealed that people thought the covers, which usually featured scenes of blood and gore, were nothing like the Christie stories at all (see fig. 4.2). Surprisingly, the fact that cover designs had gradually become more gruesome over the years was not a result of any definite policy decision. Designs had simply been influenced by the rising tide of horror books. Nevertheless, the problem facing Collins was a classic example of the double turn-off. The horror-style covers were repelling Christie's natural market of readers who liked her 'nice' murders. At the same time, the readers who were attracted by the gruesome covers were probably disappointed by the lack of gory details in her stories.

Collins reacted quickly. It was not physically possible to change all of their 68 Christie titles immediately but they quickly brought out six new cover designs based on the ideas raised in the discussions. These were then tested on four new groups of Christie readers who found them to be intriguing and subtle which was, of course, a far better reflection of the Christie style.

The launch, backed by a £25 000 sales campaign aimed at the

Fig. 4.2 Agatha Christie Books

retail trade, produced an immediate response. In fact, orders from booksellers were coming in so fast that Collins could not afford to delay changing the rest of the covers. As a result, there was no time to carry out the follow-up quantitative study which was originally planned. In theory, the results from discussion groups should always be confirmed by quantitative research before business decisions are made. But in the real world, this is not always possible.

In this case, the response to the new cover design was too positive to ignore. The impact was such that sales of Agatha Christie paperbacks increased by 40 per cent during the first year following the changes – from 1 million to 1.4 million. They have since remained buoyant at around 1.2 million a year. The boost in sales also encouraged the Christie estate to hand over to Collins the ten remaining paperbacks which had previously been handled by another publisher.

The legendary Miss Marples and Hercule Poirot would probably have been the first to agree that the detailed research investigation which led to this sales success rivalled in many ways some of their own best detective work!

Source: Adapted from *The Mystery of the Declining Sales*, Sue Williams, *Survey* magazine, Summer 1989.

4.4 Defining research objectives

There are two types of research objectives: problems and opportunities. A problem-based research project might be set up with the objective of discovering why sales of a previously successful product are starting to decline. An opportunity-based research project, on the other hand, might involve assessing the potential consumer acceptance for a proposed new product. See fig. 4.3.

In practice, of course, the two categories are often interrelated. The marketing moral in the old saying that 'Problems are really opportunities in disguise' is neatly made in the well-worn story of the two sales representatives from rival watch manufacturers who are sent to assess the market potential of some remote Pacific islands. One sends back a telegram, 'Regret no one here wears a watch. Stop. Returning at once.' The other sends the message, 'No one here has a watch. Stop. Send all available stock.' Firms can, in much the same way, turn what seem to be potential problems into opportunities.

Types of data
After the research objectives have been agreed, the next step is to decide what sources of data should be used and how the data should be obtained. Researchers have the option of using two types of data:

(i) Secondary data   Data which has been previously collected by others. The process of collecting this data is called **desk research**. It is available either from internal sources within the firm such as sales reports, account records and so on, or from external sources outside the firm such as government and other official publications, trade journals, research reports as well as market studies by commercial research organizations. Much of this data is available as continuous research.

(ii) Primary data   Data which has been collected firsthand from consumers. There are three principal methods of collecting primary data: survey, observation and experiment. The process of collecting this data involves conducting original **field research**. Unlike continuous research, it is generally carried out on an ad-hoc or occasional basis, in order to obtain the kind of information that is not available from 'off-the-peg' desk research.

4.5 Desk research

(i) Internal sources   Firms generally start by looking at the existing information available internally within the firm such as accounts records, reports from service engineers and sales representatives, as well as more informally reported feedback from buyers, customer service departments and so on. This information can show:

- whether sales fall into a clear pattern by type of product, by customer, by geographical area or by season;

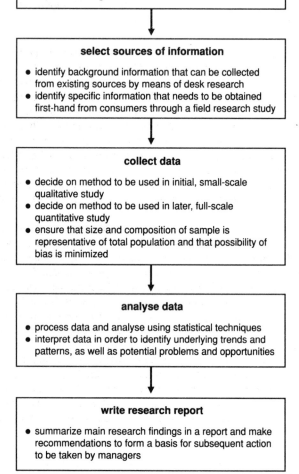

Fig. 4.3 Stages in the marketing research process

- which product lines are most/least profitable;
- which customers account for most/least sales revenue;
- how sales vary in different parts of the country;
- how sales vary at different times of the year;
- what proportion of sales quotations result in actual orders;

● whether the company is becoming too dependent on a few customers or products;
● which methods of promotion were most/least effective.

However, internal sources can only provide a limited amount of information, which means firms then have to look at the published data available from external sources.

(ii) External sources The range of data published by outside agencies is vast. Some of the most commonly used sources are listed in fig. 4.4.

Of the government publications, the national population census carried out every ten years provides marketers with invaluable information on the age, sex, social class and racial composition of households as well as occupation and employment details. The *General Household Survey* and *Family Expenditure Survey* also provide much useful information on the characteristics of households. The *Business Monitor* series of reports, produced quarterly, provides detailed information on specific industrial markets together with more general figures on imports and exports, employment and inflation rates. *British Business*, available weekly, is perhaps the best source of official statistics published recently.

Information on specific companies can be obtained from the *Kompass Register* and *Who Owns Whom* as well as from Companies House, whilst Extel Services hold details from the published accounts of companies. *The Times 1000*, published annually, ranks the largest companies in Britain on the basis of their turnover and briefly summarizes their financial performance.

The huge range of trade and professional association journals are a rich source of information on specific markets. Up-to-date information on the economy and specific markets and industries can also be gained from some of the national 'quality' newspapers and magazines.

Commercial research agencies produce reports on particular markets which are available on payment of a subscription fee. Mintel reports on a particular product would cover areas such as the market share of the main competitors, the total size of the market and projected growth levels together with details of changing trends. *Retail Business* produces similar reports specializing in retailing.

Market information is also provided by **retail audits**, such as the Neilsen Retail Audit, which measure the performance of products sold through the retail chains. The collection of sales data has been transformed in recent years by the widespread use of electronic point of sales (EPOS) tills at checkouts which record sales automatically. The data enables manufacturers to monitor the performance of their products relative to those of competitors and to assess the impact of changes in advertising, packaging, price or any other factor.

Details on purchasing behaviour can also be obtained from the published surveys of **consumer panels**, who record their purchases or viewing habits in a diary. The data collected is analysed in order to determine the characteristics

General Government Publications	Specialized Government Publications
Annual Abstract of Statistics *Abstract of Regional Statistics* *Monthly Digest of Statistics* *Regional Trends* *Social Trends* *Economic Trends* *Statistical News* *Overseas Trade Statistics* *National Income & Expenditure*	*Employment Gazette* *National Food Survey* *General Household Survey* *Family Expenditure Survey* *Business Monitor* Series *Census of Population* *Financial Statistics* *Transport Statistics*

Other Official Publications	Quasi-Official Publications

British Business
Inland Revenue Statistics
Monopolies Commission Report
Also reports by the Departments of
Trade and Industry, Health,
    Transport, etc.
	Trade Association Year Books
	Who Owns Whom (Dun & Bradstreet)
	Kompass Register
	Stock Exchange Year Book
	The Times 1000
	Bank Reviews
	Extel Services
	Trades Union Congress (TUC) Reports
	Confederation of British Industry
	    (CBI) Reports

Commercial Research Reports	Industrial/Trade Journals
Mintel *Keynote* *Euromonitor* *Retail Business*	*The Grocer* *Cabinet Maker and Retail Furnisher* *The Engineer* *Petroleum Review*

National Press/Magazines	Professional/Management Journals
Financial Times *The Economist* *Investors' Chronicle*	*Director* *Management Today* *Marketing Week* *Accountancy Age*

Fig. 4.4 Some of the commonly used sources of secondary data

of the heavy users of each brand or product. Marketers can then design their advertising with the 'typical' buyers of their brands in mind.

Other studies measure TV audience levels (BARB) and readership levels of newspapers and magazines (JICNARS). All these studies are examples of **continuous research** and enable marketers to monitor changing trends and forecast future trends. The principal market tracking studies are shown in Table 4.2.

Table 4.2 The principal market tracking studies

Name of study	Size of sample	Data collection method	Type of data collected	Reporting period
Superpanel National Shopping Monitor AGB Market Information	8500 households	Home equipment scans bar codes, sends information directly to central computer	Purchasing patterns in relation to goods in 350 product fields. Groceries, toiletries, appliances, etc.	Weekly and four-weekly reports
Target Group Index (TGI) British Market Research Bureau (BMRB)	24 000 consumers New sample every year	Self-completion questionnaire	Purchasing patterns in relation to a sample of 4500 brands in 500 fields. Also information relating to media habits	Bi-annual and annual reports
TV Audience Levels Broadcasters Audience Research Bureau (BARB) in conjunction with AGB	4500 households 9000 consumers classified by demographic characteristics	Device plugged into the TV set records when the set is switched on and which channel is being watched by particular household members	Measures viewing audience for each channel broken down by demographic composition	Weekly and monthly reports
Target Group Ratings (TGR) BMRB/BARB	9000 consumers	Links purchase data from part of the TGI sample with TV viewing audience data from BARB	Links the purchasing patterns of consumers with their media habits. Enables marketers to target their advertising very specifically i.e. brands can be advertised during programmes which are popular with their heaviest users	Bi-annual reports. Interim updates every six weeks
The National Readership Survey (NRS) JICNARS Research Services Ltd	28 000 consumers classified by demographic characteristics	Face-to-face questionnaire by in-home interview	Readership patterns of approximately 250 newspapers and magazines	Bi-annual and annual reports

Desk research plays an important role in 'setting the scene' by providing background information and is, therefore, a useful starting point in any research investigation.

This information can show:

- the size of the market;
- whether it is expanding or declining;
- the market shares held by the main competitors;
- changing trends in the economy as a whole;
- changing trends in consumer behaviour;
- the demographic composition of markets.

Much of this background information, details on competitors' performance, for instance, could not be obtained from field research. The fact that most secondary data is carried out on a continuous research basis and is published at regular intervals enables marketers to monitor changing conditions and forecast future trends. As desk research involves using data collected by others, it also has the benefit of being much quicker and cheaper than field research.

However, it is precisely because the data is collected by outside agencies, for their own purposes, that it may not be directly relevant or sufficiently detailed. It may also be out of date or biased in some way.

If the secondary data collected does prove to be inadequate for whatever reason, firms usually then undertake some field research in order to obtain primary data firsthand from consumers.

4.6 Field research

(a) Observation

This method of collecting data involves a trained observer (or hidden camera) being used to watch consumer behaviour unobtrusively. In a supermarket, it can be used to record how customers move around the aisles, whether they react to special displays and promotions and how they scan items on shelves before selecting what to buy. Observation can provide the answers to such questions as: How long do shoppers stand in front of a display? Which shelves do they look at? How many brands do they pick up?

In recent years, specially designed cameras have been developed which track the eye movements of people when they are reading a newspaper or magazine or watching a television advertisement. The position of the pupils is measured at short intervals by a beam of infra-red light and is recorded onto a computer tape. When the tape is connected to a video and played back, a bouncing ball of light shows where the eyes were positioned on the page or TV screen and how long they stopped there.

The fact that researchers can follow the way in which people have read a newspaper or magazine or watched a commercial on television enables them to measure the impact of advertisements in terms of the attention they have attracted. It can also help to identify which parts of an advertisement have succeeded in grabbing people's attention and which have not. One company decided to remove the famous (and very expensive) celebrity they had been using in their advertisement, after eye-tracking tests revealed that the star had not attracted any more attention than an ordinary actor.

The main advantage of observation methods is that they measure what people actually do rather than what they say they do. This distinction is clearly illustrated by a piece of research quoted in *The Want Makers* by Eric Clark. A New York based research company put TV cameras into 150 homes in a project for a group of electricity supply companies who were concerned as to why their projections about the amount of fuel people would use were constantly below the real figures. The research company's findings after studying the video films was that, 'people might say they kept the thermostats at sixty-eight degrees, but it turned out they fiddled with them all day. Older relatives and kids – especially teenagers – tended to turn them up, and so did cleaning ladies. Even visitors did it. In a lot of homes, it was guerrilla warfare over the thermostat between the person who paid the bills and everyone else.'

In distinguishing between *claimed* behaviour and *actual* behaviour, observational methods are therefore more objective and valid than consumer's own reports on their behaviour. However, it is this very objectivity which also constitutes their main limitation. Observational methods merely record what people do. They cannot explain why people do what they do – the underlying thought process, attitudes, opinions and values which motivate their behaviour or the influence exerted by lifestyle and other factors.

(b) Experimentation

The experimental method aims to discover the influence of one particular factor on another, in order to discover possible cause and effect relationships between them. Firms usually carry out experiments when they want to gauge the effect of a change in some aspect of the marketing mix – such as a change in the ingredients, design or packaging of the product itself, the price it is sold for or the way it is advertised.

The method works best when one or two changes only are tested and the influence of other factors is held constant or controlled, which means 'all other things being equal'. For example, a firm making soft drinks may think that a 20 per cent increase in sales of its fruit juices is due to a recent change in advertising. However, if other factors were not controlled, the sales increase could just as easily have been created by an exceptionally hot summer, a rise in the price of competitors' products and so on.

In order to avoid the distorting effect of random factors, most experiments are based on the scientific principles adopted in laboratory experiments and clinical drug trials.

The stimulus being tested is applied to an **experimental group** but not to the **control group**. The composition of the control group is matched as closely as possible to the experimental group in order to avoid possible bias. Companies can then determine the impact of a given stimulus, such as a new product formulation or price change, by comparing the effect on sales in the experimental and control groups.

However, in the real business world, where laboratory conditions cannot be replicated exactly, it is very difficult, and sometimes impossible, to ensure that all other factors remain constant.

(c) Survey methods

The survey is the most commonly used method of collecting primary data. In theory, the total potential target group for a particular product or service is capable of being surveyed. This is known as the total population or **universe**. However, it is clearly impractical to survey all members of such large groups as married women, car owners or businesses with large numbers of employees. It makes sense, therefore, for researchers to survey a small **sample** of the potential universe. The characteristics of the sample should ideally be representative of the total population and the size of the sample should be large enough to give a statistically valid result. Researchers have the option of using two methods:

- **probability or random samples**　All members of the universe have an equal or known chance of being included in the sample as the selection is made randomly, often from electoral registers or telephone directories. However, it is important to remember that both these commonly used sources are not completely random. The electoral register eliminates those under 17 and the homeless. The telephone directory, by definition, includes only those households with a telephone and is therefore biased towards higher-income households. The results obtained can be used to predict the way the total universe will behave to within a certain margin of statistical error, the degree of accuracy varying according to the size of sample.
- **Non-probability samples**　All members of the universe do not have an equal or known chance of being included in the sample as the selection is made by the researchers. The data cannot, therefore, be regarded as statistically valid because of the possibility of bias.

(i) Probability or random samples

- **simple random samples**　This is where the sample is drawn at random from names or numbers, which are nowadays usually generated from computer lists.
- **systematic random samples**　This is where every nth name is selected from a list. In the case of a market with a total population of 4000 people, it might be decided to survey a sample of 100 people. When the target market of 4000 is divided by the sample size of 100, it can be seen that there are 100 groups of 40 people in all. In order to produce a systematic random sample of 100, a number is first chosen between 1 and 40. If the number 18 is chosen, for instance, the researcher would need to include in the sample the people who are 18th, 58th, 98th, 138th and so on, within the list of 4000 people.
- **stratified random samples**　Both these methods do not, however, discriminate well in markets where some customers account for a higher proportion of sales than others. A simple random sample or systematic random

sample is unlikely to reflect exactly the make-up of a population or universe. A stratified random sample can, on the other hand, be designed so that the sample selected matches the population in some important respects, such as the proportion of 18 to 35 year olds. For example, to discover the proportion of frequent cinema goers in the population, it would be important to ensure that the sample is made up of the same proportion of 16 to 20 year olds as there are in the population.

This is of course based on the assumption that most cinema-goers are 16 to 20 year olds. The accuracy of any stratified sample obviously depends on the relevance of the stratification criteria which have been chosen. In practice, researchers frequently do not know what the important stratification criteria are for the particular market they are investigating, so they tend to use common discriminating factors such as age, sex, geographical location and so on.

- **cluster samples** In theory, a truly random nationwide sample would include consumers from all over the country. However, it is obviously very difficult, time consuming and expensive to survey a sample of people who are scattered so far apart. For this reason, researchers will often draw samples from a small number of accessible areas or clusters, which are considered to be representative of the market being studied.

(ii) Non-probability samples

- **judgement samples** The selection of which people are to be included in the sample is based on the researchers knowledge and judgement that those consumers accurately represent the market being investigated. For instance, in testing a new brand of convenience meals it might be decided to interview only married women who work full time as they might be regarded as the most likely buyers of convenience meals.

  However, the main drawback of this method is that in making this kind of assumption the researcher may well be excluding other groups of potential buyers. A high proportion of elderly people, single people and students are also likely to buy ready meals as are many full time housewives.

- **convenience samples** The choice of people to be included in the sample is based on the researchers choosing any convenient area where large groups of people are to be found. The sample could be made up of passers by at a nearby shopping centre or of people going to and from places like railway stations, office buildings and so on.

- **quota samples** The sample is composed of a certain number of people from each particular group, usually divided up on the basis of factors relevant to the market being researched, such as heavy users of a particular product or people who fall into a particular age or socio-economic group. For example, an interviewer might be given a quota of 20 people who use Brand *x* more than once a week to interview.

  In theory, the setting of quotas should reduce the possiblility of bias.

However, in practice, bias can still be introduced because interviewers differ in the way they interpret and collect quota samples. For example, interviewers might draw their entire quotas from one place – a university, army barracks or hospital, which would obviously have the effect of making the sample unrepresentative.

Generally, quota sampling is chosen in preference to other methods when time and cost are important considerations. Unlike random sampling methods, in quota sampling interviewers do not have to spend time and money contacting selected people.

4.7 Collecting survey data

There are three basic types of survey methods used to collect primary data. The advantages and disadvantages of each method are shown in Table 4.3.

Table 4.3 Types of survey methods

	Advantages	Disadvantages
Postal surveys	• This is the cheapest method of surveying large numbers of people. • Samples can be drawn nationally or even internationally. • There is no danger of interviewer bias. • Answers tend to be accurate and truthful as the questionnaires are generally completed anonymously.	• The responses take a long time to collect. • It is an inefficient method of collecting data as the response rate tends to be very low, generally between 5–20 per cent. However, the response rate can be increased if an incentive is offered like the chance of winning in a prize draw. Alternatively, people can be rung beforehand to check whether they are willing to respond. • There is a danger of bias because of the large proportion of people in the sample who do not respond. • Questions need to be short and simple as interviewers are not available to deal with any queries that may arise. • Questionnaires need to be short if the response rate is to be increased. • Data may be incomplete if questions are left out or answered wrongly.

	Advantages	Disadvantages
Personal interviews	● Interviews are carried out face-to-face so interviewers can give explanations where necessary. ● This method produces the best quality and quantity of data. In qualitative interviews, the questions are open, enabling valuable insights to be gained, although the data obtained is difficult to collate. In quantitative interviews, the questions are closed, allowing a limited number of possible answers, which makes the data easy to collate. ● Product samples, photographs or other objects may be used to stimulate responses.	● It is an expensive method to administer, particularly if the required sample is time-consuming to collect. ● There is a danger of interviewer bias. ● Some people may be embarrassed to answer truthfully in front of the interviewer. ● Some people may give the answers they think the interviewer expects them to give.
Telephone interviews	● This is the most efficient method of surveying large numbers of people quickly. ● Samples can be drawn nationally or even internationally. ● It is a fairly inexpensive method. ● Interviews can be conducted quickly. ● Interviews are carried out over the telephone so interviewers can give explanations where necessary. ● Answers can be keyed directly into the computer database, which saves the time and money spent in-putting data at a later stage, as with the paper-based questionnaires used in the other two methods.	● The sample is restricted to those people with telephones. ● It is very common for companies to give a list of their customers' phone numbers to the research agency. Agencies also have systems for random dialling of phone numbers. ● Questions need to be kept short and simple as respondents may become impatient and cut short the interview. ● Some people may refuse to participate if they have previously experienced callers using market research as a pretext for selling double glazing, life insurance and so on.

It is worth remembering that the results from all three survey methods are biased to a certain extent in that the samples consist only of people willing to be interviewed or willing to fill in a postal questionnaire. These respondents may not be representative of all consumers.

A much greater degree of bias can be introduced if the interviewers themselves are inexperienced, careless or even downright dishonest. It is not unknown for interviewers to fake the answers to their questionnaires!

To ensure the reliability of data from personal or telephone surveys most research firms train their interviewers thoroughly. They usually also operate a follow-up system to supervise their interviewers which involves writing to, or telephoning, about 10 per cent of the sample to check on how the interview was conducted.

Questionnaire design

Having decided on the size of the sample and the method which is to be used for collecting the data, the next step is to design the questionnaire. There are three types of questions which may be used:

(i) Structured or closed questions   These demand short, specific answers. **Dichotomous questions** are commonly used which allow only two possible answers – often 'yes' or 'no'. Multiple choice questions and check-list questions are used occasionally. Various ranking techniques are used when researchers want to measure the strength of a preference.

The data obtained from closed questions is easy to collate because the range of possible answers is limited. The results are therefore clear-cut and unambiguous. However, the questions cannot yield any unexpected insights.

(ii) Unstructured or open questions   These allow respondents complete freedom to express their answers in any way they wish. Picture completion and story completion are examples of techniques used. Open-ended questions are very useful for probing consumers' attitudes, opinions and feelings. Valuable insights are also gained because respondents are not channelled by a set of predetermined answers.

However, the data obtained from open questions is difficult to collate because of the tremendous variety of answers received. The results need to be analysed by trained researchers who are skilled at interpreting the pattern of responses.

(iii) Semi-structured questions   These are structured questions which allow a certain amount of freedom in answering. The most frequently used techniques involve sentence completion and word association.

Examples of these different types of question are shown in Table 4.4.

Once the type of question to be used has been chosen, the questions are arranged so that the information is collected in a logical order. Care is also taken to ensure that the questionnaire does not take too long to complete. Standard questions on age, income and so on tend to be placed at the end since they are of little interest to the person being interviewed. Any difficult questions are more likely to be answered if they also occur at the end, at a stage when respondents are committed psychologically to finishing having already got that far. Most importantly, the actual wording of the questions needs to be checked carefully. There are four main pitfalls to be avoided:

- **leading questions** Biased questions which lead people into answering a certain way. For example, 'Should British people buy high quality home-produced washing machines rather than imported foreign washing machines?'
- **ambiguous questions** Vague or misleading questions which do not make it clear what information is required, and which can therefore be answered in many different ways. For example, 'What kind of car do you own?' (A Ford? A sports car? A new car?)
- **unanswerable questions** Specific and detailed questions which respondents cannot be expected to know or remember. For example, 'How many packets of crisps have you bought in the last six months?' 'What brand of after-shave does your father use?'
- **questions that respondents are unwilling to answer** Difficult questions which pry into sensitive areas of people's personal and private lives. For example, 'How often do you have a bath or shower?' 'How much money do you have saved?'

These kinds of flawed questions, particularly misleading questions, can easily slip through without being detected. However, potential problems can be avoided if the questionnaire is first piloted with a small sample before being used on the full sample.

4.8 Analysing survey data

Once all the data has been gathered together, the responses are fed into a computer database to be processed. It is then ready for analysis, which is generally done by a series of complex statistical techniques. It is important that the analysis requirements are considered when the research is first designed to ensure that the right sort of questions are asked and that a sufficient number of respondents are questioned.

It is only when data has been analysed and interpreted that it becomes converted into information. Until the underlying trends and patterns are revealed, data remains a meaningless jumble of facts and figures. The process of analysis and interpretation highlights potential problems and opportunities and enables changing trends to be identified. At this stage, the implications of the results can be translated by researchers into recommendations for action.

These proposals provide managers with a sound basis for decision making. However, before going ahead with any decisions made on the strength of research findings, it is important for managers to establish that the research methods which have been used are valid for their purposes and that the correct conclusions have been drawn from the results.

Table 4.4 Questionnaire techniques

	Types of question	How answer to question is chosen	Examples of question
STRUCTURED QUESTIONS	Dichotomous	One of two answers	Have you used the bus service for this journey before? Yes. . . . . . . No. . . . .
	Checklist	Any number of applicable statements	Why did you use the bus service for this journey today? Direct service from home —— Cheapness of bus fares —— Quickest form of transport —— Do not drive —— Have a bus pass ——
	Multiple choice	One answer from four or five answers	How far did you travel on this journey? Less than 1 mile —— 1–3 miles —— 3–7 miles —— Over 7 miles ——
	Likert scale	One statement indicating the extent of agreement or disagreement	I would use the bus service to make this journey again. Strongly Disagree —— Disagree —— No opinion —— Agree —— Strongly Agree ——

Semantic differential	One point on a scale between two opposing statements	Did you find the bus on this journey: Crowded ---:---: Uncrowded On time ---:---: Delayed Clean ---:---: Dirty Comfortable ---:---: Uncomfortable
Ranking scale	One statement indicating the strength of preference	The attitude of the bus driver on this journey was: Excellent _____ Very Good _____ Good _____ Fair _____ Poor _____
SEMI-STRUCTURED QUESTIONS		
Word association	First word that springs to mind associated with a word or phrase	State the first word you think of when you hear the following: bus shelters; bus conductors; smoking on buses; bus fares; bus timetables; dangers on buses.
Sentence completion	The remaining part of a sentence is completed	The worst aspect of this bus journey was . . .
UNSTRUCTURED QUESTIONS		
Story completion	A story is composed based around a few opening lines which have been provided	When I eventually managed to get on the bus that day I felt angry because all the buses were late again. They should do something about it. . . .
Picture completion	The conversation featured between two characters in a scene is continued	

Case study   *Coca-Cola*   **A classic move?**   In April 1985 the
Coca-Cola Corporation announced that for the first time in 99
years it was changing the flavour of the most popular soft drink
in the world.

The change did not come suddenly or cheaply. Between 1981
and 1984 Coca-Cola secretly carried out a massive secret taste-
testing programme, involving some 190 000 respondents in twenty-
five cities in the USA and Canada, and costing about $4 million.
In announcing the new formula, the company revealed that in
various blind tests the new flavour beat the old by a 55:45 ratio,
and when tested against Pepsi the ratio was 56:44. While many
companies would not proceed with anything less than 60:40, Coca-
Cola decided the new flavour was 'it'.

After three months, when Coke's original formula – re-named
Coca-Cola Classic – was brought back after a storm of protest
from Coke fans, *Fortune* magazine reported, 'In what will go
down as one of the classic marketing retreats in the annals of
business, Coca Cola admitted it had goofed by taking old Coke
off the market.'

In 1985 *Fortune* proclaimed, 'Testing must be properly conducted and interpreted to have value. Coca-Cola's recent débâcle
is a classic study in how not to do it. The Company decided to retire
its flagship Coke formula on the basis of taste tests that did not
discriminate between Coke junkies – the six-pack-a-day types –
and occasional sippers. Coca-Cola management not only ignored
its best customers, but also failed to anticipate how the public
would react to the end of a 99-year symbol of American spirit.'

Ironically Coca-Cola may have emerged from the débâcle in a
stronger position to counter the momentum of Pepsi. For several
months afterwards the media argument was about new Coke
versus old Coke, not Coke versus Pepsi.

Source: Adapted from *The New Marketing*,
Richard W. Brookes, Gower Publishing Group.

What lessons can be drawn from the introduction of new Coke? How did
a marketing giant like Coca-Cola manage to get it so wrong? Yet Coca-Cola's
action in changing the formula of old Coke was certainly not taken lightly. The
decision was made in response to intensive market research testing, involving
what was by any standards a large sample.

Coca-Cola's experience in launching new Coke does not, of course, mean
that market research surveys cannot be relied upon to predict consumer
behaviour accurately. Their decision to use **blind tests** when new Coke was
taste-tested stemmed from the need, as with any new product, to maintain complete secrecy. The affair does, however, pin-point the importance of interpreting research findings in the context of the survey method used. Potential
distorting factors can thus be identified. Coca-Cola's experience also highlights

the need for research to ask the right kind of questions from a sample made up of the right sort of respondents.

An executive assistant at Coca-Cola is quoted in a January 1989 article in *Marketing* magazine as saying, 'The problem was that the research was top secret – in effect, the product was being blind tested. People preferred the new formula, but had no idea they were rejecting Coca-Cola. No one asked: "If we changed Coke, would you still buy it?" Consequently, we completely missed the depth of brand loyalty to Coke.'

Market segmentation

5.1 Is segmentation necessary?

It was in the 1920s when Henry Ford made his famous statement that customers could have any colour of car they wanted – as long as it was black. From Ford's point of view it probably seemed perfectly logical to dismiss customer preferences. This was the era when demand exceeded supply – his cars were being snapped up as fast as he could turn them out. Why, then, should he bother to offer customers any choice?

The assembly line method of mass production which he had pioneered in 1913 for the Model T Ford meant that production costs were lowered to the point where a car could be afforded by almost anyone – no longer just the very rich. In the space of the next two decades 15 million Model Ts were sold, creating one of the first **mass market** products.

Yet despite having the distinct early advantage of being the lowest cost producer, it was Henry Ford's unwillingness to offer anything other than one model in one colour which allowed the company to fall behind. Ford's dominant position as market leader was eventually overtaken by General Motors (GM), whose policy of providing 'A car for every purse and every purpose', was an early example of **market segmentation**.

GM had realized that customers have different needs and requirements and therefore want different benefits from a car. Their five models, starting from the basic Chevrolet to the top of the range Cadillac, offered a variety of styles, sizes and levels of luxury to suit a range of tastes and pockets.

Although this strategy made their cars more expensive it enabled GM to gain a market lead which has been maintained to this day. It also established the principle that companies which recognize and cater for different consumer needs will inevitably gain a competitive edge over rival firms who have not segmented their markets and who regard their customers as an identical mass.

Certainly today all car manufacturers cater for consumer wishes to an extent that Henry Ford could never have forseen. Those buying a new car can choose from a wide range of models and decide not only the colour but also the type of upholstery and whether to have sports wheels, power steering, anti-lock brakes, a sun roof and so on. With the help of sophisticated IT systems, Volvo can now offer something like 20 000 variations on its cars to suit the needs of different customers. At the 'luxury' end of the market some customers ordering a new Porsche have even been known to ask the paint-shop to match the colour of their favourite lipstick!

Clearly, market demand no longer exceeds supply as it did when Henry Ford first brought out his Model T. The **production orientation** he demonstrated, where firms produce what they want to make, has been replaced by a **marketing orientation** where firms produce what customers want to buy. It follows from this that firms today recognize that it is unrealistic to presume that one product or service will be suitable for all customers as the groups of people which make up a market all have different needs.

In his book *The Third Wave*, Alvin Toffler has argued that the mass-market society created by the industrial revolution is splintering more and more into a 'de-massified' society. According to Toffler, 'the mass-market has split into ever-multiplying, ever-changing sets of mini-markets that demand a continually expanding range of options, models, types, sizes, colours and customizations'.

So who are these different groups? Certain easily recognized groups have, of course, always been given evocative, if rather imprecise, labels by the popular press. The YUPPIES (Young Urban Professionals) with their designer clothes, mobile phones and obligatory Filofax achieved almost cult status a while back. Since then, new groups such as the GREENS (conservationists) and GREYS (over fifties) have been recognized, not to mention DINKIES (Dual Income, No Kids), WOOPIES (Well Off Older People) and DUMPIES (Desperately Underfinanced Mortgage Paupers).

Though such labels might be a convenient shorthand in the advertising agency world, marketers generally define groups of buyers rather more precisely! Classifications can be based on demographic factors such as people's age, income and social class, and on the type of geographical area they live in. More recently, classifications have distinguished between the kind of lifestyle they lead and attitudes they hold. Increasingly, classifications based on a combination of these factors are being used to discriminate more finely between groups of consumers. The main ways in which markets are segmented are covered later on in the unit. First we need to look at how segmentation is carried out and why it is necessary.

5.2 The process of segmentation

The first step in this process is to conduct research which analyses the market in order to identify groups of buyers within the overall market who share similar needs and have certain behavioural characteristics in common, which distinguish them from other groups of customers.

Once these groups of buyers or **market segments** have been isolated, firms can then decide which segments are likely to contain the most buyers, or the most profitable buyers (who may well be quite a small segment), for their products or services. It is important to remember that the concept of market segmentation is equally applicable to companies providing services. For example, British Airways now treats each class of travel in the same way as manufacturing companies treat their products. In recent years, British Airways has redesigned its Concorde, First Class, Club, Business, Shuttle and Economy Class services to cater for different groups of customers.

Identifying market segments enables firms to establish the position of their products or services in the market relative to those of competitors. For example, *The Sun* has a different **market positioning** to *The Guardian*. Kwik-Save 'no nonsense' foodstores are clearly positioned further 'downmarket' than Sainsbury's or Tesco. In the personal toiletries market, the Body Shop occupies a very different positioning to Boots.

The analysis could also reveal a segment of potential buyers with needs which are not being catered for as yet by products or services currently on the market. The success of Golden Wonder's entry into the UK crisp market in 1960 provides a classic example. Whereas Smiths had traditionally sold crisps through pubs and therefore mainly to men, Golden Wonder identified an undeveloped market segment – housewives buying crisps through grocery shops for domestic consumption. By concentrating its marketing effort on this segment instead (promoting the image of crisps as a nourishing snack food in its television advertisements, using its sales force to persuade more grocery shops to stock crisps and so on), Golden Wonder was successful in penetrating the market. In the process it was responsible for the UK crisp market, worth £40 million in 1960, increasing to £80 million in just five years.

However, although it would present an ideal marketing opportunity, finding such an unexploited 'gap' in the market is becoming increasingly difficult. Nevertheless, it can still be done. The Next empire started from the standpoint that there was a dissatisfied consumer group too old for the boutique but not wild about moving on to Marks and Spencer.

Identifying the most potentially profitable segments means that the marketing effort can be aimed by means of a 'rifle shot' approach directly at the segments selected as worth pursuing. These segments are designated as the firm's **target markets**. This rifle-shot approach is far more effective in reaching buyers and is a less wasteful use of resources than the 'shotgun' approach which scatters the marketing effort across all buyers at random.

Within the car market there are various segments of buyers including those on a budget who buy small cars as well as those who buy family estate cars, company fleet cars, prestige executive cars and so on. A segmented marketing

Fig. 5.1 Shotgun approach

approach could be directed, for instance, at buyers of family estate cars and more specifically at buyers of family estate cars who want a car with a good safety record and even more specifically at such buyers who want a car with a low petrol consumption which is economic to run. This sort of detailed breakdown of the market allows very precise targeting.

However, there is a danger that markets which are segmented ever more finely will, in time, become subdivided to the point where companies may find it uneconomic to cater for such small segments. This **fragmentation** often occurs in crowded markets with many competitors who are all trying to differentiate their products or services from the rest.

5.3 The advantages of segmentation

By using a market segmentation strategy firms can:

- **Define their markets more precisely** Gain a better understanding of the needs and buying behaviour of consumers who make up the markets in which they operate.
- **Devise effective strategies and plans** Meet and satisfy the particular needs of the market segments which are being targeted.
- **Analyse their main competitors** Assess their own strengths and weaknesses in relation to those of their competitors in order to identify any segments where the market leader is so dominant that it is not worth wasting resources in trying to compete.
- **Respond rapidly to changing market trends** Monitor the changing tastes and preferences within a small, precisely defined group. This can be done more easily for a small group than for the population as a whole. Closeness to the needs of their target markets means changes can be identified and acted on quickly.
- **Allocate their resources efficiently** Distribute resources so that they are concentrated on the particular groups of consumers who have been defined as forming the target markets. This is far better than wasting resources, such as the money spent on advertising or the efforts of the sales force, by spreading them over the entire market.
- **Identify gaps in the market** Discover areas of the market where customers' needs are not being catered for as yet.

In view of these advantages the majority of firms do, in fact, divide the overall market into segments in order to concentrate on the target groups which are likely to prove most worthwhile. However, a segmentation strategy is not worthwhile in three situations:

- where the heavy users account for such a high proportion of sales that they are the only segment worth targeting;
- where the dominant product or brand accounts for such a high proportion of sales that there is no point in segmenting the market any further;
- where the total market is in itself worth so little that it is not economic to pursue sales in smaller market segments.

5.4 Methods of segmenting consumer markets

The majority of firms generally do adopt a segmentation strategy. The next step is to decide which method of grouping customers they will use. Some of the main options available to them are shown in fig. 5.2.

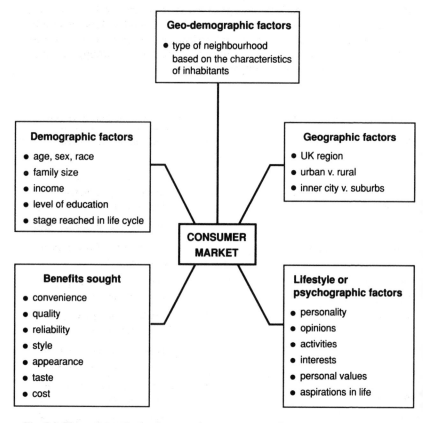

Fig. 5.2 The main methods of segmenting consumer markets

(a) Demographic segmentation
This is the earliest and most commonly used method and involves dividing up the market into categories of people based on their age, sex, income, level of education and socio-economic group.

A glance along the magazine shelves of any newsagent or bookshop illustrates clearly the segmentation of a market by demographic factors. The *Beano* and *Smash Hits* cater for very different age groups in the same way as *GQ* and *Woman's Own* cater for different male and female readerships. Compare the income levels of people reading *Horse and Hound* with that of *Bella* readers. Those reading *The Economist* are likely to have a very different level of education from those reading *Tit Bits*. The *Tatler* and *Harpers and Queen* are aimed at members of a different socio-economic group to readers of *Do It Yourself* magazine.

Marketers are well aware of the different readerships these magazines target and this is reflected in the sorts of products and services advertised within their pages. Similarly, the markets for a great variety of other goods and services including clothes, toiletries, records, electrical goods and holidays can also be divided up on the basis of one or more demographic factors. The market segments catered for by retail outlets within the Burton Group, shown in Table 5.1, provides a good example.

Table 5.1 Market segments catered for by retail outlets within the Burton Group

Retail outlet	Target market group	Age of target market	Fashion profile segment
Dorothy Perkins	women	18–40	Main-stream fashion at mid-range prices
Top Shop	women	15–25	High fashion at popular prices
Principles	women	25–45	Sophisticated classic fashion at higher prices
Evans Collection	women	25–60	Women's wear sizes 14+ at mid-range prices
Burton	men	20–45	Main-stream fashion at mid-range prices
Top Man	men	15–25	High fashion and moderate fashion at popular prices
Principles For Men	men	20–45	Up-dated classic fashion at higher prices
Champion Sport	men, women and children	15–35	Fashionable sportswear and equipment
Debenhams	men, women and children	all ages	Main-stream mass market fashion for the individual and home

Segmentation by socio-economic group has been used widely by marketers as it links aspects of both income and level of education to purchasing behaviour. The classification of social grades shown in Table 5.2 is the standard classification which is in common usage.

Table 5.2 Social grade definitions

Social grade	Social status	Occupation	Percentage of all adults over 15 years
A	Upper middle class	Higher managerial, administrative or professional.	2.6
B	Middle class	Intermediate managerial, administrative or professional.	13.9
C1	Lower middle class	Supervisory or clerical, and junior managerial, administrative or professional.	26.8
C2	Skilled working class	Skilled manual workers.	25.5
D	Working class	Semi and unskilled manual workers.	19.4
E	Those at lowest level of subsistence	State pensioners or widows (no other earner), casual or lowest-grade workers.	11.8

Source: *JICNARS National Readership Survey*, July 1989–June 1990.

Some examples of typical occupations in each category are shown in Table 5.3 opposite.

Critics argue that the National Readership Survey (NRS) method of segmentation has outlived its usefulness as class divisions have become more and more blurred in the forty years since the classification was first developed. For instance, many of the skilled working class in group D have a high enough income to purchase the types of cars, household goods and holidays that were once the exclusive preserve of the middle class in Group B. In addition, there are many old-age pensioners and widows who are not dependent on state benefits and who do not live at the lowest level of subsistence.

The second major criticism of the NRS method is that the classification is based solely on the male 'head of the household' with the occupation of the female only being considered in households where there is no male. However, this assumption is clearly out-dated in view of the high proportion of married women found in the workforce today. Some of these may have a higher income than the male head of the household and some may well be the only wage earners, especially in areas of high unemployment.

In any case, given that the full-time housewife and 'Mum' is fast becoming

Table 5.3 Typical occupations in each social grade

Social class grade	Example of occupations
A Upper middle class	Chief executives and company directors; owners of a business with more than 25 employees; senior civil servants; doctors; headteachers; bishops; pilots; barristers; architects; navy commanders; police chief constables.
B Middle class	Senior managers in industry; owners of a business with 5–24 employees; senior local government officers; pharmacists; older teachers; journalists; accountants; vicars; managers of large firms; police inspectors; navy lieutenants; army captains or majors.
C1 Lower middle class	Junior managers in industry; owners of a business with 1–4 employees; civil servants; bank clerks; social workers; library assistants; nurses; younger teachers; curates; clerical 'white collar' workers in general.
C2 Skilled working class	Foremen responsible for up to 24 employees; plumbers; carpenters; electricians; bricklayers; print workers; skilled coal miners; bus and train drivers; police constables; army corporals.
D Working class	Bus conductors; shop assistants; postmen; farm labourers; fishermen; cleaners; gardeners.
E Those at the lowest levels of subsistence	Old-age pensioners or widows; those dependent on sickness, unemployment or supplementary benefits; casual labourers.

an endangered species, it seems likely that the purchasing power of many households will continue to stem from the joint income of both partners.

In the light of a growing body of evidence confirming the inadequacy of this system of social grading, the stage reached in the **family life cycle** has come to be regarded as a better indicator of consumer behaviour. For instance, it is far more logical to group a couple in their twenties and one in their forties who both have young toddlers as part of the same segment in terms of the stage reached in their life cycle, rather than in two separate segments on the basis of their different ages.

As both couples have reached the stage in their life cycle of starting a family they will have the same needs and requirements – for nappies, baby food, cots, life insurance and so on. They are also similar in facing a drop in disposable income compared to couples who have no children or whose children have grown up and left home.

The most widely used model of the stages which people pass through during their adult lives is that shown in Table 5.4.

Table 5.4 Family life cycles

Age	Developmental level	Stage in the family life cycle
18–34	Early adulthood	1. The bachelor stage: young, single people. 2. Newly married couples: young, no children. 3. The full nest I: young married couples with dependent children (a) youngest child under six; (b) youngest child over six.
35–54	Middle adulthood	4. The full nest II: older married couples with dependent children.
55 and older	Later adulthood	5. The empty nest: older married couples with no children living with them (a) head in labour force; (b) head retired. 6. The solitary survivors: older single people (a) in labour force; (b) retired.

Source: *Consumer Behaviour*, D. Reynolds and W. Wells, McGraw Hill, 1977.

(b) Geographic segmentation

Marked contrasts exist in consumer behaviour between countries. The French, for instance, drink more wine per head of the population and the Germans more beer. Quite large variations in consumption patterns can also be found between different regions of Britain for everything from whisky to white bread. It makes sense, therefore, to segment markets by geographical area.

Most firms allocate their advertising budgets across the country and generally use the areas covered by ITV regions as a convenient basis for dividing Britain into broad geographical areas, as shown in Table 5.5.

On a smaller scale, however, this method does not provide a fine enough distinction between the often starkly contrasting localities which exist within regions – such as the contrasts between densely populated urban areas and thinly populated rural areas or between the decaying, impoverished inner city areas and the prosperous outer suburbs.

(c) Geo-demographic segmentation

A growing awareness of the fact that every regional market is made up of a complex mosaic of local neighbourhoods, each with their own patterns of consumer behaviour, has encouraged marketers to devise a more revealing method of dissecting markets than the classification based on socio-economic grades.

The geo-demographic method is based on the principle that 'people like us live next door to people like us'. In other words, the people found in a particular geographical neighbourhood who live in similar housing will tend to share

Table 5.5 ITV regions

ITV area	TV company
London	Carlton TV/LWT
Midlands	Central TV
North West	Granada TV
Yorkshire/North East	Yorkshire-Tyne Tees TV
Wales and West	HTV
South and South East	Meridian Broadcasting
East	Anglia TV
South West	Westcountry TV
N. Ireland	Ulster TV
Border	Border TV
Central Scotland	Scottish TV
N. Scotland	Grampian TV

many demographic characteristics in common such as age, income, race and so on.

The two geo-demographic systems most commonly used include ACORN (A Classification of Residential Neighbourhoods) which was developed in the late 1970s, and PIN (Pinpoint Identified Neighbourhoods). Geo-demographic systems use data from the census carried out every 10 years, the last one being in 1991, to produce a classification of residential neighbourhoods in the UK. In the Acorn classification, 38 neighbourhood types grouped into 11 broad types were identified, whilst the PIN system adopted a classification of 25 neighbourhood types.

The 11 main Acorn groups are shown in Table 5.6.

Table 5.6 Acorn profile of Great Britain

Acorn groups
Agricultural areas
Modern family housing, higher incomes
Older housing of indeterminate status
Older terraced housing
Council estates — category I
Council estates — category II
Council estates — category III
Mixed inner metropolitan areas
High status non-family areas
Affluent suburban housing
Better-off retirement areas
Unclassified

Source: *CACI Market Analysis.*

Initially, geo-demographic classifications were based on the smallest area for which census data is collected, i.e. the enumeration district, each of which contains about 150 households. However, as these districts are rather small to target economically, they tend now to be grouped into postcode sectors, each of which contains on average between 2000 and 2500 households.

Given that particular types of neighbourhoods are likely to be made up of people with similar demographic characteristics, it was logical for marketers to assume that they would also be likely to contain people with similar lifestyles and buying habits.

A number of systems have been developed based on this principle, including MOSAIC (which identifies 58 lifestyle types), the Littlewoods' SUPER-PROFILES system, and the new ACORN LIFESTYLES. In addition, a host of more specific systems have been developed which classify customers according to their credit rating, the types of savings accounts they hold and so on. The most recent of the so-called 'psychographic classifications' is called PER-SONA. This system has been developed in conjunction with the National Shoppers Survey (NSS), which has a database on the shopping habits of three million households. It defines households on the electoral roll by categories which relate to consumers' priorities and lifestyles.

Another development has been the way classifications such as ACORN, PIN and MOSAIC have been linked with data from other research sources. When used in conjunction with data from surveys of consumer purchasing habits such as the Target Group Index (TGI), this allows very detailed profiles to be drawn up of the typical users of individual brands.

All these methods offer marketers more detailed information than can be gleaned simply from the ABC socio-economic grades. Those six categories seem very basic indeed when compared to the 38 neighbourhood types of the ACORN classifications or the 58 lifestyle groups of the MOSAIC classification which enable markets to be dissected in very fine detail right down to postcode level. When combined with research from other sources, targeting can be aimed even more precisely at individual households on the electoral roll.

As targeting becomes increasingly accurate, companies using **direct mail** techniques to promote their goods and services are less likely to find their material consigned to the waste-paper bin as 'junk mail'. This is an important consideration, particularly when you consider that, in 1990, 2.3 million mail shots were sent out in the UK, equivalent to an average of 38 items per head. There will be far less wastage when companies distribute samples and money-off coupons to encourage trial usage of their products. These methods have also proved useful in helping retail firms to decide if they should set up in a particular location. By analysing the neighbourhood around the projected store, retail chains can assess whether there are enough customers of the right type in the surrounding catchment area.

(d) Lifestyle segmentation
According to a typical demographic study, Mrs X the average heavy user of 'Dazzle' furniture polish might be 35 years old with 2.4 children, living in the suburbs in a semi-detached house with 3.4 bedrooms, 1.8 television sets and

1.3 cars – hardly the most revealing or useful portrait! Of course, the great appeal of demographic classifications is their simplicity and ease of use. But it is this very simplicity which also constitutes their main weakness in that they paint a rather sterile picture of the typical consumer for a particular product or service. It is hardly surprising, therefore, that marketers have gone beyond the kind of bland information provided by demographic studies, and looked instead at lifestyle studies to provide them with a more realistic profile of their customers.

Lifestyle analysis describes people in terms of their interests, personalities, opinions, values and day-to-day activities. This information is gained by asking a sample of people to respond to a list of lifestyle statements by stating how well each one describes themselves – very well, fairly well, not very well or not at all. The pattern of answers that emerges reveals a set of beliefs, values and personality traits which can be used to build a profile of that consumer.

One of the classic lifestyle studies was carried out by advertising agency Leo Burnett for the Schlitz brewing company in the USA. In order to create a suitable campaign they decided to develop a profile of the typical heavy beer drinker at whom the advertising was to be targeted. This was an essential first step in the light of their preliminary market research which showed that heavy drinkers can get through as much as a case of beer a day on their own!

Based on the initial research the agency then wrote a series of lifestyle statements such as:

- 'Beer is a real man's drink.'
- 'Men should not do the dishes.'
- 'I usually read the sports pages.'
- 'I would do better than average in a fist fight.'
- 'I like war stories.'
- 'I like to play poker.'
- 'I smoke too much.'
- 'I'm not very good at saving money.'

The heavy beer drinkers said that statements of this kind described them 'very well' or 'fairly well', whereas few light beer drinkers identified with such statements. The series of advertisements subsequently developed by Leo Burnett, which ran successfully for many years, appealed to this rather 'macho', pleasure-seeking lifestyle by picturing rugged, 'he-man' types in various sporty settings accompanied by slogans such as, 'You only go around once in life – so grab all the fun you can.'

Lifestyle classifications have been developed not just for targeting heavy users of a product but also more generally for identifying broad groups of consumers within the population as a whole. One of the best known examples of this type of classification is known as VALS (values and lifestyles), based on a survey carried out in the USA which grouped together people who had similar profiles of responses to a list of 60 statements. The characteristics of each group are shown in Table 5.7 overleaf.

The idea of this kind of study is to find out what factors motivate these different groups of people to buy. In the car market, for instance, the 'achievers'

Table 5.7 The characteristics of lifestyle groups

Survivors 4 per cent
The most disadvantaged group. The old, poor, sick and those with little education.

Sustainers 7 per cent
Those who live on the edge of poverty. They do not suffer from the depression and hopelessness of survivors and aim to 'get on'. Many operate in the underground economy.

Belongers 39 per cent
The large group who make up the solid middle class. They are stable, patriotic, conservative and content with their lives. Their key drive is to fit in and not stand out.

Emulators 8 per cent
They are ambitious, upwardly mobile, status conscious, competitive and want to 'make it big'. Mainly young, they have little faith in 'the system'.

Achievers 20 per cent
These are the leaders in society. Mainly middle aged. Affluent, successful, hard working and materialistic, they would defend the economic status quo.

I-am-me 3 per cent
They are young, impulsive and individualistic.

Experiential 6 per cent
They are passionately involved with others and tend to be attracted to the strange, mystic or natural. Often the most artistic people.

Societally conscious 11 per cent
They have a high sense of social responsibility. Often do volunteer work and live simple, frugal lives. Tend to support causes.

Integrated 2 per cent
They are psychologically mature. Self-assured. Well-balanced and able to see many sides of an issue.

Source: Adapted from *Values and Lifestyles of Americans*, SRI International, 1983.

would buy luxury cars as status symbols, whilst 'belongers' are likely to buy practical, family cars and would probably not dream of buying a foreign car. Groups such as the 'societally conscious' would look for cars that use less fuel.

A more recent classification of lifestyle groups is that developed by market research company Taylor Nelson. They identified three broad groups of people with distinctive lifestyles and social values, which were then further subdivided into seven groups in all. The social values which characterize each group are shown in Table 5.8 opposite.

Classifications which are even more detailed can be compiled. These identify the purchasing habits of consumers in relation to a specific product. An example of this type of classification is the survey carried out by Taylor Nelson for Volkswagen UK. They identified six lifestyle segments for car buyers in the UK based on demographic factors and lifestyle characteristics, linked to their attitudes to cars and to driving.

Table 5.8 The characteristics of lifestyle groups

I The sustenance driven

Aimless 5 per cent of the population.
Often young, unemployed, anti-authority and occasionally violent. Tend to live from day to day looking for excitement or 'kicks'. May get involved in petty crime.

Survivors 16 per cent of the population
Hard-working and stable with a strong community spirit, placing great emphasis on traditional working class values. They look for security and stability above all and as consumers prefer the safety of long established goods and services and reputable brand names.

II The outer directed

Belongers 18 per cent of the population.
Hard-working and traditional, they value home and family life above all else and are concerned to 'fit in'. They are generally house owners with savings and tend to be willing to forgo short-term pleasure in order to achieve long-term aims. As consumers, they are very cautious and risk-averse, preferring to make 'sensible' purchases.

Conspicuous consumers 19 per cent of the population.
Hard working and traditional, they are also concerned to conform but in a more materialistic sense. Concerned with success, this group looks for the good things in life that money can buy. They want to get on at work and socially and therefore look for maximum impact in whatever they buy as a visible display of their achievements.

III The inner directed

Social resisters 11 per cent of the population.
Caring people whose prime concern is improving the quality of life. They are likely to be passionately involved in supporting 'causes' — issues such as environmental protection, disarmament, aid for the third world and so on.

Experimentalists 14 per cent of the population.
Also caring and concerned people, they value individual freedom and self-expression above all, often rejecting traditional values. They are materialistic, open-minded towards change and willing to experiment with new products.

Self-explorers 16 per cent of the population.
Again caring and concerned people, they tend to be more conformist than the social resisters and less materialistic than the experimentalists. As consumers, they are broad-minded and highly discerning.

Source: Adapted from *Social Value Groups,* Applied Futures Unit, Taylor Nelson.

The six groups of car owners they described were: 'Frightened', 'Sunday Driver', 'Small is Beautiful', 'Car Disinterested', 'Pro-Am' and 'Boy Racer'. The labels given to each group reflected their differing attitudes towards cars and to driving in general. 'Boy Racers' are clearly not going to buy the same models as 'Sunday Drivers'! These contrasting attitudes highlight why the advertising campaign for any particular product is likely to be ineffective unless it is targeted specifically at the appropriate segment of buyers.

Case study   Using database marketing to target customers
Should you buy a new car from Saab, be prepared to disclose a
little more than your name and address. Saab will want to know
whether you are single, married or divorced. Have you any
children? Do you enjoy music, rock-climbing or parachuting?
Where do you take your holidays? Which newspapers and
magazines do you read? What are your favourite TV programmes?
And incidentally, why did you choose a Saab?

This interrogation may seem like a gross invasion of privacy, but
no one is obliged to answer Saab's questionnaire. In fact, 95 per
cent of customers fill in the form, says Chris Owens, the company's
UK advertising and direct marketing manager.

Follow-up questionnaires are sent out every six months and
analysed to maintain a comprehensive and up-to-date profile of
typical Saab owners. Customers are asked how frequently they
expect to change their car, and whether they look for safety, performance, innovation or economy when buying a new vehicle.

Owens uses the responses to focus his direct mail and promotional activities on the right audience. 'With only 12 000 new cars
sold each year, 78 per cent to previous customers, our volumes are
small. It is more sensible for us to look for closely targeted campaigns rather than broadcasting our message to the masses with
reams of advertising. The only way we can do it is to obtain an
accurate profile of our existing customers.'

The database enables Saab to measure the effectiveness of
advertising, direct marketing, sponsorship, exhibitions and
coupon mailshots. 'We can find out which promotion pulls in the
best results, and use this knowledge to refine the database for
future use,' Owens says. 'For example, if we had been advertising
in *Gardening World*, and I discovered that none of our customers
were reading it, I'd immediately cross it off our advertising
programme.'

Owens uses his database for joint promotions with companies
whose products are targeted at the same socio-economic group. 'It
also helps us to spot sponsorship opportunities, if, for example,
we find people show a preference for off-shore power-boat racing,
water-skiing, sailing or golf,' he says. The detailed customer profile enables Owens to rent other similar customer lists, thereby
expanding his audience. They also help identify and attack market
opportunities. A series of questions on customers' thoughts about
their car services provides feedback on the quality of Saab's dealer-
ship franchises.

Many companies are expected to adopt similar research techniques during the next few years. Analysts forecast that the £1.7
billion that UK companies spent in 1990 on the use of IT for sales
and marketing will grow at an annual 30 per cent. But if you are

one of those who curse when the letter-box is full of unsolicited catalogues and brochures, take heart. Database marketing should result in less, or at least more appropriate communications. According to one database consultant, 'It means companies can analyse your consumer characteristics and know who is interested in receiving what information. The whole idea is to stop hassling people with junk mail.'

Source: Adapted from *Targeting customers*, Jane Bird, *Management Today*, November 1991.

(e) Benefit segmentation
Another useful method of classification is to divide the market on the basis of the benefits sought by consumers when purchasing a product. An early survey of a group of toothpaste users showed that those who worried about decay prevention tended to choose a brand like Crest whereas those who were more concerned about the brightness of their teeth preferred brands like Macleans and Ultra Brite. In contrast, for those who bought brands such as spearmint flavoured Colgate, the principal benefit being sought was fresh breath.

Benefit segmentation applies to many other products. In the market for watches, for example, young children, trendy teenagers, sporty people, elegant women, divers and those on a limited budget will all be looking for particular benefits in the watch they would choose to buy. Each group will therefore constitute a distinct market segment in terms of the benefits they require.

5.5 Are chosen segments valid?

Whatever method of segmentation is chosen, the next step for marketers is to check whether the segments which have been chosen as target groups actually do warrant the investment which is to be made in them. For segments to be considered worthwhile they must be:

- **Substantial** Of a sufficient size to justify the effort of exploiting them. Even small segments can prove a viable proposition for firms offering expensive goods or services – providing they contain enough people with a high purchasing power.
- **Measurable** Capable of being identified using data which is available or which can be collected through market research.
- **Accessible** Capable of being reached through the normal channels of distribution, for example, shops, supermarkets and the usual media channels such as television, magazines and so on.
- **Unique** Able to respond in a different way to any other segment and therefore require their own marketing approach.

5.6 Segmentation strategies

Once markets have been segmented, by whatever method, firms then need to choose which of the three possible segmentation strategies they intend to adopt.

(a) Mass marketing or undifferentiated marketing

This is where one product or service is sold to the entire market, e.g. Heinz baked beans. Costs are kept low because of the economies of scale which are made possible as a result of producing in huge volumes. It is rare to find this strategy being adopted today – even Coca-Cola, which for many years was the classic example of an undifferentiated product, now offers a range of products aimed at different segments – the health conscious (caffeine free Coke), weight watchers (diet Coke) as well as a range of flavours such as Cherry Coke.

(b) Selective marketing or differentiated marketing

This is where a number of products or services are sold to selected market segments in order to increase overall sales. Costs are, however, higher than in mass marketing. Most large firms target many segments with a range of models, as IBM have done in the computer market. This is true of the large firms in many other industries such as cars, electronics, detergents and packaged food. Increasingly, services are also being differentiated into segments.

(c) Niche marketing or concentrated marketing

This is where firms concentrate on selling to a small market segment or **niche**. Costs can be kept low because of the savings made as a result of specialization. It is a strategy commonly adopted by smaller companies who, although they are not able to compete in the wider mass market, can concentrate their limited resources on establishing a strong image and dominant market position within their chosen niche. Niche marketers also benefit from the absence of large firms as competitors, who would not generally contemplate chasing the low sales volume yielded by a small segment. Rolls Royce, for instance, have successfully carved themselves a profitable niche in the car industry without any competition from the giant manufacturers.

5.7 Market positioning

Once a strategy has been chosen, the firm then has to decide what **market position** each of its products or services will occupy, relative to those of its competitors, within a particular market segment. Ideally, any product or service should stand out from the competition and thus occupy a unique position in the market by virtue of its better quality, design, performance, reliability or some other advantage. In other words, it should offer a **unique selling proposition (USP)**: an aspect or feature which sets it apart from the rest of the competition.

In reality, products which have been on the market for some time invariably become very similar to each other as each firm has time to find out exactly what features the market wants. Many products are now so similar in all important respects that they are essentially **parity products**, i.e. products that are 'at par' with each other. Brands of shampoo, for instance, are all basically the same apart from slight variations in additives. The differences lie more in the way each shampoo is packaged, priced and advertised. Yet these superficial changes are enough to give each brand a distinctive image in the minds of consumers.

This suggests that it probably does not matter too much if the features which distinguish a product from its competitors are real or merely *perceived* differences – providing the consumer believes the product is unique in some way. Nevertheless, as market segments become ever more crowded and competitive, the need for products to establish a unique position has never been greater.

5.8 Why does re-positioning occur?

When Johnson and Johnson discovered that sales of their baby powder and baby lotion were exceeding the levels that could be expected purely from babycare use it became obvious that a much wider market was being tapped. Subsequent research revealed that women were buying these products because they had assumed, logically enough, that any product which was gentle enough for a baby's skin would probably also be kind to their skin.

As a result of this discovery, Johnson and Johnson launched an advertising campaign aimed at women. This exploited the company's strength in the babycare market with appeals such as 'Baby yourself – be a Johnson's baby'. Later campaigns targeted men when it was realized they were also using baby products. Johnson and Johnson capitalized on the discovery that their products appealed to adults and were able, as a result, to **re-position** their products in these new segments.

In this case, the re-positioning occurred because the products came to be used in a number of segments within the toiletries market and no longer just in the babycare segment. In other cases, re-positioning may be necessary when shifts in taste, technological advances or the introduction of a successful competitive product result in a product becoming seen as out of date.

A classic example of a product which became hugely successful once it was re-positioned is the Marlboro brand. Formerly marketed as a filter cigarette aimed at women, the 1954 re-positioning, linked to a new advertising campaign featuring the familiar Marlboro cowboy, created the second most widely-recognized brand name in the world, after Coca-Cola. In recent years, the successful re-positioning of Lucozade, which transformed the brand into a main-stream soft drink product, provides one of the best examples of this strategy.

> **Case study The revival of *Lucozade*** There will come a point, with any well-established brand that has been on the market for some time, when a decision has to be taken as to its future. Should the product be allowed to fade into obscurity or should an effort be made to rejuvenate sales in some way? This was the dilemma

SmithKline Beecham faced in the early 1980s with their long running Lucozade brand.

Lucozade was introduced back in 1927. By the early 1980s, after such a long life, it might well have been thought that Lucozade was heading towards an honourable retirement. Sales levels were static and showed no signs of increasing. The decline seemed unstoppable. Or was it? Could it be simply that the brand's image was in danger of becoming a bit dated? After all, Lucozade had always been positioned as a drink purely for convalescents and marketed accordingly, on the basis of advertising appeals such as 'Lucozade aids recovery'. Perhaps this traditional message had narrowed consumers' perceptions too much and it was time a different marketing strategy was adopted.

The decision by SmithKline Beecham to re-position Lucozade as an energy-giving drink was a bold move, aimed at exploiting a much wider target market – teenagers and young adults. At the same time, Lucozade was also repackaged in small 'one-shot' bottles and cans in recognition of the fact that 'on the street' consumption was becoming an increasingly important part of today's fast-moving pace of life.

The creation of a new advertising campaign was central to the re-positioning strategy. To this end, a memorable new campaign was developed with their advertising agency, Ogilvy and Mather, which used the outstanding athlete Daley Thompson to symbolize Lucozade's new image and emphasize its energy-replacing benefits. He was to prove an excellent choice.

When SmithKline Beecham first made their decision to adopt this strategy, they expected that sales would increase. In the event, the effect on Lucozade of taking it out of the medicine chest and into the world of soft drinks could not have been more dramatic. Lucozade is now the third largest selling carbonated drink in the UK (after Coca-Cola and Pepsi-Cola). The re-positioning brought about a remarkable transformation in the brand's fortunes, with sales accelerating from a mere £15 million in 1980 to a massive £143 million by 1991.

Lucozade provides a classic example of a product which has been given a new lease of life through being positioned on a different platform in the market. The success of the strategy has prompted SmithKline Beecham to launch a host of product variants: Orange Lemon and Tropical Barley and a Light version, as well as the new Lucozade Sport which is endorsed by footballer John Barnes.

Fig. 5.3 Daley Thompson, chosen by SmithKline Beecham to symbolize Lucozade's new 'high-energy' image

The marketing plan

6.1 What business are we really in?

Before firms can begin to prepare their marketing plans, the first thing they need to establish is, 'what business are we really in?' Firms that identify their business incorrectly or define their market too narrowly run the risk of misjudging who their real competitors and customers are. As a result, they may adopt strategies which are inappropriate to the business in which they are actually operating. For example, if manufacturers of typewriters regard themselves simply as being in the typewriter business, they could fail to see the introduction of word-processors as a threat to their market.

In his article, *Marketing Myopia*, Ted Levitt has made this point in relation to the decline of the railroads. 'The railroads did not stop growing because the need for passenger and freight transportation declined. That grew. The railroads are in trouble today not because the need was filled by others (cars, trucks, airplanes, even telephones), but because it was not filled by the railroads themselves. They let others take customers away from them because they assumed themselves to be in the railroad business rather than in the transportation business. The reason they defined their industry wrongly was because they were railroad-orientated instead of transportation-orientated; they were product-orientated instead of customer-orientated.'

Having defined their business correctly, firms need to analyse the competition. They also need to establish who their most important customers are using the **Pareto effect**. Carrying out a **SWOT analysis** enables them to take stock of the existing situation by identifying internal strengths and weaknesses as well as external opportunities and threats. They are then in a position to decide on a product/market strategy using the **Ansoff matrix**. The next step is to choose the correct market segment at which the marketing effort is to be targeted. However, before going ahead with any decisions firms need to analyse the market. Forecasting techniques are used to determine the level of sales that is likely to be achieved. The marketing planning process describes how this information is used in achieving the firm's objectives. Finally, the marketing mix co-ordinates strategies involving the four elements of product, price, promotion and place, each of which is described in more detail in units 7, 8, 10, and 11.

6.2 Analysing the competition

Firms do not operate in isolation. The activity of competitors is a major factor determining success or failure. Firms thrive where competition is weak or non-existent. Conversely, strong competition can force a firm out of business through the use of tactics like price undercutting or simply by virtue of the large market share held which can make it impossible for firms to break into a market. There are three types of competition.

(a) Direct competition
Firms experience direct competition from other organizations providing the same or similar products and services. In today's affluent society, most firms have to contend with a whole host of competitors. Consumers make their purchasing decisions on the basis of real (or perceived) differences between brands which are generally of a comparable specification and quality.

(b) Indirect competition
Firms experience indirect competition from less obvious sources. Manufacturers of knitwear may experience competition at Christmas from the makers of pens, records, cigarette lighters and after-shave. In short, they experience competition from firms making other items which can be given as gifts as well as from rival knitwear manufacturers. The business traveller can choose between several different methods of travel. Airlines therefore have to contend with indirect competition from British Rail, coach firms and car manufacturers, in addition to the direct competition they face from other airlines.

(c) Need competition
This is where firms experience competition from other needs that consumers may wish to fulfil. The UK tourist industry often competes not only with overseas package holidays but also with painters and decorators, car manufacturers and kitchen designers. The need to have a holiday may conflict with the need to buy a new car, have the house repainted, or have a new kitchen fitted.

6.3 The Pareto effect: who are a firm's most important customers?

One of the most important tasks of marketers is to identify their best customers in order that they can decide where to concentrate the majority of their efforts. Within the UK book market, for instance, just 27 per cent of the population makes 80 per cent of the purchases. It is a common characteristic of all types of markets that a small proportion of customers accounts for a large proportion of sales. This phenomenon is known as the 80/20 rule or **Pareto effect**.

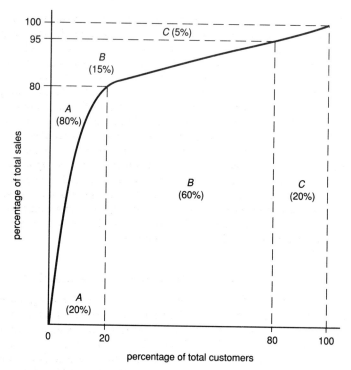

Fig. 6.1 The Pareto effect (or 80/20 rule)

The typical ratio of sales to customer groups found in markets demonstrating the Pareto effect is shown in fig. 6.1. The *A* group constitutes only 20 per cent of customers but accounts for 80 per cent of sales. The *B* group customers make up 60 per cent of customers and account for 15 per cent of total sales, whilst the *C* group, who represent 20 per cent of all customers, accounts for only 5 per cent of total sales.

What are the implications for marketers experiencing this phenomenon? Clearly, firms that are successful in identifying the key *A* group customers can improve the effectiveness of their marketing effort by targeting the sales and promotional effort directly at these important customers. For example, advertising campaigns can be designed to appeal specifically to this group. Similarly, *A* group category customers can be allocated more frequent visits from sales representatives than *C* group customers. Orders from *A* group customers may be given priority in times of shortage. Orders can also be dealt with more urgently even on a routine basis. The company's pricing policy can be adjusted to give higher discounts to the *A* group customers who account for the largest sales volumes.

However, whilst the 80/20 rule is a useful tool for marketers, enabling them to analyse their markets and target the marketing effort at the most valuable customers, great care should be taken not to apply the rule too rigidly. For instance, even though most of a company's costs are incurred by the 80 per cent of its customers who account for only 20 per cent of sales, this does not mean that a company should promptly drop 80 per cent of its customers. If this were to happen it would be an extremely dangerous situation. Apart from anything else, the sales volume contributed by this mass of smaller customers makes a valuable contribution to the overheads of the business (see page 153). In reality, most firms should only get rid of their smallest, least profitable customers.

The main limitation of this kind of analysis is that it does not take into account changing market conditions. Marketers should be aware that *B* and *C* group customers might increase in importance in future years. Equally, *A* group customers could decline in importance at any time. Just as important is the fact that some *B* and *C* group customers have the potential to become *A* group customers if they are given the right level of service and attention. In any event, it is also worth remembering that the customers who generate most sales do not necessarily generate most profit. Some of the low volume *B* and *C* customer accounts may actually be very profitable.

6.4 SWOT analysis: taking stock of the existing situation

Before deciding on the marketing strategy that is to be followed, managers need first to take stock of the situation in which they find themselves. Firms need to be aware of the factors which affect their operations both internally within the company itself (see fig. 6.2 overleaf) and also externally in the wider business environment. This kind of analysis enables firms to identify not only the internal strengths and weaknesses over which they have a high degree of control, but also the external opportunities and threats over which they have very little control. The most widely used technique is called **SWOT analysis**, i.e. strengths, weaknesses, opportunities, and threats.

The great appeal of SWOT analysis is that it prevents firms from becoming too insular and complacent by alerting them to potential threats posed by the outside environment. Of equal benefit is the fact that firms have to evaluate critically the strengths and weaknesses within their own operations. Armed with this information, firms should then be able to match their internal strengths to the external opportunities that have been identified. It is worth remembering, however, that opportunities are only worth pursuing if they are realistically achievable, i.e. within the resources and capabilities of the firm.

(a) Internal factors: strengths and weaknesses

- Size of market share held; a dominant market share gives firms the power to influence prices. High sales volumes enable firms to reduce their unit costs which means that they can survive when market prices fall. High sales volumes are also more efficient because they allow the firm to operate at or near full production capacity.
- Degree of profit made; linked in turn to the level of sales volume achieved and to the costs incurred.

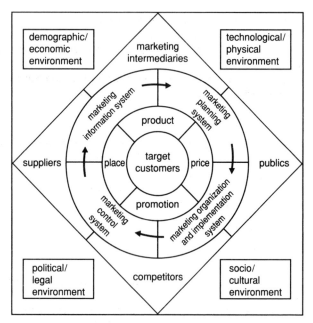

Source: Philip Kotler, *Marketing Management*, Prentice Hall 1984.

Fig. 6.2 Factors influencing company marketing strategy

- Types of sales made; companies may have strengths (or weaknesses) in relation to certain industries, geographical areas, suppliers or customers.
- Accuracy and relevance of data obtained from marketing research.
- Effectiveness of the marketing strategies themselves.
- Quality, design, reliability and technological superiority of products. The innovativeness of new products and the speed with which they are launched onto the market.
- Suitability of prices for target market segments. Attractiveness of any discounts and credit facilities which are offered.
- Effectiveness of advertising campaigns, sales promotions and public relations activities in generating sales and building brand identity.
- Suitability of physical distribution channels, methods of transport and choice of retail outlets.

(b) External factors: opportunities and threats

(i) Business climate

- Political, e.g. inflation and interest rates, taxation levels, regional grants, tariffs on foreign imports, etc.
- Legal, e.g. Health and Safety legislation, employment contracts, environmental protection, advertising standards, etc.
- Economic, e.g. unemployment levels, mortgage rates, wage levels, raw

material costs, availability of investment finance, etc.
- Demographic, e.g. age/sex distribution, etc.
- Socio-cultural, e.g. social class, education, religion, racial background, lifestyle, etc.
- Technological, e.g. advances in raw materials, production equipment and processes, product design, etc.

(ii) Nature of the competition

- Competitiveness of a firm's products, prices, promotional techniques and distribution systems relative to those of rival firms.
- Intensity of competition encountered.
- Size of market shares held by the major competitors.
- Opportunities for creating niche markets.
- Ease with which new entrants can join the market.

(iii) Nature of the market

- Total size of the market.
- Growth potential of the market, i.e. whether it is expanding or already saturated.
- Changing trends (both present and forecast) within the market.
- Differing needs and purchasing patterns of distinct segments of buyers.
- Influence of trade unions and professional associations and of any other bodies and organizations, e.g. OPEC.
- Degree of purchasing power exerted by marketing intermediaries such as wholesalers and retailers.

6.5 The Ansoff matrix

The most widely used framework for classifying the strategies adopted by a firm is that developed by Ansoff (see fig. 6.3). Most marketing objectives such as to improve profitability, expand market share or increase sales revolve around the interaction of two key dimensions: what the company sells, i.e. its

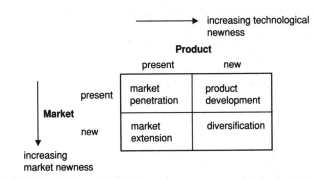

Fig. 6.3 The Ansoff matrix

products and who it sells them to, i.e. its markets. There are, in practice, only four possible combinations of these factors. According to Ansoff, the four strategies that firms can follow are:

- selling existing products to existing markets (market penetration);
- selling existing products to new markets (market extension);
- developing new products for existing markets (product development);
- developing new products for new markets (diversification).

However, the simple four-box matrix is not an infallible classification as the strategies adopted by firms do not always fall neatly into these four distinct categories. Each axis is, in reality, a scale or continuum because there are varying degrees of technological newness or market newness. This means that permutations of these four options can be classified at a number of points along each axis, as shown in fig. 6.4.

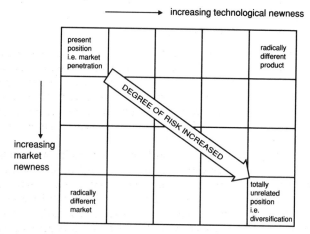

Fig. 6.4 Product/market strategies

Companies that move further away from their present position towards more unrelated positions inevitably increase their chances of failure. Equally, companies that stick to the safe option of selling existing products to existing markets are likely to stagnate in the long term. In any case, if they wish to maintain sales and profits when their products are nearing the end of their life cycles, firms often have no choice but to adopt one of the high-risk strategies.

6.6 Choosing the correct market segment

Firms obviously need to choose the right market segment on which to concentrate their marketing efforts. Ideally, the segment chosen should be one where the firm is able to demonstrate distinctive competence in one or more important respects. This means the firm must possess strengths which allow it to gain an advantage over its rivals.

It follows that a firm is most likely to succeed in a market segment with which it is familiar, where it knows the customers and understands their needs and requirements. It is worth remembering, however, that the segment which offers the most potential for one firm may not necessarily be the best choice for another with very different resources and capabilities.

The most promising segments tend, as a rule, to be found within rapidly expanding growth markets, particularly those where the large corporations have not yet gained a stranglehold. Segments to avoid are those in 'mature' industries where sales are declining, saturated markets and markets which are difficult to break into because of the high capital investment and degree of technological competence required.

Firms do not, of course, continue to operate within the same segment indefinitely. Firms need to re-evaluate their choice of segment constantly in line with changing market conditions.

6.7 Analysing the market

If preliminary estimates suggest that there might be a promising market opportunity, planners will generally carry out a full-scale analysis of the market before going ahead with any decisions designed to exploit that opportunity, such as launching a new product or entering a new market. The market analysis involves the use of a variety of **forecasting techniques** which aim to predict the level of sales that is likely to be achieved in a particular market under a given set of conditions.

The first step in preparing a sales forecast is to estimate the **total market potential**. This is the total possible sales of a product by all competitors in the market, assuming that each competitor makes the maximum marketing effort.

In reality, however, competitors rarely manage to fulfil the total market potential. The **total market demand** for a product by a particular target group is invariably less than potential demand. This discrepancy occurs because competitors do not make the maximum marketing effort and some consumers are therefore unaware of the existence and benefits of the product. In fact, achieving total market potential is not a desirable goal because the additional cost of reaching the last remaining consumers in a market lowers profits on those marginal sales to the point where they are not worthwhile.

Given that it is impractical and uneconomic to aim at satisfying total market potential, firms will instead prepare a **sales forecast** which provides a realistic indication of the sales they hope to make. Sales projections tend to be expressed in volume rather than value terms. Sales volume is a more reliable indicator of market demand because sales value figures can be affected by factors such as the level of inflation.

Forecasts are generally prepared for each product line assuming that it is geared to the needs of a chosen market segment, and is sold over a specified time period, within a defined geographical region and backed with a specified level of marketing effort. When preparing their forecasts, marketers also need to consider the impact on sales of external factors such as the state of the economy, government legislation, demographic trends, technological break-throughs and competitor activity. Sales do not take place in a vacuum and forecasts that make no allowance for these factors are meaningless.

Having specified the assumptions that have been taken into account, marketers then prepare three forecasts – a 'most likely' forecast that is considered realistically achievable, together with an optimistic and pessimistic version. These take account of favourable or unfavourable eventualities that may occur.

Once the potential size of the market has been estimated, marketers can compare the existing market size with the potential size, which then enables them to prepare projected annual growth figures for the entire market. If marketers have some idea of the market share held by their products, projected sales figures for individual products can also be calculated in this way.

The **forecasting techniques** used to prepare these figures vary in complexity from simple **judgemental methods** to mathematically complex **quantitative methods**. The type of method chosen depends on factors such as the availability of historical data and the degree of accuracy required.

6.8 Judgemental methods

(a) Market research surveys

These are used to predict the level of sales likely to be achieved by a new product. Asking a sample of potential buyers whether they would buy the new product when it becomes available and if so, how often, and in what quantities enables marketers to forecast the eventual sales pattern. This is particularly useful in the case of innovative products, where there are no similar products to provide an indication of potential sales.

However, forecasts based solely on the results of consumer market research surveys have to be interpreted with a degree of caution. As a rule, stated 'intention to purchase' figures exceed the actual sales that are achieved, often by a large margin. The fact is people do not always do what they say they are going to do – witness the conspicuous failure of the polls to predict the UK election results in 1992. It goes without saying that there are many reasons why people may change their minds about a purchase decision (pages 13–14).

Nevertheless, the existence of this marked discrepancy does not invalidate the survey method, providing marketers take account of this phenomenon and reduce their projections accordingly. In the case of established products, sales data from previous years can be used to moderate projections that are over-optimistic, but this is obviously not possible for innovative products which have no precedents. In view of these limitations, firms tend to use the survey method in conjunction with the **Delphi approach** and sales staff forecasts. Obtaining the opinions of experts and their own sales force enables firms to exercise human judgement in analysing the results of market research surveys.

(b) The Delphi approach

This approach, named after the famous oracle which the Ancient Greeks used to consult for advice, also involves using experts to predict the likely course of events. The experts consulted may include the company's own senior executives, as well as other eminent figures such as industry leaders, economists, consultants, journalists and members of professional associations such as the CBI. This method is known as **top-down forecasting**.

In some cases, the experts may be asked to meet as a panel in order to discuss their opinions and arrive at a consensus viewpoint. More often, however, their opinions are sought independently by means of postal questionnaires. This is an effective method given the cost and practical difficulties of bringing a panel like this together in one place. Questionnaires completed individually also avoid the possibility of members being influenced by the opinions of powerful or dominant personalities on the panel, which is a potential source of bias in face-to-face discussions.

(c) Projections by the sales force

This is where firms ask each member of the sales force to prepare projected figures for their own particular sales territories. Each area forecast is then combined into a regional forecast. These regional forecasts are in turn amalgamated to produce a national forecast. This method is often known as **bottom-up forecasting**.

The main disadvantage of this kind of forecast is that sales representatives invariably have a large proportion of their salary dependent on meeting sales quotas set by the company. They may have a vested interest in making low predictions and thus reducing the sales targets they are expected to reach. However, the method does tend to prove quite accurate, particularly in sales-orientated companies. The sales force are, after all, closest to the marketplace and are therefore in an ideal position to prepare realistic sales forecasts.

Nevertheless, all three judgemental methods are subjective to a greater or lesser extent. In order to improve the accuracy of their sales forecasts, firms use a variety of quantitative techniques. These are based on historical sales data and are therefore more objective.

6.9 Quantitative methods

(a) Moving averages

Using historical sales data, if the series of figures shows a fluctuating pattern of sales, the **moving average** can be calculated in order to highlight the basic underlying trend. When sales are changing constantly, calculating the moving average makes it possible to establish whether sales are staying constant, increasing or decreasing. In the example shown in Table 6.1 and fig. 6.5 (overleaf) the monthly moving average for sales of sports shoes over the previous 12 months provides a more accurate indication of the underlying trend in monthly sales because it averages out seasonal variations.

Table 6.1 The calculation of the moving average for sales of sports shoes

| Month | Sales of sports shoes | |
	Monthly sales	Moving average
Jul.	327	
Aug.	229	
Sep.	175	
Oct.	191	
Nov.	208	
Dec.	322	
Jan.	316	
Feb.	167	
Mar.	193	
Apr.	187	
May.	212	
Jun.	241	231
Jul.	348	232

new sports centre opens

Aug.	366	244
Sep.	315	256
Oct.	382	271
Nov.	457	292
Dec.	676	322
Jan.	663	351
Feb.	334	365
Mar.	367	379
Apr.	336	391
May.	339	402
Jun.	386	414
Jul.	522	429
Aug.	321	425
Sep.	228	418
Oct.	248	406
Nov.	270	391
Dec.	419	369

(b) Exponential smoothing

However, the moving average may not reflect fully the impact on sales of new developments. In the example shown in Table 6.2 (on page 98) **exponential smoothing** is used because it takes into account the effect that the new sports centre is likely to have from now on. The technique involves giving a greater weighting to more recent sales, which obviously then results in more optimistic sales forecasts. In reality, of course, the weighting will need to be re-assessed periodically. In this example, sales of sports shoes have tailed off after the initial burst of sales created by the opening of the new sports centre, which means that the weighting should now be reduced. The forecaster's skill in

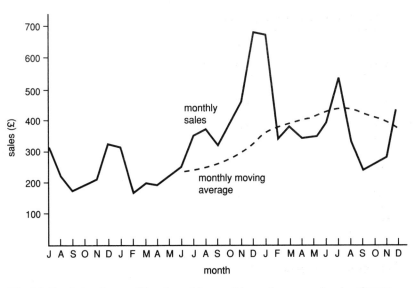

Fig. 6.5 Graph showing monthly sales and the monthly moving average in sales of sports shoes over the previous 12 months

allocating different weightings is obviously crucial to the successful use of this technique. Inevitably, however, there is an element of subjectivity involved as the weightings given depend on the forecaster's judgement in assessing the importance of particular factors.

Both these techniques are examples of **time series analysis**, i.e. they attempt to identify the underlying trend behind a series of fluctuating figures over a period of time. The analysis can prove complex, particularly when multiple forecasting techniques are used, which is why it is now generally done by computer.

6.10 The marketing planning process

In his book *Marketing Plans* Malcolm McDonald points out that 'During periods of high economic prosperity there was little pressure on companies to do anything other than solve operational problems as they arose. Careful planning for the future seemed unnecessary. However, most companies today find themselves in increasingly competitive markets, and there is a growing realization that success in the future will come only from patient and meticulous planning and market preparation.' What, then, does planning involve?

In contrast to the day-to-day matters which need to be dealt with immediately, planning focuses attention on issues that are likely to be important in the future. Working towards goals that have been set forces managers to look beyond the pressing operational problems which can so easily occupy all their energies. Companies that adopt such a **proactive** approach towards change,

Table 6.2 The calculation of the exponential trend in sales of sports shoes

		Sales of sports shoes		
Month	Monthly sales	Moving average	Weight	Exponential trend
Jul.	327		1.00	
Aug.	229		1.00	
Sep.	175		1.00	
Oct.	191		1.00	
Nov.	208		1.00	
Dec.	322		1.00	
Jan.	316		1.00	
Feb.	167		1.00	
Mar.	193		1.00	
Apr.	187		1.00	
May.	212		1.00	
Jun.	241	231	1.00	231
Jul.	348	232	1.00	232

new sports centre opens

Aug.	366	244	1.25	251
Sep.	315	256	1.25	270
Oct.	382	271	1.25	294
Nov.	457	292	1.25	324
Dec.	676	322	1.25	367
Jan.	663	351	1.25	410
Feb.	334	365	1.25	431
Mar.	367	379	1.25	453
Apr.	336	391	1.25	473
May.	339	402	1.25	490
Jun.	386	414	1.25	510
Jul.	522	429	1.25	536
Aug.	321	425	1.25	531
Sep.	228	418	1.25	522
Oct.	248	406	1.25	508
Nov.	270	391	1.25	489
Dec.	419	369	1.25	462

which means that they anticipate rather than merely react to change, are obviously in an ideal position to exploit any new market opportunities that may arise. This forward-looking orientation results in managers having a better long-term vision of where the company is going.

Unfortunately, however, what often passes for marketing planning is simply sales budgeting and forecasting. In some cases, managers set arbitrary profit goals without any thought as to how these targets are to be achieved (see fig. 6.6).

Marketing planning involves gathering information on an existing situation, analysing both the internal and external factors affecting the company's performance, and making some basic assumptions about external trends that are

Fig. 6.6 How not to carry out marketing planning from *The Marketing Plan*, M.H.B. McDonald and P. Morris, Heinemann Professional Publishing.

likely to occur in the future. The results or objectives that firms hope to achieve and the actions or strategies that are needed to implement these are then decided. Finally, the strategies adopted are evaluated in relation to the desired objectives. These stages are shown in fig. 6.7. The time scales involved vary greatly from industry to industry. The entire planning process may take as little as three to six months in the case of the fashion clothing industry, whereas the introduction of a new jet engine, high speed train or car may require planning over a period of fifteen years or more.

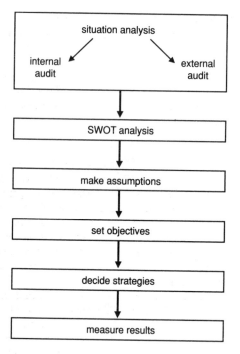

Fig. 6.7 The marketing planning process

(a) Situation analysis

The first step in the marketing planning process is to examine the firm's existing situation, which essentially means finding out, 'Where are we now?' This involves carrying out an **internal audit** of the organization's own resources and capabilities, together with an **external audit** of the factors in the wider business environment which are likely to affect the company's performance.

(b) SWOT analysis

When all the information has been gathered together, it is then subjected to a SWOT analysis. The aim of this is to pick out from the mass of data collected the factors which relate most closely to the company's activities. The SWOT analysis (which is described in detail on pages 89–91) highlights only the important internal strengths and weaknesses as well as the key external opportunities and threats.

(c) Make assumptions

At this point, it is usually necessary to make some assumptions about external factors which are likely to affect the company's performance. For example, decisions will vary greatly depending on whether it is assumed that prices are likely to increase by 15 per cent or decrease by 15 per cent in the next few years.

Assumptions might include statements like: 'The level of imported goods is likely to increase by 10 per cent during the next two years' or 'The entry of several new competitors into the market over the next five years is likely to force prices down by 20 per cent'.

Assumptions should be as accurate and specific as possible as decisions obviously cannot be made on the basis of vague suppositions. Only those factors which are likely to have a critical impact on the firm's performance should be taken into account.

(d) Set objectives

The setting of objectives enables firms to answer the key question of 'Where do we want to.go?' People are much more motivated when they are working towards a particular goal like passing an examination, getting a promotion, saving up to buy a car and so on. Organizations benefit from setting and pursuing goals in the same way as individuals do. On a practical level, the existence of clear objectives improves co-ordination between departments and prevents potentially disastrous situations like the personnel department reducing production staff at a time when the marketing department has introduced a new advertising campaign designed to boost sales.

Most well-run companies set objectives which are challenging yet realistic and try to involve staff at all levels in formulating these objectives, although broad strategic objectives, such as a decision to expand market share in Europe would invariably be decided by senior management at corporate level.

Marketing plays a central role in achieving any business objective. If one accepts, like management writer Peter Drucker, 'that the purpose of business is to create a customer', it becomes clear that marketing is the key element in all business objectives. In fact, it is difficult to see how any overall corporate objective, such as improving profitability, could be achieved without the involvement of marketing. In other words, an improvement in profitability will only occur if specific marketing objectives have been achieved, e.g. increasing sales volume, improving advertising effectiveness and so on.

If these marketing objectives are to be implemented fully, it is important that they are stated in terms which are quantifiable, i.e. capable of measurement. An example might be to 'increase the market share of product A by 10 per cent within the next two years'. Objectives need to be worded as precisely as possible otherwise it is impossible for staff to know when they have been achieved.

(e) Decide strategies

Once definite marketing objectives have been agreed, the next step is to decide on the strategies that will need to be adopted in order to achieve those objectives. This involves the firm working out 'How do we get where we want to go?' Strategies are the actions and decisions which need to be taken in order for the eventual objectives to be accomplished. Strategies are in turn translated into tactics. These are the detailed actions and decisions, taken on a day-to-day basis, which are needed to implement the strategies. In practice, marketing strategies tend to revolve only around products and markets. The strategies which can be adopted by firms include:

● Selling existing products to existing markets
● Selling existing products to new markets
● Developing new products for existing markets
● Developing new products for new markets.

These options, summarized in a framework called The Ansoff matrix, are described in more detail on pages 91-2. Strategies relating to any element of the marketing mix (i.e. product, price, place and promotion) ultimately relate to these four strategies. For example, the decision to introduce a price discount might be taken as a result of a firm deciding to sell an existing product to new markets.

(f) Measure results
Once the marketing plan is in operation, the results are monitored closely in order to assess whether the original objectives have been achieved. This will establish whether, for example, Product *A* actually did increase its market share by 10 per cent within two years. If the results reveal that there is a marked discrepancy between actual and planned performance, the entire planning process would be analysed in order to determine the reasons for the variations. The process may then need to be modified at one or more stages in the light of these findings.

6.11 The marketing mix

Having been through the overall process of marketing planning, marketers then need to prepare the short-term **operational plan** which will enable the company to achieve its long-term goals and objectives in terms of improved market share, sales volume, profitability and so on. This operational plan consists mainly of the tactics needed to implement the marketing plan, together with sales forecasts and estimates of the likely budgets and timescales needed.

How do companies go about achieving their marketing objectives? It is widely accepted that the key factor determining success in the marketplace is the ability to satisfy consumer needs and wants profitably (page 9). To this end, the strategies adopted by marketers aimed at maximizing consumer satisfaction revolve around the key factors of product, price, place and promotion. These four elements make up what is commonly known as the **marketing mix** or the 'four Ps'. The elements of the mix can be combined in different ways just as the ingredients of a cake can be varied in different recipes (fig. 6.8).

Marketers can expect to have little or no control over factors in the external marketing environment such as political, demographic, technological and social forces (Unit 3). However, marketers obviously do have an influence on internal decisions concerning the nature of the product and the way it is priced, distributed and promoted. As marketing tools, the attraction of the

Fig. 6.8 The 'ingredients' of the marketing mix

four Ps therefore stems from the fact that these are the only variables which are capable of being directly manipulated by marketers. As Philip Kotler has pointed out, 'The marketing mix is the set of **controllable variables** that firms can use to influence the buyer's response.'

A marketing-orientated approach involves providing consumers with a total offer – a package of benefits which caters for their needs and wants, based on a balanced combination of all four elements. As a whole, the marketing mix provides a potentially far more powerful tool than the sum of its component parts. Used in isolation, each element of the mix is relatively ineffective. For example, sales of an expensive product will be reduced if the high price is not reinforced by other elements of the mix, for instance, if the quality of the product is poor, it is sold through places like discount outlets and is promoted by a 'downmarket' advertising campaign. Where the balance of the mix is inconsistent, as in this case, the customer is presented with a disjointed image of the product.

If the marketing effort is not integrated from the outset, the full sales potential of a product may never be realized. An uncoordinated effort will almost certainly result in a substantial waste of company resources. It is pointless wasting advertising expenditure on an inferior product, for example.

Marketers need, therefore, to ensure that the four key elements are mixed together in order to present a co-ordinated offering to the customer, consisting of the right product, at the right price, in the right place and supported by the right promotion. The four elements are also inter-dependent, which means that if one element is changed in any way, it will automatically have a knock-on effect on the others in the mix.

It is essential, therefore, that the elements of the mix are managed as an integrated whole. This does not mean of course that the way in which the elements are combined should remain static, although some degree of continuity is obviously important in order to maintain customer loyalty in the long term. The optimum combination of the elements is in any case bound to change as the product moves through the different stages of its life cycle (page 124). In addition, the mix may need to be altered as factors like economic, social and technical changes alter the level of demand.

In recent years some authors have suggested that the four Ps should be extended to include other aspects of marketing such as packaging. Whilst the case for factors such as packaging is less clear-cut, there is a growing body of support for the inclusion of people as a fifth 'P'. The standard of customer service provided is increasingly recognized as a key factor in determining a company's success or failure. Authors like Peters and Waterman pin-pointed the way in which a company's employees behave as the main factor distinguishing their successful American companies – a finding that has since been confirmed by other studies in Britain and elsewhere.

6.12 Strategies involving the elements of the marketing mix

(a) Product

- Introduce new product;
- delete old product line;
- modify product design;
- change packaging;
- improve product specification.

(b) Price

- Increase price to exploit innovative product or re-inforce quality image;
- lower price to penetrate new market or undercut competitors;
- change level of discount.

(c) Place

- Change type of outlets through which product is sold;
- change method of transport used;
- reduce delivery times;
- improve storage and warehousing facilities.

(d) Promotion

- Invest in new advertising campaign;
- design new advertising to re-position product;
- introduce new sales promotion offers;
- expand public relations activities;
- improve training of sales force.

> **Case study   Using the full power of the marketing mix**   There is a lot of nonsense being spouted about the issue of tobacco promotion. On the one hand there are those who see it as an issue of principle – as long as tobacco is legally on sale, it should be provided 'freedom of commercial speech'. On the other side, and equally absurd, are those who see the banning of tobacco advertising (and perhaps sponsorship) as the be all and end all of their campaign.
>
> Yet it is utter nonsense to think that Silk Cut and Marlboro would stop selling if all advertising was banned. The brands are far too powerful. Which gets us to the real point: the power of marketing as a whole, as opposed to mere advertising. Anyone serious about being anti-tobacco would use all the Ps to undermine cigarette brands, just as marketers use all the Ps to build them.
>
> The product could be made less appealing and less dangerous by making it smaller. They would look less elegant and twenty a day would mean less tobacco. Legislation on packaging could really undermine cigarette brands. What would happen if manufacturers were forced to sell their goods in packs without a logo, called perhaps, '20 Government standard, Type A, Low Tar'?
>
> Then there is the price. How about putting up the price to pay for a powerful anti-smoking campaign? The sponsorship problem would disappear. Few manufacturers would want to sponsor the 'Imperial Type B Snooker Championships'.
>
> How about the place? Ban cigarette sales from everywhere but confectioners and tobacconists and extend the current bans on smoking in public places. Add all these together, and the hotly debated 'principles' paraded about tobacco advertising would all but disappear. The real principle, a political decision about society's attitude towards the product, would come to the fore.
>
> The point of all this? To show that those who really want to tackle an issue such as tobacco should think in terms of marketing, rather than advertising, which is after all only one (albeit important) component of the marketing mix.
>
> Source: Adapted from *No smoke without brand fire*, Alan Mitchell, *Marketing*, 28 February 1991.

The right product

7.1 What is a product?

When we think of products we usually think of tangible, physical objects like a can of soup, a pair of jeans or a washing machine. In fact, products also encompass many other intangible things such as services (e.g. dry cleaning and life insurance); organizations (e.g. British Telecom and Greenpeace); places (Milton Keynes and Barbados) and even ideas (e.g. the 'Buy British' campaign). In addition, whilst they might not like to think of themselves in this light, people such as politicians and pop stars are often packaged as products, in terms of the public image they project. The American election campaigns would convince even the most hardened sceptics that people can be marketed as products!

Yet whatever the type of product or brand that is purchased, consumers generally expect to receive a variety of benefits from their purchases. For example, when you buy a bottle of shampoo you take it for granted that it will fulfil its **core benefit** of cleaning your hair. The chances are you will probably also expect it to be gentle on your hair, add shine and body and smell fresh. This is quite apart from any expectations concerning the price and packaging, not to mention the often highly evocative brand image created by the advertising. The campaign for Timotei shampoo is a classic example, portraying an idealized image of natural beauty and health.

In the case of major purchases like electrical goods, consumers often expect extra product features, good reliability and long service contracts. For items like expensive perfumes and designer clothes, the expectation of quality created by the brand name and image can be as important as the products themselves. In short, consumers today expect to be offered much more than the basic product. Marketing expert Ted Levitt maintains that products can be offered at four levels:

(a) Generic product
This is the basic product. In the past, household goods such as soap, flour and tea were sold loose in grocery shops. Today supermarkets still sell some goods

which customers can weigh and pack but most tend to be offered in the form
of packaged and branded products.

(b) Expected product
This is the product with features which have, over a period of time, become
the standard specification. For example, consumers would be surprised to find
a video cassette recorder these days that did not have an electronic remote control. Competition has intensified to the point where features which were once
regarded as radical new extras (such as VCRs with Nicam digital stereo) have
very rapidly become the industry *norm*.

(c) Augmented product
Firms accept that, in the markets of today, technological superiority cannot be
maintained for long. They therefore strive to gain a competitive edge by adding
to, or augmenting, the attractiveness of their product in other less tangible
ways. This can be done by improving the quality of after-sales service, reducing
delivery times and by extending guarantee periods. In recent years, firms have
also started to offer credit facilities such as zero per cent finance deals.

(d) Potential product
Inevitably, it is not long before even these initiatives are adopted by competitors. Firms are then faced with trying to unlock the full potential of their
products by discovering new ways of attracting and holding customers. In the
case of banks, this has led to the introduction of Saturday opening and of
interest-earning current accounts – moves designed to stem the inroads made
by building societies into areas that were once the traditional province of the
banking sector. In the final analysis, measures aimed at improving the potential
of any product succeed only if they manage to add value to the product in the
eyes of consumers so that it is then perceived as the best purchase.

Levitt argues that firms are facing a new kind of competition today. 'Not
competition between what companies produce in their factories, but between
what they add to their factory output in the form of packaging, services, advertising, customer advice, financing, delivery arrangements, warehousing and
other things people value.'

7.2 What makes a successful product?

The product is generally acknowledged to be the most important element of
the marketing mix. There are many instances of good products succeeding
despite being priced, promoted or distributed incorrectly. By the same token,
indifferent products invariably seem to fall by the wayside, even when the other
aspects of the marketing mix are properly organized. So, what factors determine whether or not a product is successful?

One of the most important factors is that a product must be geared to satisfying the existing needs and wants of consumers. Alternatively, it should be
capable of stimulating entirely new *latent* needs and wants, as is the case with

innovative products. If a new product is launched without any reference to consumer requirements (perhaps because the need for secrecy precludes market research) then there is a high likelihood that it will fail; witness the Sinclair C5 fiasco (page 7). After all, as Ted Levitt points out, customers buy $\frac{1}{4}$-inch holes not $\frac{1}{4}$-inch drill bits – the implication being that consumers do not buy products as such, but the benefits provided by those products.

Once firms have established that their products can satisfy the needs and wants of consumers, the next step is for them to decide whether the product is capable of meeting those needs or wants economically. In his book, *The Supermarketers*, Robert Heller makes this point in relation to the costs (put at some £900 million) of developing Concorde. 'By definition, a marketing need that can't be economically serviced might as well not exist. No more striking proof of this point will ever be provided than that of the supersonic airliner Concorde. Forgetting its relatively cramped interior, this is plainly a superior product. . . . Real product superiority invariably has the sublime virtue of attracting a premium price. But the premium can't be scaled-up indefinitely. Nor will it necessarily reach a level at which prices cover the costs of the superiority.' It is interesting to speculate whether Concorde would have survived had it been subject to normal market forces without the benefit of subsidies.

Clearly, then, the ability to satisfy consumer needs, and to make a profit from doing so, is fundamental to the success of a new product. Yet this process, which seems relatively straightforward, is in reality fraught with difficulties. For instance, evidence suggests that many new products fail simply because they are not distinctive enough. Consumers are not prepared to switch from a product which they find satisfactory, if it appears that the new product is no better than the one they use normally. Thus, in order to succeed, a product should have certain features which enable it to stand out from the crowd so that it forms a **unique selling proposition (USP)**. In other words, it should offer the consumer some unique benefit which distinguishes it from rival products and motivates consumers to switch from their existing brands or products. **Product differentiation** has now become the main basis for competition between firms as a means of providing consumers with a reason for preferring one product over other similar products.

There is, in fact, very little variation (apart from minor additives) between the different types of lager, shampoo or washing powder, yet the way each is priced, packaged and advertised creates a unique image and identity which positions them in the market and pin-points them as being aimed at a particular type of consumer. Without a distinctive personality maintained and, in the case of products like mineral water, largely created by advertising, the new product will fail, as it will be only a matter of time before it is copied by competitors.

However, the rewards can be high for firms that do manage to create a unique platform for their products in the market. Focusing on the convenience aspect of being able to use just one product instead of a separate shampoo and conditioner, Vidal Sassoon's Wash & Go has proved a phenomenal success. Launched as recently as 1989, Wash & Go is credited with creating a whole new sector of the hair care market – a sector that it still dominates, despite the 'copycat' or me-too products which followed hard on its heels.

This need to create a distinctive personality and image is as important for the service industries as it is for firms providing more tangible products. The banking industry illustrates this clearly. It is not surprising that the four large clearing banks should offer very similar services and charge almost identical interest rates – a policy which avoids the destructive price-cutting that would result if they tried to compete by undercutting each other. However, according to an article in *Marketing* magazine in September 1990, this has made their advertising and image building all the more important as they try to differentiate themselves in the eyes of consumers by building on their own particular strengths.

Griffin advertising by the Midland bank in the mid-eighties is widely regarded as having broken the mould in an attempt to focus on factors such as friendliness, helpfulness and reassurance. National Westminster has gone for a single and simple message: 'The Action Bank'. From its research Barclays found that its name is extremely powerful. It has tried to meet consumer misconceptions of banks as faceless monoliths with its slogan, 'You're better off talking to Barclays'. Meanwhile, Lloyds has tried to distinguish itself by building on its more up-market base, hence, 'A thoroughbred bank'.

In addition to creating a strong USP, companies can also increase their chances of success by speeding up the time it takes to develop and introduce new products. The 'First is best' principle holds true in most markets today. Being first in a market enables a company to capture a substantial market share. This is why Honda have chopped their five-year cycle of development for new car models down to three years and why Olivetti can now produce a new typewriter design in two months instead of two years. Nor does speed of introduction necessarily mean inferior products. For instance, Xerox created a new photocopier in twenty-eight days that has since earned them £3 billion.

Development times can be cut by using Computer Aided Design (CAD) techniques and by setting up cross-functional development teams where design, production and marketing departments work together *simultaneously* on a project instead of being brought in one after the other, as in the traditional *sequential* method. Co-operation between departments from the outset reduces costs by preventing the need for multiple re-design. Most importantly, it results in a better product.

Nevertheless, even when a new product scores highly on all the factors discussed previously, i.e. it is geared to satisfying a particular consumer need or want, is capable of producing a profit, provides a real consumer point of difference and is introduced onto the market quickly, there are still no guarantees that it will succeed – even if it is plainly better than a rival product. Market conditions are complex and there are many reasons why even products that are technologically superior do not automatically win out.

In the case of the Apple Mackintosh computer, what should have been a huge sales advantage (i.e. that anyone, not just computer buffs, could learn how to operate the computer in as little as twenty minutes), counted for very little in a market where the need for IBM compatibility, particularly in terms of software, was a major consideration.

Similarly, it was an issue completely unconnected with the merits of the product itself which was to ruin the chances of the Betamax video system developed by Sony becoming the industry standard. According to Nigel Cope in an article in *Business* magazine, March 1990, 'In the 1970s Sony produced their Betamax video system, expecting it to become the industry standard. It did not. Rivals such as JVC threw their weight behind the technically inferior but cheaper VHS format. JVC allowed its systems to be widely licensed; Sony insisted that its sets be sold under the Sony brand name. The result: more VHS systems were sold, so more films were offered on that format; Betamax withered and died. Sony had to swallow its pride and start manufacturing VHS.'

7.3 The importance of new product development

'Our job', according to Sony's chairman, Akio Morita, 'is to make our products obsolete before our competitors do.' As Morita recognizes, companies which do not regard new product development as essential for long term survival run the risk of being overtaken by their competitors. Ultimately, those that do not innovate face an uncertain future as they are pushed out of markets where their products have been superseded. How, then, should firms go about developing new products?

In reality, new product ideas that are radically different are few and far between. A new invention such as the telephone, microwave oven, photocopier or hovercraft does not come along every day. Most 'new' products are simply improvements to existing products, copies of competitors' products or **line extensions**. The costs of developing and advertising a new product from scratch have escalated in recent years to the point where marketing managers tend to concentrate increasingly on developing new products under an existing brand name with a proven record of success. Mars Bar ice-cream is a classic example.

For many companies today, the process of new product development could perhaps be described more properly as the process of old product development. A survey carried out by Booz, Allen and Hamilton in the USA, which studied 13 000 new products introduced during the five-year period ending in 1981, found that only 10 per cent of the products surveyed were true innovations.

This does not necessarily mean, of course, that the other 90 per cent, i.e. the modifications and variations of existing products, were poor introductions. In fact, the majority of successful new products stem from a gradual evolutionary process of development rather than from the type of technological breakthrough that represents a quantum leap forward. This applies even in the case of a product like the Sony Walkman, which seems, on the face of it, to be the classic example of a technologically innovative product. Yet as Akio Morita points out, 'There was no new technology involved in the Sony Walkman. What we did was see the technology we had already in a totally new configuration.'

At the end of 1990 and a decade after it was first launched, the Sony Walkman held an impressive 26 per cent share of the personal stereo market which it had created – a market worth £100 million at the time.

Case study   The Sony Walkman   **A runaway success**   Tim Steel, the UK Managing Director of Sony Consumer Products from 1979 to 1983, remembers the first time he saw a Sony Walkman. 'It was at a product briefing in Tokyo. They passed this thing round and everyone shook their heads and said: "You're kidding. It's got no record mechanism, only one person can listen to it and we don't think much of the name."'

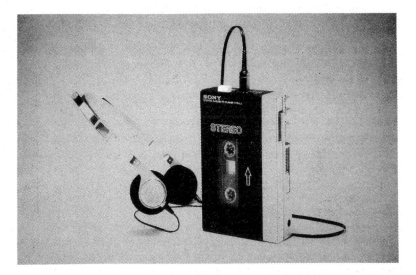

Fig. 7.1. Sony Walkman

The reaction was not surprising. From a company whose name had become synonymous with innovation, the Walkman was a technological throwback. The innovation lay only in the miniaturized parts to make the machine portable. It was a marketing coup rather than a technological breakthrough.

Credit for the initial idea must go to Akio Morita. After hearing complaints from Sony's co-founder about the weight of his tape recorder and headphones, Morita immediately put his engineers to work on making them smaller. He had a hard time, he says, getting the product through. 'It seemed as if no one liked it.'

Few liked the name either. Pressman, Soundabout and Stowaway were all suggested. According to Morita, Walkman was coined 'by some young people while I was away on a trip'.

If Sony was unsure what to call its baby, it was even less certain about its chances of reaching adulthood. Sales forecasts were so cautious that it allowed an advertising budget of just £25 000 to launch the innovation. 'With that kind of money we couldn't do anything,' recalls the former head of marketing. 'Certainly no television.' Instead he opted for a publicity stunt, taking journalists out to a park in Tokyo where he had hired school children to roller-skate around wearing Walkmans. 'The reporters got the idea,' he says. 'We were selling a lifestyle.'

That lifestyle, as every commuter knows, took off to become one of the greatest marketing successes of the 1980s. Since 1979, Sony has sold more than 50 million Walkmans and still makes one million a month. Endless variations followed: the splashproof sports model, the sandproof model, the childproof version called My First Sony.

Hits such as the Walkman are a result, some say, of Morita's view that a company should not be afraid of failure. 'Don't worry,' he apparently remarked to Yasuo Kuroki, the man given a Y20 million budget to design the Walkman. 'If it fails, we can always take it out of your salary.'

Source: Adapted from *Walkmen's Global Stride*, Nigel Cope,
Business magazine, March 1990.

7.4 The process of new product development

(a) Generation of ideas
A constant supply of ideas is needed in order that some will survive the process of new product development shown in fig. 7.2. Potential losers are weeded out at each stage and very few make it through the entire development process to reach the market. For a product that fails at a particular stage, the process may need to revert back to an earlier stage, perhaps even to the point of beginning with a new idea.

Ideas for new products or **concepts** can come from almost anywhere. Customers and retailers often suggest ways in which existing products can be adapted. Employees can also generate useful ideas through processes such as suggestion boxes, brainstorming sessions and so on. Then there is the sales force, who effectively function as the 'eyes and ears' of the company in the marketplace. Being in direct contact with customers they are in an ideal position to recommend improvements to products. Most importantly, they can identify potential gaps in the market where consumer needs have yet to be satisfied.

Larger companies tend to carry out their own research and development (R & D) progranmes. Those who operate at the leading edge of technology in industries such as aeronautics, electronics and pharmaceuticals view their often considerable investment in R & D as an essential investment in the future. Marketing research can be useful in identifying unsatisfied consumer

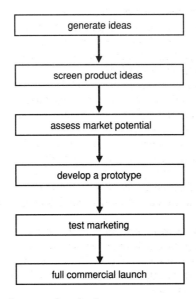

Fig. 7.2 The process of new product development

needs – though research is less useful in the case of highly innovative products which exploit latent needs, largely because consumers find it difficult to evaluate an idea which is completely new to them.

Companies can also pick up ideas by scouring the literature of competitors. It is well documented that the Japanese firm of Seiko acquired their knowledge of quartz watch technology by studying freely-available Swiss technical journals. More companies than would openly admit to doing so obtain ideas from competitors' products. For example, many electronics manufacturers practise **reverse engineering**. This is where competitors' products are stripped down to the smallest component so that any superior features which are found can be improved on and incorporated in their own version.

Ideally, the 'new' version should not be an exact copy of the competitor's product. Such **me-too products** are rarely successful, unless they offer a significant improvement on the earlier model. Nevertheless, me-too products have become a fact of life. In the nature of things it is perhaps inevitable that successful products are going to attract competition. However, it is the sheer scale of this competition that has left observers gasping. As Richard Brooks points out in his book, *The New Marketing*, 'Five years after the launch of its personal computer, IBM was fighting a new PC battle – not with the Japanese, as everyone originally expected, but with low-wage companies in Taiwan and South Korea. By 1986 IBM's PC had become a commodity product and was being copied by more than two hundred firms.'

(b) Product concept screening

The aim of the **screening process** is to narrow down the list of ideas generated to a small number of concepts which are worth investigating further. Some product ideas are sifted out simply because they are inappropriate to the strengths and weaknesses of the company. For instance, it is unlikely that a company making fashion clothing will start to make microwave ovens as it will not have the skilled labour, production facilities or distribution channels needed to produce the ovens. Alternatively, ideas may be rejected purely on the basis that they are incompatible with the company's existing range of products.

Once a product concept is considered a serious prospect, the company may decide to carry out a **value engineering** study in order to weed out products which might be too impractical or uneconomic. This involves looking into the availability of raw materials and components, probable manufacturing costs and so on.

Assuming that the product is a feasible proposition from the company's point of view, the next step is to assess whether the proposed new product is likely to appeal to customers. Detailed drawings or scale models of the concept are prepared. These are inexpensive for the company to produce yet realistic enough for consumers to get a good idea of what the product would be like. In order to evaluate the likely benefits of the product, respondents are also asked to imagine what it can do for them. **Concept testing** therefore makes it possible to evaluate consumers' reactions to a new idea before the company has committed itself to the expense of actually making the product.

(c) Assessing market potential

The next stage involves carrying out a detailed analysis of the product's market potential. The marketing department calculates sales forecasts and market share projections, estimates the advertising and promotional budgets that will be needed and recommends the prices that should be set. They also receive estimates from the production department as to the availability and cost of raw materials, packaging and production equipment, etc.

In addition, a break-even analysis is performed (page 150) to establish the point at which the product would begin to make a profit. Most importantly, marketers can use the forecasts to determine whether the volume of sales would be sufficient to cover development costs and provide a healthy profit margin in the long term.

Thorough and detailed analysis of this nature is expensive and time-consuming. Nevertheless, it is money well spent if it enables companies to decide at this early stage that a product is not commercially viable. This is particularly important as costs of development begin to escalate greatly at this stage.

(d) Developing a prototype

Given that the company has eliminated any unrealistic product ideas and carried out a thorough analysis of market potential, it will now be in a position to develop a **prototype product**. The main advantage of building a prototype is that designers and engineers can see potential manufacturing problems much more easily when they have a tangible, physical product before them.

Increasingly, however, the number of prototypes needed in testing is being reduced (or even eliminated) by the use of computer simulation techniques. Simulations allow the performance characteristics of the computer model, such as its resistance to stress, to be analysed accurately. Whereas in the past a company like Rolls Royce would have built as many as 39 test engines when developing a new aero engine, today 8 or 10 would be enough as the majority of the early testing is done by computer simulation.

(e) Test marketing
Providing that the prototype performs satisfactorily, the next stage is for the product to be sold in a **test market**, which is usually a town or small TV region. For example, Tyne-Tees was used as a test market for the launch of Wispa chocolate bars because it is a fairly neat, self-contained region, representing 5 per cent of UK spending power. Undertaking a small-scale trial enables the company to assess the degree of consumer acceptance for a new product without incurring the expense of a full national launch.

If the product does not realize its full potential, companies can cut their losses fairly easily. Linked to this is the fact that if the product fails dismally, then any damage to the company's reputation and image is limited to a small geographical area and thus a small number of potential purchasers.

Test marketing also benefits successful products in that it enables initial teething problems to be dealt with at the outset. However, test marketing is not possible for all new products; the need for secrecy can be vital to prevent rival firms getting wind of a launch. For example, whilst a US firm researched its new brand of chocolate-chip cookies in Kansas City, competitors Nabisco and Keebler rushed to launch their own versions nationwide, stealing the initiative (and much of the early sales advantage) from the pioneering brand.

(f) Full commercial launch
Once a product has proved to be successful in test markets, it is then ready for full commercial launch. Production capacity is increased to cope with the projected national level of demand. Final modifications are made to the product formulation, packaging and price, as well as to the promotional campaign. Advertising is booked, the sales force trained and distribution channels set in place.

The new product is then ready for national **roll out**. It is introduced first into one region, then a few months later into a second region. Firms thus have an opportunity to fine-tune any aspect of the marketing mix. At the same time, they have a chance to build up stock levels to meet the rising level of demand as the launch proceeds nationwide.

7.5 The failure rate of new products

It can be seen, then, that the entire product development process is geared to minimizing the risk of potential losers slipping through. Many products are rejected by the weeding-out process that takes place at each stage of development. For example, each year the pharmaceutical division of ICI considers approximately 10 000 new chemical compounds. Probably no more than four of these will be taken into development and only about one in ten eventually make it through to full commercial launch.

Even then, there is no guarantee of success for products which do reach the market. A recent study has shown that despite an explosion in the number of new products launched, on average less than a third actually survive their first two years in the market, let alone start to pay back development costs. As a result, companies do not get a chance to recover their investment in developing these new products, which normally requires a **payback period** of at least seven years. This is quite apart from the marketing and other costs incurred over that time period. However, the survival rate of new products varies for different categories of goods. Household goods actually have the highest failure rate with only one in ten new products surviving for two years.

What, then, are the prospects for the future? All the signs suggest that the failure rate, particularly in the fast-moving consumer goods market, looks set to increase. Sophisticated stock control systems, linked to electronic point of sale (EPOS) checkout tills, have enabled supermarkets and stores to root out slow moving lines. As competition for shelf space intensifies with the growing number of products on the market, those that fail to achieve a high sales volume initially are not allowed to gather dust for long.

Firms today are therefore faced with an impossible paradox. If they do not innovate they will inevitably be left behind by their competitors. On the other hand, if they do launch new products they stand to lose vast sums as the chances of failure are high. As Philip Kotler points out, 'Under modern conditions of competition, it is becoming increasingly risky not to innovate. . . . At the same time, it is extremely expensive and risky to innovate. The main reasons are:

- Most product ideas which go into product development never reach the market.
- Many of the products that reach the market are not successful.
- Successful products tend to have a shorter life than new products once had.'

7.6 Adoption and diffusion of innovations

If an innovative product is to be successful it must first be bought or adopted by individual consumers, households and organizations. Diffusion occurs only once acceptance of the product spreads through whole segments of society over a period of time. This would seem to suggest that there is an automatic progression from adoption to diffusion. The reality is, of course, very different. So, why is it that some newly launched products are adopted by the market more rapidly than others? Everett Rogers has outlined the factors influencing the rate at which innovative products are adopted and diffused. He argued that products achieve rapid acceptance when they have the following characteristics:

(i) Relative advantage The products can offer superior benefits in relation to existing products, e.g. colour television sets had a dramatic advantage over black-and-white television sets.

(ii) Compatibility The products are compatible with existing equipment and systems, e.g. radial tyres were quickly accepted because they could be fitted to cars in the same way as ordinary tyres.

(iii) Communicability Consumers find it easy to learn about the existence of the product and of its benefits which is why products often achieve rapid acceptance where they can use advertising of the 'Brand *x* washes whiter' variety.

(iv) Simplicity The products are simple to understand and use. For example, disposable lighters and razors work on the same principle as ordinary lighters and razors.

(v) Divisibility The products can be tried out before purchase. It is particularly important to reduce the level of perceived risk associated with items requiring a major financial commitment. For example, prospective purchasers can test drive a new car and try out a computer in the showroom.

According to Rogers, when the majority of these factors are positive adoption and diffusion is rapid. It is worth remembering, however, that some innovations may achieve rapid acceptance despite certain factors working against them. For example, computers were complicated to understand, represented a high-risk purchase and were not compatible with traditional methods of accounting and administration. Nevertheless, their obvious advantages were enough to outweigh these negative factors. In the event, computers have been adopted and diffused to the point where they have revolutionized every aspect of our lives.

The rate of adoption and diffusion is also influenced by whether the new product is evolutionary or revolutionary in nature. In general, **continuous innovations**, such as push-button telephones, tend to be accepted readily because they are usually modifications of existing products and so do not require consumers to change their behaviour drastically. Conversely, the telephone itself is a classic example of a **discontinuous innovation**, i.e. one which was quite different to any existing product. Discontinuous innovations are not adopted as readily because they alter profoundly the way we behave, unless of course the benefits are so dramatic, as with televisions and computers, that consumers do not resist the changes involved.

Ultimately, however, people vary greatly in their reactions to innovations. Why is it that some people rush to buy a new product the minute it comes onto

the market while others wait to see what everyone else does? Rogers identified
several different categories of people based on the ease with which they adopted
new products. The percentage of the population found in each of these groups
is shown in fig. 7.3.

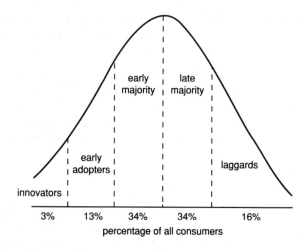

Fig. 7.3 The diffusion of innovations to different consumer categories

(i) Innovators   Innovators think for themselves and are willing to take risks.
They will often buy products simply because they are new. Sales to this group
are therefore not a reliable indication of a product's future potential.

(ii) Early adopters   Early adopters are willing to try new products before they
have achieved widespread acceptance. They have status in society and are often
regarded as opinion leaders which makes acceptance by this group crucial to
the success of a product.

(iii) Early majority   The early majority are cautious and risk-averse and will
only adopt the product once it becomes socially acceptable. Adoption by this
large group determines whether the product will gain widespread acceptance
and succeed as a mass-market product or whether it will survive merely as a
specialist product catering for a small market niche.

(iv) Late majority   The late majority are even more risk-averse than the early
majority. They will only consider adopting the product after overwhelming
evidence from others overcomes their reservations. At this stage the product
has become well established.

(v) Laggards   The laggards are individuals or organizations who resist the
new product and may never adopt it. They are generally timid and cautious by
nature, though this does not necessarily explain why they reject the innovation.

For instance, some products may be of little interest to particular consumers, e.g. sportswear will not interest those people who do not play any sports. In some cases the products may simply not be needed, e.g. garden equipment for people who live in flats. Alternatively, some people may find the product too expensive, too complex and so on.

The categories of adopters will, in any case, vary according to the type of product. For instance, innovators are not always the same people in each market. Some people may be early adopters in the computer market and laggards in the health food market.

The research carried out by Rogers into the adoption and diffusion of innovations has important implications for marketers. Once the characteristics of people in each category of adopters are known, then the advertising and sales effort can be targeted directly at them. The novelty aspect of the new product can be emphasized to the innovators, for instance, with a different emphasis being chosen for each group of adopters during the life cycle of a product.

7.7 The importance of branding

What's in a name? Until recently, the answer from many firms would have been 'not much'. But the takeover of Rowntree Mackintosh by Swiss confectionery firm Nestlé has finally put paid to all such notions. The fact that Nestlé was prepared to pay £2.3 billion for a firm which just six months earlier had been valued by the City at £1 billion was a clear indication of the importance it attached to such established **brand names** as Kit Kat, Polo, Smarties and After Eight.

In line with accounting practice at the time, Rowntree had never included a valuation for their brands in the company accounts. Not surprisingly, however, the Nestlé acquisition stimulated a flurry of activity as firms raced to include their brands as assets on the balance sheet so that they could then be reflected in the value of the company. For example, Rank Hovis McDougall valued its brands, among them Hovis, Mr Kipling and Bisto, as having a combined worth of £678 million. When Whyte and Mackay paid £33 million in 1990 for the Vladivar Vodka brand (without the bottling plant), this was further evidence that brand names have a market value over and above the intrinsic value of the products themselves.

If the prices at which brand names have recently been changing hands were not evidence enough, support for the fact that successful brands can be a firm's most important asset comes in a statement issued by the legal department at Coca-Cola: 'The production plants and inventories of the Coca-Cola company could go up in flames one night, yet the following morning there is not one bank in New York or any other place that would not lend this company the funds necessary for re-building, accepting as security only the goodwill of its trademark.'

Brands have evolved considerably since the late nineteenth century when the first manufacturers began to give their products names in order to distinguish them from the unpackaged goods available in general stores. For example,

William Lever first brought out his Sunlight soap in 1880, at a time when soap was still being cut from a slab, weighed and wrapped in brown paper. The new factory owners could take advantage of the mass-production techniques just developed. This, together with the growth of the railway network and spread of newspaper advertising, enabled them to produce in one location, yet win customers from anywhere in the country.

However, once face-to-face contact between sellers and buyers had been lost branding became essential; first, to distinguish the branded products (which were sometimes protected by legal patents) from unbranded products, and second, to provide consumers with a guarantee that the branded product was of a uniformly high quality as opposed to the often quite variable quality of unbranded products.

Today, the differences in quality are more marginal. Yet branded products consistently outsell their 'own label' counterparts in supermarkets. Clearly, a brand is much more than just a registered trademark. In fact, the imagery created by brands is so powerful that it is debatable whether buying decisions can ever be completely rational. In any case, human nature is such that in the same way as people tend to form irrational attachments towards scruffy old jumpers, comfortable arm-chairs and favourite books or records, they can also have illogical preferences for products on supermarket shelves.

Market research involving blind tests provides overwhelming evidence that brand names exert a strong influence on buying decisions. In the well-known Coca-Cola/Pepsi-Cola blind tests, people found little difference in taste between the two when they did not know whether they were drinking Coke or Pepsi. Yet when the test was repeated with the labels visible, 65 per cent of the sample then claimed to prefer Coca-Cola!

What, then, is the real attraction of a brand for consumers? A tube of toothpaste is merely a product. All toothpastes have the functional benefit of cleaning teeth, but a particular brand of toothpaste offers some additional benefit which differentiates it from its competitors – fewer fillings (Crest) brighter teeth (Ultra Bright), fresh breath (Aquafresh), etc. When building new brands manufacturers try to endow each one with a distinctive personality which is designed to set it apart from rival brands. Galaxy, Cadbury's Dairy Milk and Yorkie all have individual personalities and very different target audiences. Yet all three are just chocolate blocks.

The fact that brands provide some additional benefits compared with those offered by the basic products enables them to acquire an **added value** because of what consumers perceive as their extra worth. The **price-pain limit** is therefore raised as consumers are willing to pay more for what they regard as the 'better' branded product.

This is why so many products have now been branded; even typical **commodity products** like flour and sugar. Take Perrier, which must rank as one of the most phenomenal branding success stories of our time. A whole new market for bottled mineral waters was created from nowhere. Those who thought water was surely one of the last remaining 'unbrandable' commodities must be left wondering 'What next?'

Brands which become most powerful are those where a high level of repeat purchases are made by consumers who exhibit **brand loyalty**. If brands are to achieve this kind of loyal following, marketers must succeed in making consumers feel better towards their brand than those of competitors.

In time, brands can become successful to the point where the brand name passes into common usage and becomes adopted for all the products in that category – even those of rival firms. Walkman, Sellotape and Biro are all examples of such **generic brands**. In other words, people often say Hoover when they want a vacuum cleaner and Biro when they want a ball-point pen.

The most successful brands are, by definition, generally also the most profitable. For this reason, most large companies do not see any point in operating in a particular market unless they own the most successful brand leader with a dominant share of that market. This is not corporate arrogance but sound business strategy. Studies have shown that the brand leader in a market tends to earn an 18 per cent return after tax, with the number two brand producing only a 3 per cent return and the rest losing money. In apparent contradiction to this principle, the many small firms who manage to survive do so because they have actually gained a dominant share of a smaller, more specialized **market niche**.

Brands that achieve a leading market share are often remarkably long-lived. When consultants Booz, Allen and Hamilton looked at how twenty-four leading brands of 1923 had fared by 1983, they found that nineteen of the twenty-four were still market leaders sixty years later!

7.8 Why do brands disappear?

With the exception of the elite minority that seem almost immortal, the majority of brands do in fact have a finite economic life, succumbing to a variety of marketing pitfalls or often just being superseded as lifestyles and fashions change and new technologies are introduced. Remember Treets, Quattro, Farley's Rusks and the Ford Capri?

So why are brands withdrawn? In the case of Cadbury's Aztec, which was designed to compete with the Mars Bar, the problem was that it was just not distinctive enough. Others are withdrawn because of more subtle problems such as their public image becoming tainted. This happened to Watney's Red Barrel which sold in large quantities initially; until it became synonymous with everything cheap and nasty and the butt of jokes by drinkers belonging to organizations such as the Campaign for Real Ale.

Then there is disastrous advertising. Strand cigarettes fell victim to an infamous campaign with the slogan, 'You're never alone with a Strand' – interpreted universally as people with no friends smoke Strand cigarettes!

Changes in fashions and lifestyles help kill off many brands. Bronco hard toilet-roll paper, which was around for a hundred years, was obviously part of a bygone era. Similarly, the development of new models which make the old ones obsolete explains the disappearance of cars such as the Ford Cortina and the Vauxhall Viva.

This does not mean of course that brands disappear only because they have failed in the marketplace or reached the end of their lives. Today, the development costs for new brands are such that even brands which have been selling well can be withdrawn, purely because they did not meet the demanding sales targets which were set for them.

Consequently, there has been an increase in the use of **umbrella branding**. This is where the original strong brand name is transferred to a host of other related products, thus saving the cost of developing new brands from scratch.

Proctor and Gamble's Fairy Liquid is a case in point. The original product – household soap – is dead, but the brand name lives on as washing-up liquid, toilet soap and, more recently, as automatic washing liquid. This raises the question of whether brands can survive indefinitely. Perhaps brands only die if the company is not prepared to invest money in keeping them alive?

> **Case study** *PG Tips* **The impact of branding** Imagine the scene: a nervous account executive is presenting a new advertising idea to a major client for its tea brand. 'Well you see, er, we thought it might be a good idea to have these chimpanzees in a board-room meeting, sitting around in pin-stripe suits and reading the *Financial Times*. Then another chimpanzee dressed as a secretary brings in the tea and, er, they all drink it and agree what nice tea it is.' Exit red-faced account executive (client shouting, '. . . and don't come back!').
>
> The ultra-sophisticated advertising industry of today would no doubt throw its hands up in horror if the PG Tips monkeys were proposed for their screen debut in 1990. But as it is the 'PG chimps' have dominated the tricky world of tea marketing for 35 years.
>
> Their good work for the Brooke Bond PG Tips brand was recognized this year when it was awarded top prize in the Institute for Practitioners in Advertising's annual Advertising Effectiveness awards.
>
> Prior to a 1955 re-launch, the tea was known as Pre-Gestive (hence the PG) and was promoted for its medicinal qualities rather than its taste. The chimpanzees were brought in to lift the brand from its fourth position in the tea market.
>
> The first chimps advertisement featured a tea party at a stately home, with a voice-over by Peter Sellers. The simple proposition was that monkey antics on television would generate public warmth towards the brand. It was an immediate success and within two years PG Tips had reached the number one position in the market, pushing ahead of Typhoo, Lyons and Brooke Bond Dividend. The chimps stayed and to date have appeared in 110 commercials, keeping the brand ahead of the efforts of rival characters such as the Tetley Teafolk.
>
> Considering the turnover in advertising ideas, it is amazing that the campaign has been so popular for so long. Part of the reason

is undoubtedly the topicality of many of the scripts. One recent advertisement sends up the Channel tunnel project, with the British diggers emerging this side of the Channel.

However, the old scripts are best-remembered. Perhaps the two classics are the 1972 'Mr Shifter' advertisement ('Dad, do you know the piano's on my foot?' 'You hum it son, I'll play it.'), and the later 'Tour de France' advertisement which immortalized the lines, 'Avez-vous un cuppa?' and 'Can you ride tandem?'

The campaign, although undoubtedly popular with the public, is regularly scrutinized by Brooke Bond to evaluate its performance. Sales in the tea market have been declining steadily, from 156 million kg in 1964 to 110 million kg in 1989.

Since 1956, PG Tips has had to withstand two principal changes in the market: one was the advent of the teabag in 1963, when Tetley first put its perforated bags before the public; the second was the rise in popularity of own-brand teas. Despite sporadic blitzes by rival brands attempting to re-launch, PG Tips has retained its position at the top of the market. This, argues the advertising agency, has been achieved largely by a policy of consistent advertising.

Perhaps the power of advertising and branding was most clearly demonstrated by the fact that in blind tastings, the results showed people were unable to detect anything more than slight variations between brands, while branded tests had people rating PG Tips as the best-tasting tea. In marketing jargon this is known as **perceived added quality** – in other words, people imagine the product to be better because of its branding.

The long-running campaign has now passed into advertising folklore. Before the recent revival of 'Mr Shifter', research groups would claim to have seen the advertisement recently whereas it had not been on air for several years.

The PG Tips chimps clearly have something of a monopoly on recall and branding; how long the campaign will continue to be a success is impossible to tell, but it will be a brave marketing director who scraps them in favour of something more sensible.

Source: Adapted from *Thirty-five years of monkey business*, Emily Bell, *Observer*, Sunday, 11 November 1990.

7.9 A typical product life cycle

In our fast-changing society nothing stands still for long. We expect to see individual products and brands, and occasionally even whole product groups, come and go over a period of time. Inevitably, however, individual timespans vary greatly, ranging from the chart-topping records, ultra-trendy fashion crazes and fads like skateboards and frisbees, which may be 'out' as fast as they are 'in', to an elite minority of products which look like surviving forever.

Benedictine liqueur, now owned by Martini, was made by the monks centuries ago. Gilbey Gin was first introduced back in 1876, Hovis bread in 1895 and Cadbury's Dairy Milk in 1905. Much can happen to products in their lifetime, but it seems that the hardiest survivors can look forward to a long and profitable old age. The chances are products like Fairy Liquid, Nescafé, Kit Kat, Oxo, Colgate and Gillette, which seem to have an enduring appeal for successive generations of consumers, will probably still be around in 50 to 80 years time. It remains to be seen how many of the strong new brands to emerge in recent years, such as Ariel, Flora, Perrier, Nike and Foster's, will be able to match the performance of these long-running favourites.

However, with the exception of the premier brands, the development of new technologies, activity of competitors and changes in tastes and fashions all contribute towards making lesser products obsolete more quickly than ever before. Product life cycles are therefore getting shorter and shorter, particularly within the high technology industries such as electronics. Within the car industry, for instance, even a highly innovative product like the Leyland Mini, which was a huge success in its day, was not manufactured indefinitely. In contrast, products in the low-technology markets such as food, toiletries or household cleaning materials do not date easily, which explains why the successful ones can often enjoy very long life cycles. However, it is worth remembering that although long life cycles do offer more potential for making profits as a rule, short life cycles are not necessarily disastrous. For example, Golden Wonder's Pot Noodles had only a fleeting moment of glory but proved extremely profitable at the height of their popularity.

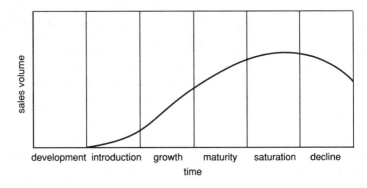

Fig. 7.4 Stages in a typical product life cycle

Yet whether they live for a century or more, or sink into obscurity within a short time, all products will nevertheless pass through a series of stages during their life span. They are born, grow rapidly in the early years then slow down as they reach maturity, until they eventually become old and die. In the same way, fig. 7.4 shows that the sales of a newly-launched product will increase rapidly during the growth period until competitors enter the market, causing the rate of growth to slow down. When almost all potential customers have been exploited, the market can expand no further and becomes saturated. Once sales begin to decline, possibly because the product has lost its appeal or has been overtaken by a rival product, it then becomes unprofitable to continue and the product is withdrawn.

The characteristic features of each stage, in terms of the level of demand, degree of competition and resulting share of the market, type of pricing policy and promotional methods adopted, as well as the level of profit which can be expected are outlined in Table 7.1.

Given that the conditions experienced in each stage are so different, it is obviously important for companies to know which stage their products have reached in order to make the best planning decisions. This has implications for such issues as deciding when to invest (essential in the growth period), when to charge high prices (impossible in the growth period when competition is intense) and when to expect a profit (not in the period of introduction when investment costs have yet to be recovered).

7.10 Extending the product life cycle

The standard sequence of stages described in the typical product life cycle presumes that the life of a product ends when sales have stagnated to the point where it is uneconomic to continue production. In reality, however, a product is not necessarily withdrawn even if sales have declined dramatically. For instance, it may be left on the market and 'milked' of any remaining profits, in which case any expenditure on maintaining it in terms of advertising and sales promotions would obviously be cut to a minimum. It goes without saying that the product would be removed very quickly if it started to damage the company's image and prejudice the introduction of new products.

Alternatively, companies may decide to keep an ailing product on the market in order to retain a complete range of products, or perhaps because the product still makes a contribution to overhead costs. Less rationally, an ailing product, which was once a best-seller, may be left on the market because the decision to drop it is a difficult one to take. The stance taken by Volkswagen towards the Beetle in former years is a prime example. As Robert Heller points out in his book, *The Supermarketers*, 'It had lived for far, far too long with the entire company's fortunes pinned to its snub nose, because the management couldn't bring itself to admit that its beloved Beetle was obsolete – or to agree on how to replace it.'

Table 7.1 Characteristics of the stages in a typical product life cycle

Characteristic	Introduction	Growth	Maturity	Saturation	Decline
	Innovators	Early adopters	Early majority	Late majority	Laggards
Type of customer					
Demand and level of sales	Sales growth is slow at first because people tend to be wary of new products. Firm assesses level of market demand and decides whether product is commercially viable.	Demand takes off and sales increase rapidly. The pioneering firm may not be able to meet the level of demand for the new product.	Sales continue to increase for a while (though less steeply than before) until they reach a peak. They then start to level off.	Demand decreases as there are fewer potential customers because the market has expanded to its full extent.	Sales begin to decline when changes in fashion, technological advances, or the introduction of superior products by rival firms make the product out of date.
Degree of competition	Few or no competitors, especially if product is innovative.	Competitors are attracted by the growth in sales. The shortfalls in supply provide them with an easy opening into the market. Aggressive competitors may offer products with superior features, perhaps even at a lower price.	Competition intensifies. Market leaders consolidate their position making it difficult for new entrants. Firms specialize to meet the needs of specific segments.	Few new competitors enter as the market is no longer growing. It is also expensive for new firms to break in. There is a 'shake out' as some firms drop out of the market.	The one or two remaining firms may not retaliate against new competition if they have already decided to withdraw their declining brands. Small firms may continue to survive by catering for specialized niche markets.
Aims of promotion	Informative advertising is used to create awareness. Promotions such as free samples may be used to encourage trial usage.	There is a shift from informative to persuasive advertising in an attempt to build brand preferences relative to competitors' products.	Increased spending on advertising is needed to maintain brand loyalty. Competitive advertising is used to defend market position.	Advertising aims to sustain habit buying. Advertising is also used to publicize 'new' or 'improved' versions which may be brought out in an attempt to extend the life of the product.	Advertising aims to slow down the rate of decline. Some firms may stop supporting their products altogether if they intend to let them die.

Share of the market	If the new product becomes accepted the pioneering firm can capture the entire market for a time.	The pioneering firm loses some market share as competitors enter and the total market is expanded.	The market expands to its full potential, then stabilizes with a few companies dominating the market.	Some competitors drop out of the market as their profits decrease.	Some firms may maintain their market share even when sales decline in order to retain a complete range of products.
Type of pricing policy	If the product is innovative high prices can be set to 'skim off' profits quickly before competitors enter the market. An alternative strategy is to set low prices in order to build market share rapidly.	Prices remain high initially then start to fall as competition intensifies with new entrants setting low prices in order to penetrate the market.	Prices level off as consumer buying patterns become stable and there is more resistance to price increases which are perceived as unnecessary. Price cuts may be needed to maintain sales.	Prices tend to fall as price wars break out with firms trying to undercut each other.	Pricing policy tends to be defensive and related to what competitors are charging. Over-capacity means that frequent price cuts are used to generate sales.
Level of profit	A loss is made to begin with as investment and development costs of research, production and marketing have yet to be recovered. Low sales volumes mean that production costs are also high.	Profit levels increase to a peak as the market grows and sales increase. Development costs begin to be recouped.	The market leaders make their highest profits in this phase, though the rest of the competition may only make marginal profits.	Profits decrease because of the reducing returns on each unit sold as it becomes more and more expensive to make any additional sales.	Profits fall as sales decline. The product may be 'milked' or withdrawn altogether if the firm has new products to take over from it.

In some cases, companies may make a conscious decision to invest in a product and attempt to raise a flagging sales curve by the use of various **extension strategies**. These include:

- making purely cosmetic changes to the product's shape, colour or packaging;
- changing the formulation, e.g. by removing artificial preservatives, introducing 'Diet' or 'Light' versions, etc;
- adding a new ingredient, e.g. a fluoride stripe to toothpaste;
- changing the price;
- changing the kind of retail outlets through which the product is distributed;
- adding new accessories;
- bringing out new product variants, e.g. fun-size Mars Bars, tinted light bulbs;
- designing a new advertising campaign;
- finding new customers, e.g. by opening up export markets.

In these ways, the original product or brand can be 'stretched' to support several variations on a theme thus prolonging the mature stage of the life cycle for as long as possible. The changes are often quite marginal, witness the many 'new' or 'improved' products, launched amidst a blaze of publicity, which invariably turn out to be virtually identical **line extensions** of the original product.

In addition, marketers need to be aware of the danger of **cannibalization**. With any new product that is launched, there is a danger that it will steal sales away from the brand leader which usually has a higher profit margin – this was the effect diet Coke had on sales of Coke. There is also the danger of diluting the brand name, which can occur when products that are launched subsequently under the same umbrella brand do not perform as well as the original parent brand.

Ironically, new versions sometimes become far more successful than their parents. Mini-cheddars, sold as small cheese snacks in a crisp-style packet, are a classic example. United Biscuits sold the product for years in a conventional roll pack as biscuits for eating with cheese. Now, scaled down and presented as snacks, they sell at twice the price per gram as the standard biscuit pack. The product is the same – the differences are purely cosmetic, i.e. in the size, shape and packaging.

A product which is given a new lease of life for any reason will experience a **recycled product life cycle**, as shown in fig. 7.5. In other words the flagging sales curve is rejuvenated and lifted upwards as the increase in sales creates a new period of growth.

A new advertising campaign which changes the image of the product, and therefore its market positioning, can ward off decline and lead to a very successful recycle. The dramatic transformation in both the sales and image of Lucozade, into what is now a mainstream soft-drink product, is a case in point (case study on pages 83–4). Repackaging packet tea into tea bags which could

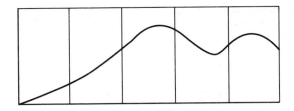

Fig. 7.5 The recycled product life cycle

then compete with the convenience of instant coffee, revived the fortunes of the entire tea industry. A recycled product life cycle can also occur when new markets are found for a product whose present market is saturated. For instance, Raleigh established successful new markets in third world countries for its bicycles and continued selling in those markets long after sales in the UK had declined dramatically.

With some products, new market uses are found which stave off eventual decline and cause a step-up in the product life cycle as sales escalate periodically with each new use that is discovered. Du Pont's handling of nylon is a good example. Originally developed for the parachute industry, nylon would have gone into decline after the Second World War had Du Pont not found a new use for it in women's stockings. They have since found new uses in clothes, ropes, fishing nets, tyres and more recently in carpets. This **staircase effect** product life cycle is shown in fig. 7.6.

Fig. 7.6 The staircase effect product life cycle

Other products are replaced at intervals by newer models with superior features. This applies particularly to goods such as cars, domestic appliances, computers, hi-fi equipment and so on. This **leapfrog effect** product life cycle is shown in fig. 7.7.

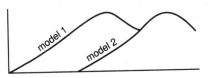

Fig. 7.7 The leapfrog effect product life cycle

7.11 The need for a balanced product portfolio

Firms are only too aware that even the most successful products cannot last forever. For this reason they generally attempt to build a balanced **product portfolio**, consisting of a range of products which are all at different stages in their life cycles. If firms relied solely on their established products they could face cash flow problems in the future when those 'mature' products inevitably begin to decline. Conversely, an over-reliance on 'young' products could prove equally dangerous because of the heavy financial burdens created by the cash injections which growing products require. The survival rate of newly-launched products is in any case notoriously low and many do not last long enough to repay the investment made in them.

However, by ensuring that they have a balanced product portfolio, with some established products to generate cash in the present and some growth products as an investment for the future, firms are in effect avoiding the risks associated with having 'all your eggs in one basket'. Portfolio analysis can also help firms to identify those products which are going to need extra resources in order to improve their performance, as well as those which are performing so badly that they need to be dropped altogether.

One of the earliest and most influential methods of portfolio analysis is that devised by the Boston Consulting Group in the USA during the 1960s. This technique enables firms to assess whether they have a balanced range of products by classifying products on the basis of two key factors – **relative market share** and **market growth**.

(a) Relative market share

Relative market share (RMS) is in many ways a more useful concept than market share (MS). RMS is calculated by dividing the market share of a firm by the market share of its largest competitor. For example, a firm may have a 25 per cent MS. If its closest rival has a MS of 5 per cent this means that the firm has a RMS of 5 (i.e. $25 \div 5 = 5$). If on the other hand the firm has a 25 per cent MS and its closest rival has a MS of 50 per cent, the firm then has a RMS of only 0.5 (i.e. $25 \div 50 = 0.5$). In other words a percentage MS can mean very different things in different markets. The great appeal of RMS, however, is that it indicates the position of a firm in the market relative to its largest competitor.

It is essential that the RMS held by each product in the portfolio is known. After all, any firm which manages to capture the highest share of a market relative to its main competitors will, by definition, have the largest sales volume and will therefore be able to produce its goods most cheaply. Cost savings result from the firm moving down the **experience curve**. As output increases costs fall, partly because of the **learning curve** where workers become more efficient and specialized in what they do, and partly because of the **economies of scale** which produce lower operating costs. According to the Boston Consulting Group, costs can decline by as much as 30 per cent for every cumulative doubling of output. It follows that a firm which has achieved the highest RMS in any particular market is bound to become more profitable than its competitors simply because it has the lowest unit costs.

(b) Market growth

The second factor considered in portfolio analysis is market growth. Firms need to know whether their products are sold into high or low growth markets. (Actual percentage growth rates will of course vary according to the market. For instance, a growth rate of 15 per cent may be considered high in the mature market for breakfast cereals but low in a growing market like that of home computers.) In general, firms prefer to invest in growth markets because these obviously offer more potential for products to succeed than declining or static markets.

Growth markets are also more attractive to firms who wish to improve the market share of their products. In fact, a company must improve its market share during a period of high market growth as it is extremely expensive, if not impossible, to gain share from the established market leaders later on as growth slows down. There is a great danger of being forced out of the market if this is not done, which is, in fact, exactly what happened to the British motorcycle industry. Whereas the Japanese increased their market share dramatically during a period of rapid growth, the output of British firms remained static. When the rate of market growth fell inevitably and consumers became more price sensitive, the Japanese were able to reduce their prices (because of their lower costs and higher profit margins). The British firms could not compete and died out.

7.12 The Boston matrix

This simple matrix developed by the Boston Consulting Group enables firms to classify their products according to two key variables: relative market share and market growth (fig. 7.8). Each category is given a descriptive title which summarizes the ability of the product to generate cash (cash flow is usually a more accurate indication of healthy performance than profits). The categories equate neatly to the stages in the life cycle of a typical product. A 'Question mark', for example, is a product introduced recently which has not yet established itself, hence the doubt as to its future. If it passes through the growth stage successfully, it may become a 'star' and then a 'cash cow' as it reaches maturity. Once it passes into decline it becomes a 'dog'.

(a) Question marks

These are products with a low relative market share in a high-growth market. Question marks have not yet captured a high market share, often because they have been launched recently. They require a high level of funding to maintain their position within a high-growth market and are therefore a drain on the company's resources. Question marks have an uncertain future. Some may succeed, increasing their market share and becoming stars, particularly if management thinks they have potential and are prepared to invest cash in developing them. However, if question marks are allowed to slide without being given any support, they can decline rapidly and become dogs.

(b) Star
These are products which have generally been introduced recently, and which have achieved high relative share in a high-growth market. Stars may not actually produce much surplus cash (despite generating large amounts), simply because they require a great deal to finance their rapid growth. As they mature, stars should eventually turn into cash cows, though if funds are not invested in defending their market share against the competition, they may well regress to becoming question marks once again.

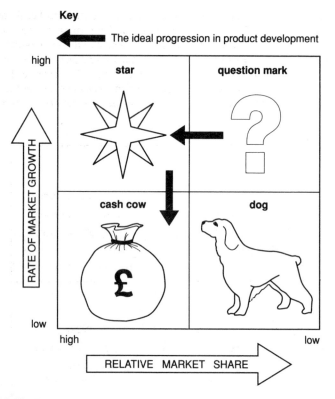

Fig. 7.8 The Boston matrix

(c) Cash cows
Products become cash cows once they hold a high relative market share in a low growth market. Cash cows such as the IBM main-frame computer and the Philip's light bulb are market leaders that generate large amounts of revenue,

which can be 'milked' to fund the development of question marks and the growth of stars. They require minimal re-investment because of being in a stable, mature market where their established market position does not need to be defended. They have the potential to become stars again if their life is prolonged by recycling, perhaps because of the discovery of new uses or markets or perhaps because management has decided to adopt extension strategies such as creating a different advertising campaign. However, cash cows can only become stars again if initiatives such as these can rejuvenate products to the point where the entire market is stimulated and the growth rate of the market begins to increase.

(d) Dogs

Products are known as dogs when they have a low relative market share in a low-growth market. Dogs have little future and are often a drain on the resources of the company. Investment in them should be reduced to a minimum. Ideally, dogs should be phased-out or sold off, unless they are needed for some reason – to complete a product range, for instance. In some cases, lack-lustre products may be reprieved if management decide that they are capable of surviving within a small market niche. The decision to drop these

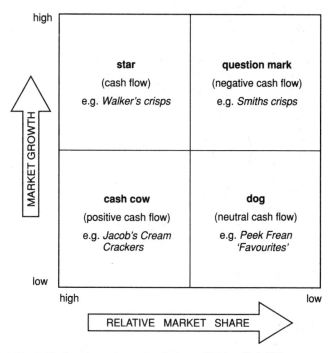

Fig. 7.9 The BCG share/growth matrix relating to Nabisco Ltd, UK
Source: *Offensive Marketing*, Hugh Davidson, Penguin Business Books.

products is never easy, especially if they were once large money-spinners or the 'baby' of a particular manager. Many such products survive, according to Peter Drucker, purely as 'investments in management ego'. The Boston matrix relating to Nabisco Ltd, UK is shown in fig. 7.9.

7.13 Using the Boston matrix to forecast the future potential of products

The Boston matrix can be used to forecast the future market position of products within a portfolio. The present and forecast positions can be represented visually on a matrix, as in the example shown in fig. 7.10. The circles represent the company's four main products, A–D, with the shaded circles showing the forecast position of the products at a given time in the future – usually a year ahead. The area of each shaded circle is proportional to the amount that each product is predicted to contribute to the sales volume.

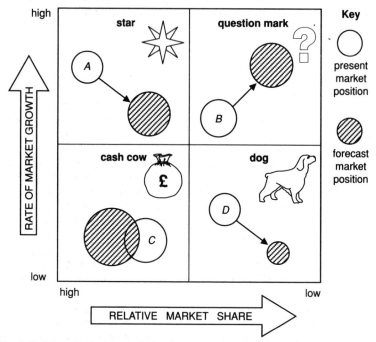

Fig. 7.10 A hypothetical example showing future market positions of a firm's products

Product *C* is obviously the best-selling line in the case of this hypothetical company. The matrix also reveals that product *A*, in spite of its increased sales volume, is likely to lose market share – a worrying trend within a high-growth market and one which would need to be rectified, if possible. However, the increase in sales anticipated for product *C* seems promising, particularly within a declining market. Product *B*, despite increasing sales slightly, is predicted to lose market share, which means it inevitably has an uncertain future. Product *D*, which looks set to lose sales as well as market share, clearly has no future at all and should be withdrawn from the market.

7.14 Strengths and weaknesses of the Boston matrix

(a) Strengths

- The matrix represents in a simple and graphic way how well a firm's products are performing in terms of the two key variables of relative market share and market growth.
- It can be used to forecast the future market potential of products.
- Managers can allocate resources on the basis of these classifications, i.e. shifting funds away from the dogs (which are due to be phased out) and cash cows (which do not require investment). These resources can then be put to better use funding the growth of stars and question marks, as well as the research and development of new products.

(b) Weaknesses

- Market growth is not the only measure of a market's attractiveness. In fact, high-growth markets are not necessarily the best markets to be in. For example, it would not make sense for a firm making agricultural machinery to enter the personal computer market purely because it is a high-growth market.
- The assumption underlying the experience curve, i.e. that the firm with the highest relative market share is always the lowest cost producer, may not always hold true. For instance, late entrants into a market may have operating costs which are lower than the established market leader because they can install the most advanced production equipment and systems.
- The approach hinges on the need to weed out products with very little potential. Companies with a high proportion of products classified as dogs cannot, however, divest themselves of these products immediately, even if they are a considerable drain on resources. After all, it would be extremely dangerous to get rid of what amounts to most of the company's product base in one fell swoop.
- Another central assumption is that products with a low market share are not financially viable. In reality, though, providing the low share products form part of a wide product range they will benefit from the economies of scale created by other products in the portfolio. For example, premium beers with a low market share are in fact extremely profitable because they are produced and distributed along with the mass market beers which enjoy high market shares.

More sophisticated techniques such as the McKinsey/General Electric matrix have since been developed, which classify products on the basis of a number of different factors, not just relative market share and market growth.

The right price

8.1 Setting the right price

Prices cannot be decided in a vacuum. Unit 9 shows how economic factors external to an organization influence the prices that are set. This unit deals with the other side of the coin – how internal factors within an organization, e.g. the type of objectives set by firms, the kinds of strategies adopted to achieve those objectives and the different techniques used to determine costs and revenue, all influence the prices which are chosen.

Decisions concerning price cannot, in any case, be made in isolation from other elements of the marketing mix. There would be no point, for instance, in offering an upmarket perfume which retails through specialist stores and is advertised in 'quality' magazines at a very low price. The price clearly does not fit in with the other elements of the marketing mix and as a result the image projected to the consumer is confused.

What exactly is the 'right' price? Some people are prepared to pay almost any amount to get what they want – witness the Bugatti Royale that last changed hands at auction for around £10 million! When consumers can pay anything between £10 000 and upwards of £100 000 for what is essentially a metal container on wheels to take them from A to B, it becomes clear that price is the amount that consumers are prepared to exchange for what they perceive as the value of a product or service.

Whether products are perceived as good or poor value by consumers is influenced by the use to which they will be put. Consumers will pay more for products whose benefits they value highly. Much depends on the esteem in which the product or service is held. The significance of the purchase cost within individual budgets is also important.

Marketers distinguish between the basic price paid by consumers for the 'core' product and the **premium price differential**, which is the extra amount charged for the superior quality product with better features. This is illustrated by the difference in price between a Timex watch and a Rolex. But manufacturers have also been known to charge a premium price for products which are almost identical to the basic product, the only difference being in the packaging and advertising!

In deciding on a price, marketers also need to be aware of the fact that consumers often tend to judge the quality of a product by the price itself. If a price is set which is too low there is always the danger that the psychology of price may influence consumers into thinking, 'If the product is really so good, why is it so cheap?'

This was the problem with a new brand of fruit juice which when launched sold in much smaller quantities than anticipated. Market research revealed that consumers found it hard to believe that the claims on the can could be true for such a cheap product. Based on these findings, the company decided to take the fruit juice off the market and re-introduce it at twice the price. Sales increased dramatically, thus proving that the original price had been wrong. However, setting the 'right' price is never easy, as shown by the case of Nigel Wright and the company he founded to sell cut-price jeans.

Case study The shrunken dreams of Nigel Wright After storming Britain's jeans market, the founder of Dickie Dirts crashed spectacularly. Now, a wiser man, he is having another go.

In the late 1970s to early 1980s, Dickie Dirts outlets were regularly thronged with shoppers buying cut-priced jeans. Nigel Wright, the company's founder, was a former photographer who began selling shirts (dickie dirts in Cockney rhyming slang) as a sideline when commissions were slack. By a quirk of fate, the business became the Topsy of jeans retailing. It grew from almost nothing on a market stall in 1976 into a £10 million operation employing 200 staff by 1982.

It seemed that Wright's success would catapult him into the Richard Branson league. Instead, in the spring of 1982, over trading sent the company into liquidation with losses of £2 million. Wright was made personally bankrupt to the tune of £250 000. Now, aged 51, he expects to be declared solvent shortly and is making a comeback.

When Wright hit London in the late 1970s, consumers loved him, fellow retailers loathed him. Wright undermined his rivals by breaking their near-cartel on pricing, an action from which the market has not completely recovered. By driving down prices, Dickie Dirts devalued the product. 'Denim is now a low margin business, unless you have something different,' says Chris Healy, Sales and Retail Director of Falmer Jeans, one of the best-known British manufacturers.

Wright admits he took advantage of what was widely seen as overpricing in the 1970s. 'There was controversy because jeans were popular and had become very expensive,' he says. 'There was talk of an investigation into pricing, so I used that as a vehicle to promote our name.'

Cheapness was not the only attraction. Wright campaigned for late night and Sunday opening and kept his shops trading seven days a week. Growth was so rapid that he was unable to keep up. 'It sounds a wonderful dream,' Wright says, 'but we needed to hire so many staff and install so many phones that we never sat down and counted the cost. I didn't know anything about management techniques. It was just me and I was a jack of all trades, master of none.'

Looking back, a wiser Wright believes a few simple decisions could have kept him afloat. 'If we'd charged just £1 more a pair, the original company could still be in business today,' he claims.

Source: Adapted from *The shrunken dreams of Nigel Wright*, Sally Hamilton, *Business* magazine, March 1990.

8.2 Pricing objectives

The pricing objectives chosen will tend to reflect general corporate objectives. For instance, a firm which intends to become the dominant market leader within the next five years will clearly adopt very different pricing objectives to a firm which is quite content with continued gradual growth. In practice, firms tend to pursue a combination of objectives rather than a single objective. Nor do these objectives remain static for long. Competitors' activities and the ever increasing pace of technological progress means that objectives are constantly revised in line with changing conditions.

(a) Improve profitability
Profits can be made in two different ways. Firms which sell their products and services at low prices can make profits even though the profit margin on each item is small, providing a high sales volume is generated from a large turnover of goods sold.

Firms which sell their products and services at high prices can make profits because the high profit margin on each item compensates for a lower overall turnover.

Whatever approach is adopted, it is worth remembering that firms are not necessarily preoccupied with making larger profits. Much research in recent years has questioned the underlying basis of conventional price theory which assumes that **profit maximization** is the sole aim of every firm. If anything, evidence suggests that survival is now more likely to be the major preoccupation in the marketplace of the 1990s.

A proportion of firms have, in any case, always been prepared to sacrifice profits temporarily in order to achieve other objectives such as an increased market share. By undercutting competitors' profits (even to the point of making a loss for a while) they have expanded their own market share at the expense of those that have been driven out. Japanese firms have penetrated many markets by employing this strategy.

There are, of course, other reasons why firms may decide not to maximize profits. They may choose to invest heavily in land, buildings, equipment or research and development – all of which are likely to improve their profitability over the long term. This kind of investment in the future is obviously essential for the long-term health of firms. It may, however, mean they have to forgo profits in the short term.

(b) Build market share

A common objective is to set prices at a level that enables a specified share of a market to be captured. Firms in the consumer goods industries tend to use this kind of objective because it is practical and workable. It is also easy to assess whether a particular market share has been achieved by referring to one of the many officially published sources of market research. Consumer-panel studies such as the Television Consumer Audit (TCA), which monitor the purchasing behaviour of a panel of consumers, are often used for this purpose.

Firms which manage to build a large market share, such as Eastman Kodak with photographic film and Caterpillar with construction equipment, are able to operate cost-effectively because of the economies of scale made possible by a high sales volume. This enables them to become more profitable than their competitors. The dominant market position which accompanies a sizeable market share can also allow firms to dictate prices which their weaker competitors often have to follow. In the computer industry, smaller firms have tended to follow the lead set by IBM, particularly during the period of the late 1950s and 1960s when IBM held a staggering 80 per cent share of the market for main-frame computers.

Not all firms, however, strive to increase their share within the market as a whole. Whereas Texas Instruments have captured a large chunk of the pocket calculator market with their low prices over the years, Hewlett Packard have chosen instead to cater for a small, specialized segment with their expensive scientific calculators. Despite their small share of the overall market Hewlett Packard have, in fact, gained a large share of a smaller **niche market**.

(c) Achieve a return on investment

A common pricing objective is for firms to achieve a specified level of income as a **return on investment (ROI)**. In other words, they aim to get back a certain proportion of the money they have invested in land, buildings, machinery and stock or which has been held as capital. For instance, General Motors has traditionally aimed to achieve a 20 per cent ROI after tax.

(d) Maintain price stability

This is a popular objective, particularly amongst the largest firms in an **oligopoly**. Oligopolies, which are markets dominated by a handful of giant firms, are found in industries such as soaps and detergents (e.g. Unilever, Proctor and Gamble) and cigarettes (e.g. Imperial Tobacco and Gallaher).

If one firm decides to raise prices for any reason, the others immediately follow suit to avoid undercutting the new price. The oil companies provide a good example of this pattern in relation to petrol prices. The fact that they are all aware of the consequences of setting off a fruitless price war encourages price stability.

The danger of a **price cutting war** is that the firm which cuts its prices merely gains a temporary advantage as it will not be long before the other competitors are forced to retaliate by lowering their prices even more. A relentless downward spiral of prices leads ultimately to the status quo being reinstated, with all the major firms holding the same market share as they had before – but at a new lower price level. Thus, every firm involved in a price cutting war suffers in the long run.

Firms therefore avoid getting into a destructive price war which lowers profit margins for all, preferring instead a strategy of **non-price competition**. This is where firms compete by using one or more of the other elements of the marketing mix such as product, place or promotion. It is much harder to change the product itself or the places through which it is distributed so in practice non-price competition usually boils down to the creation of new advertising campaigns. These are designed to imbue each product with an original and distinctive image so that it then occupies a unique position in the marketplace.

The collapse of Laker Airways provides a powerful illustration of the pitfalls of price competition. When Freddie Laker first offered transatlantic fares at bargain prices via his Skytrain service, business flourished. However, his prices were soon matched by the larger airlines who, with their greater resources, were in a much stronger position to sustain the prolonged price war that ensued.

The lesson which can be drawn, as Robert Heller points out in his book *The Supermarketers*, is that, 'Initially, the price cutter operates and flourishes under the umbrella of the established giants whose prices he is undermining. When, eventually and inevitably, they retaliate, he loses his unique selling proposition and with it goes some of the sold-out volume that keeps down his unit costs. As his costs rise, while his prices can't, the profits get crucified.'

The American airline People Express experienced a similar fate when it challenged the prices of the established airlines. As Heller explains, 'People Express, with its notorious overbooking, the bedlam at Newark airport and no-frills (that is, minimal) service, offered a bad deal in every respect save one – price.' With their sole advantage gone, it was only a matter of time before People Express met the same fate as Laker Airways.

Clearly, it is far better for a firm to win sales by differentiating its products from those of its competitors with a fresh advertising campaign rather than on the basis of lower price; particularly in view of the market research studies carried out by firms such as A.C. Nielsen that suggest price reductions appeal mainly to those who are already regular users. In other words, the lower prices merely encourage consumers to bring forward purchases which would have been made at a later date at the normal price.

(e) Prevent competition

Mature markets for well established products, which are dominated by a few large firms, tend to be characterized by price stability. In contrast, young markets for products still in the early stages of their life cycle, often exhibit a high degree of price competition as firms jockey for position in the marketplace.

Some firms may deliberately set very low prices in order to strengthen their market share by forcing existing competitors to withdraw and discouraging potential new competitors from entering the market. This is known as **predatory pricing**.

During the early 1980s, market leaders in the personal computer market pursued an aggressive pricing strategy whereby a constant stream of technologically superior models was introduced at rock bottom prices. As a result, they were able to outsell the small firms, many of whom died out.

8.3 Pricing strategies

Once firms have defined their objectives, the next step is to establish a pricing strategy.

(a) Skimming

This is where firms set very high initial prices in order to 'skim the cream' from any profits to be made. It is a strategy adopted in both new and mature markets.

When new products are introduced, particularly if they are innovative and technologically advanced, the earliest buyers tend to be those who are prepared to pay over the odds or those who can justify paying the high prices because of the usefulness of the new product to them. For example, the high prices of car telephones meant that they could only be afforded by senior management initially. Then as prices fell many more people came to regard them as essential items.

A skimming policy has been adopted for the introduction of a whole host of products such as colour televisions, video cassette recorders, calculators, telephone answering machines, personal computers and satellite TV dishes. The Polaroid Land Camera, for instance, which was the first camera to produce instant photographs was originally sold for around £100, whereas a basic model now sells for about £10. Compact disc players, selling at around the £100 mark, are now a quarter of the price they were in 1983 when they first came onto the market.

The high profits resulting from this strategy enable research and development costs to be recovered quickly. Skimming is commonly used for products in their infancy and for those which are likely to have a short life cycle.

The fact that sales levels are low initially is actually another advantage of this strategy. Firms benefit from the breathing space which allows them to build up their production capacity to cope with the likely increase in demand. Prices are then lowered as economies of scale result in falling costs. This allows larger, price sensitive segments to be tapped.

Manufacturers of newly launched products could, at one time, count on a fairly long period of market domination before competitors were able to organize their production systems to bring out 'copycat' versions. Me-too products are, however, tending to appear increasingly rapidly, particularly from

Far Eastern competitors, shortening the crucial post-launch period when a new product is expected to yield the highest returns. The days of fat profits enjoyed over a long period, which the makers of earlier generations of electronic gadgetry experienced, have long gone. The microwave oven, for instance, was selling at a fraction of its launch price almost immediately after it appeared.

Though a skimming strategy is usually associated with new products, it has also been adopted successfully in mature markets which are highly segmented, particularly within high income segments which are not sensitive to price. The luxury end of the car market is one such example. The price of a Bentley car (in 1993) ranged from £94 000 to £170 000 for a top of the range Continental coupé. Yet even these list prices are meaningless – with a six-year waiting list, second-hand Continentals can change hands at well over £150 000!

(b) Penetration
This is where firms set low prices to capture mass markets quickly. It is a strategy often used for undifferentiated products which can be copied quickly by competitors, such as food or drink items. There is not usually a segment of buyers willing to pay premium prices for these products.

The low prices encourage rapid adoption and diffusion when these products are first launched. They also enable firms to build market share and a degree of brand loyalty before competitors have time to respond. The low prices will, in any case, often discourage potential competitors from entering the market in the first place.

However, in other respects the low prices create disadvantages for firms operating a penetration strategy. As profit margins per individual product are minimal, they need to be offset by a very high sales turnover to generate enough profit in total. Even so, it may take quite some time before firms recover their development costs and begin to make a profit.

With the exception of notable success stories such as Amstrad in the consumer electronics market, this is a strategy that holds many pitfalls for the unwary. It is extremely difficult to penetrate a market by undercutting competitors' prices and to maintain that position for long, as there will always be a firm somewhere which is prepared to offer even lower prices. Increasingly, this challenge comes from a manufacturer based in one of the low-wage producing countries of the developing world such as Taiwan, Hong Kong and more recently South Korea. British firms, with their higher operating costs, are thus likely to be far too vulnerable if they attempt to compete in today's market solely on the basis of lower prices.

So, on balance, is it better for firms to adopt a skimming or penetration strategy? This is not an easy question to answer as both approaches have their advantages. Fortunately, the choice between the two opposing strategies is not usually an either/or decision. What often happens is that firms set skimming prices initially in order to recover their development costs, switching to penetration prices later on once competitors enter the market, thus gaining the best of both worlds.

(c) Competition orientated pricing

Often known as pricing at the going rate, this is a strategy which is commonly found in price sensitive markets, particularly those involving commodity type products which are not capable of being differentiated in any way.

Firms have to charge similar prices to one another in this situation because unless their product offers customers a significant benefit it cannot command a higher price. This is why petrol companies, banks, building societies, supermarkets and high street electrical retailers, for instance, all tend to keep their prices very much in line with each other.

Competition orientated pricing is also found in industries dominated by one or two large firms where the weaker firms tend to follow the prices set by the market leaders.

(d) Price discrimination

Based on the principle that demand for a product varies according to different factors, this is now so commonplace that we almost take it for granted. We expect to pay less to use the telephone at evenings and weekends, to travel by train during the middle of the day, to watch a matinée performance at the cinema in the afternoon and to stay at a resort hotel out of season. The lower prices at these times attempt to compensate for the lack of demand outside periods of peak usage by encouraging the use of facilities that would otherwise be under-used.

Price can also vary for different groups of customers. Children, old age pensioners, students and the unemployed are all entitled to reduced rates for many facilities.

In addition, prices can vary tremendously when different market segments are catered for by slightly different versions of what is essentially the same basic product. Examples include:

- seats in a theatre - stalls, dress circle, box;
- rooms in a hotel - standard room, superior room, executive suite;
- seats in a plane - economy or tourist class, business class, first class.

> **Case study   Sugar's low prices made Amstrad a sweet success**
> By 1968, when he was barely 21 years old, Alan Sugar had earned enough money through selling car aerials from the back of an ancient van to set up his own company, AMS Trading, which was later changed to Amstrad. In the years since, Sugar has propelled Amstrad from its standing start in 1968 into a major household name, proving that a British firm is capable of taking on the giant Japanese and American firms within the cut-throat video, TV and computer markets - and winning. Amstrad has become a dominant force within consumer electronics, at one time outstripping even the mighty IBM to capture a leading share of the personal computer market in Britain.
> Few would disagree that Sugar has more than succeeded in his

original aim of 'filling the gaps in the electronics market'. In the process, he managed to build a company worth just under £700 million in June 1990. By 1988, his personal stake in Amstrad shares had reached an all time high of £597 million, making him one of the richest businessmen in Britain – an incredible achievement for a boy who grew up on one of the poorest council housing estates in the East End of London (fig. 8.1).

Fig. 8.1 Alan Sugar and the first Amstrad PC

Alan Sugar has come a long way from his days of selling at street markets. Yet those early trading experiences were undoubtedly crucial in shaping his legendary 'feel' for the kinds of products that his target customers would be likely to want. A high degree of customer orientation is obviously an essential ingredient in Amstrad's success. Sugar says he would paint pink spots on his computers if that was what the customers wanted! But in the final analysis, it was the cost cutting policies, careful sourcing of components and commitment to large production volumes that enabled products to be launched at prices designed to savagely undercut the competition which were ultimately responsible for Amstrad's phenomenal growth.

Amstrad computers are found in so many studies and bedrooms across the nation, it is easy to forget that computers were once the exclusive preserve of medium-sized companies, and came with price tags that kept them out of most people's reach. In producing a personal computer (PC) that was cheap enough for the majority of people to buy and simple enough for them to use, Amstrad stimulated such a huge demand that PCs were transformed from specialist products into mass market goods. Analysts had by then begun to call this opening up of a whole new mass market of people who could afford to buy for the first time 'the Amstrad effect'.

Sugar's first big high street success had in fact occurred much earlier, with a stackable hi-fi system launched in 1978. Called The Tower, it housed a turntable, tuner and tape deck together in one unit with a single plug. No new technology was involved but the idea was revolutionary in its simplicity as most audio equipment of the time was bought as separate items, which were complicated and time-consuming to connect together. It was a product aimed not at hi-fi buffs but at 'the truck driver and his wife', according to Sugar.

Identifying a previously untapped market segment was, of course, only the first step in producing these successful money spinners. The hard part was to deliver a product that was easy to use, represented excellent value for money and looked as if it had cost far more than it had in reality.

The success of Amstrad's first home computers, which were practically skating out of the shops when they were launched in 1984 at the startlingly low price of £299, provided the clearest evidence that Amstrad had perfected a winning formula.

A new word processor was unveiled soon afterwards aimed mainly at small businesses and the self employed. Priced at £399, which was about a quarter of the cost of its nearest rival, it showed what kind of impact 'the Amstrad effect' could have on markets. When first launched, it started selling at the rate of 50 000 units a month. This was at a time when total sales of all makes of word processors in Britain were around 30 000 units a year!

On the strength of this success Amstrad brought out its IBM PC clone, which doubled the size of the PC market within a year. The slogan used on the advertising campaign accompanying the launch, 'Compatible with you know who. Priced as only we know how', reflected the typically competitive Amstrad stance on pricing.

Sugar's strategy was based firmly on the principle that the price of his computers should reflect what they cost to make, not the price that the market could bear. Amstrad's aim was to generate high sales volumes by opening up new mass markets. This made it economic to charge low prices. At the same time production costs were cut to the minimum. But how did Amstrad manage to drive costs down to the point where profits were made despite the low prices set?

Sugar's skill in scouring the world for the cheapest components provides part of the answer. Discovering early on when buying from British firms that many of their components had been shipped in from the Far East, he decided it would be cheaper to buy direct. To this day, he maintains flexibility in sourcing, buying from whichever firms he can negotiate the best bulk discounts. Buying from a variety of firms also ensures that Amstrad does not become over dependent on any particular supplier.

The fact that manufacturing is sub-contracted to outside firms lowers overhead costs considerably. Without a fixed capital investment in factories and machinery, Amstrad has the option of abandoning markets where demand is drying up in favour of those which look more promising. Sugar's uncanny ability to sense which way the wind is blowing led him to pull out of CB radios in 1981 just before the bottom fell out of the market and to quit the colour TV and video recorder market in 1984 when he predicted a market glut and potential price war in the wake of the Japanese onslaught.

Costs are also reduced by the elimination of specialist product features that only a few people are likely to want – what Sugar scathingly dismisses as 'frills'. 'We produce what the mass market customer wants, not a boffin's ego trip,' he says. And contrary to accepted practice, Amstrad sets the price of a product before it is designed. Designers and engineers then have to make sure the product fits the price.

The winning formula developed by Amstrad paid off handsomely in creating a string of winners in the seventies and eighties. However, in the early nineties the company made a loss for the first time, partly as a result of the recession in the UK market and partly as a result of the venture into satellite dishes. Nevertheless, it seems a good bet that the man who steered Amstrad from a one man band into a multi-national empire could well have a few more surprises in store for the consumer electronics market in the future.

8.4 Moving down the experience curve

When a product is first introduced onto a market, the manufacturer does not make any profits because research and development costs have yet to be recouped. But as sales continue, the firm eventually starts to make a profit and can afford to cut prices as its costs fall, thus moving down the **experience curve**.

Being first in the market is an advantage because the firm can use what it has learnt and the experience it has gained to lower its production costs quickly. Those who enter the market later on have to start right at the top of the cost curve whereas the earliest producer has a competitive edge because of having already ridden the experience curve. It can, therefore, afford to charge very low prices (which cannot be matched by new entrants) yet still make a profit because of its lower operating costs.

Firms which adopt a penetration strategy are most likely to benefit from this process as the volume sales resulting from the low prices enable them to move down the experience curve very quickly. This is a common practice amongst firms in the electronics and computer industries. Texas Instruments provides one of the best known examples with its slashing of calculator prices.

In contrast, other firms try to maintain the original high price for as long as possible. However, the problem is a price umbrella can be created over the market under which competitors charging lower prices can flourish. There is then a very real danger that these firms may be able to move down the experience curve more quickly, capturing the market in the process. However, **umbrella pricing** has never worried the handful of large firms such as IBM, Eastman Kodak or Xerox who, until recently, dominated their markets to the point where the activity of competitors made virtually no impact.

There are, in fact, many firms who will not consider lowering prices until the market becomes much more competitive. The pricing of compact discs provides a good illustration, as shown by the following extract taken from an article which appeared in the *Observer* newspaper, February 1990.

> **Case study   Money for nothing as CDs go on spinning out the profits**   This week the compact disc, the fastest selling consumer product on the market, which provides hi-fi without the crackle, is seven years old.
>
> But the birthday celebrations for the industry's most lucrative product have been overshadowed by a furious row over pricing. Last month, in a report headlined 'Compact Disc Rip-Off', the Consumers' Association's magazine *Which?* claimed that the record industry was taking consumers for a ride by charging up to £12 for a product whose manufacturing costs were less than £1.
>
> This attack provoked a furious reaction from the British Phonographic Industry (BPI), which first threatened to sue for libel and has now complained to the Press Council.
>
> Whether or not the Consumers' Association was right to describe the compact disc market as a 'rip-off' depends on one's view of the marketplace. With disc sales growing at 40 per cent a year, the competitive pressures on manufacturers to accept lower profits are, to put it mildly, not intense. 'In all honesty', said a

record industry spokesman, 'what is the incentive to cut prices?'

The burden of the *Which*? attack is that CDs are one of the few consumer products which have gone up in price since their introduction. When CDs were first introduced in 1983, the manufacturer's price for classical discs was £5.75. It is now £7.29. This is despite the fact that the cost of manufacturing a CD has been more than halved. Last year the industry, which is dominated by six major companies – EMI, Polygram, CBS, WEA, Virgin and BMG (RCA) – sold an estimated 40 million discs, an increase of more than a third on the previous year.

Record manufacturers claim that their profits in relation to turnover are not excessive when compared to other leisure industries. Industry spokesmen also point out the costs of distribution, artists' royalties, and recording sessions have all risen steeply with inflation. The average price of a CD in 1989 was £10.50. If its price had kept pace with inflation, it should, they claim, have now been between £16 and £17.

If manufacture is such a small proportion of the retail price, why is it that a CD containing the same amount of music as an LP vinyl disc should cost £4 more? And why is it that identical CDs are almost a third cheaper in the United States than in Britain? There is only one answer to this – the marketplace there is much more competitive.

The lesson appears to be that until the marketplace becomes a great deal more competitive, British consumers will continue to have to pay more than they should for their silver disc hi-fi.

Source: Adapted from *Money for nothing as CDs go on spinning out the profits*, Adam Raphael, *Observer*, Sunday, 25 February 1990.

8.5 Pricing techniques

Firms use two main techniques to determine the prices that will most effectively achieve their objectives and strategies. Both of these techniques – the cost plus approach and break even analysis – are cost based methods. The level of costs faced by a firm has an important influence on pricing decisions and is at times the main consideration. It is essential, therefore, to understand the different types of costs incurred by firms.

(a) Types of costs

(i) **Fixed costs**   These are costs which do not immediately change with variations in the level of output. They include the cost of land, buildings, machinery and rates, all of which have to be paid for regardless of how many units are produced. These costs have to be carried even when the firm is operating at less than full **production capacity**.

Apart from fixed production costs, the cost of the **overheads** which are connected with the general administration of the firm are also usually fixed costs. These indirect costs are not associated with any particular product but stem from overall running costs. They include the cost of **indirect labour** such as secretaries, accountants, sales staff and managers as well as the cost of **indirect materials** such as the cost of word processors or advertising leaflets.

Fixed costs remain fairly static in the short term. However, if output increases greatly a point will eventually be reached when there has to be a corresponding increase in fixed costs. For example, more machines or larger premises will be required to cater for the increased production.

Total fixed costs divided by the number of units produced gives the **average fixed cost** figure, which is the proportion of fixed costs carried by each unit of production. Average fixed costs increase when output falls (as fixed costs are spread over fewer units) which is why it is important for firms to operate as near to full production capacity as possible.

(ii) Variable costs   Unlike fixed costs, these are costs which do vary directly with the level of output. They include the cost of labour, raw materials and fuel, all of which fluctuate with the amount produced, rising when output increases and falling when it decreases.

In reality, the situation is not always so clear cut. The costs of raw materials may, for instance, decrease proportionately as output rises if bulk discounts can be negotiated with suppliers. Labour costs may not necessarily decrease when output falls if union agreements exist which prevent workers being laid off.

Total variable costs divided by the number of units produced gives the **average variable cost** figure, which is the proportion of variable costs attributable to each unit of production.

(iii) Semi-variable costs   Some costs are partly fixed and partly variable. The rental of a photocopier, for example, is a fixed cost whereas the purchase of the paper is a variable cost as it depends on the volume used.

When all the fixed and variable costs are added together, the firm's **total costs** can be determined. Once the extent of the costs which they incur is known firms can then set suitable prices for their products.

(b) Cost plus

The simplest approach to price setting is the **cost plus** pricing method. Firms will obviously want to ensure that the prices which are set are high enough to cover all their costs. It is common, therefore, for firms to simply add a percentage **mark up** onto their variable costs to cover overhead costs and provide a profit margin. This method is most often adopted by retailers and wholesalers.

(c) Break even analysis

An alternative approach is the **target pricing** method which is where firms aim to achieve the target profit produced at a particular price level. The first step in this process is to carry out a **break even analysis** of the relationship between costs and revenue in order to determine the break even point (BEP). This is the lowest point at which a firm can operate without losing money, where the sales revenue received covers exactly the total costs incurred (assuming that every item produced is sold).

A typical break even graph is shown in fig. 8.2. This firm makes products which cost £2 each in terms of variable costs and which sell for £3. Each unit sold therefore makes a contribution of £1 towards fixed costs. As their fixed costs are £4000, this means that 4000 units have to be sold before the BEP is reached.

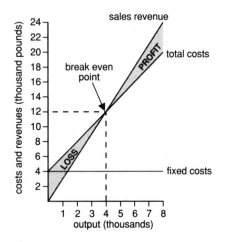

Fig. 8.2 A break even graph

Notice that the fixed cost curve stays the same whatever the size of output. The total cost curve starts from the base level provided by fixed costs. This is because even when output is nil and no variable costs are incurred, fixed costs still have to be paid.

To the left of the BEP where costs are greater than revenue a loss is made, whereas to the right of the BEP revenue is greater than costs which results in a profit being made. The greater the output the greater the profit, though a stage will be reached when fixed costs will obviously have to rise to cater for the increased production. The amount of profit or loss is greatest where the vertical distance between the two curves is furthest apart. However, it is worth remembering that a BEP will not occur automatically. If total costs remain higher than sales revenue the firm will never break even.

Once the BEP is known, a target price can be set which will produce a particular level of profit. The firm can then work towards achieving this target profit having established from the break even analysis that it will not suffer a loss or merely break even.

(d) Disadvantages of cost based methods

Both these pricing techniques suffer from the disadvantage that they only take into account the internal costs of the firm. In fact, external factors such as the actions of competitors and in particular the market demand are generally more influential in determining the 'right' price.

For instance, if new, technologically innovative products or prestige products are launched with prices derived from a cost plus basis, much potential profit may be lost from consumers who would have been prepared to pay higher premium prices. In contrast, if products are sold at an expensive price in an attempt to cover high production costs, consumers may not be willing to pay premium prices for products they regard as overpriced.

Either way, whether the price set is too low or too high, it is dangerous for firms to ignore external factors such as market demand. In the final analysis, the 'right' price should not be based solely on the firm's costs. It must relate to the price that sufficient numbers of customers are prepared to pay – i.e. the price the market will bear – which in turn reflects the way in which consumers perceive the value of the product.

8.6 Marginal analysis

Before deciding on the price to charge and on the level of production, firms need to work out what will happen to their costs and to their revenue as they produce each additional unit. They might wonder what would happen if they reduced prices by 5 per cent. The answer to such questions can be provided by marginal analysis.

If a firm making calculators sells their calculators for £10, then each time they sell another calculator their total revenue increases by £10. The increase (or decrease) in revenue obtained from the sale of an extra unit is called **marginal revenue** (MR). Total revenue divided by the number of units sold is termed **average revenue** (AR).

Under conditions of perfect competition, marginal revenue is the same as price because the firm can sell all their output without lowering their price. This means that the demand curve is the same as the marginal revenue curve. When perfect competition exists prices are constant because there is no incentive for firms to raise prices (as sales would be lost) and no need to lower prices (as they can sell all their output anyway). For these reasons the demand curve is also the same as the average revenue curve, shown in fig. 8.3.

The point at which the firm maximizes its profits will be when **marginal costs** equal marginal revenue, i.e. MC = MR, at the **equilibrium position**, shown as E, fig. 8.4. Up to point E, MR (the extra income from the sale of an additional unit) is greater than the MC curve (the extra cost of producing an additional unit). It is obviously worthwhile for the firm to increase output up to point E as each extra unit sold will increase profit.

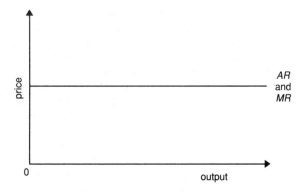

Fig. 8.3 The marginal revenue curve

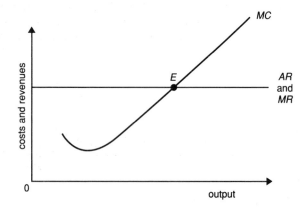

Fig. 8.4 The equilibrium position

However, past this equilibrium point the MC curve is greater than MR. The extra costs are greater than the extra revenue gained so it would be foolish to increase output further. The level of output at the point where MC = MR is therefore the equilibrium position where profits are maximized.

In the short run, any firm will continue to produce, even when it is making a loss, providing it is managing to cover its variable costs such as the cost of labour, raw materials and power, though it cannot, of course, survive over a long period on this basis. In the long run, fixed costs such as the cost of a factory, machinery, rates, etc. also have to be covered.

However, there may be times when it is sensible for a firm to accept an order even though the price offered does not cover all its costs. For example, when a firm is short of work and is operating at less than full capacity, it may take on work which covers variable costs like wages and raw materials and which makes a **contribution** towards fixed costs.

As fixed costs such as rent on the premises and loan repayments for machinery have to be paid anyway, it is worth making use of any spare capacity as even a small contribution towards fixed costs helps to minimize losses.

This principle of **marginal costing** can be seen to operate when airlines offer cheap stand-by tickets to fill seats that would otherwise be left empty. In the same way, British Rail's Supersaver fares and cheap day-returns encourage people to make use of the service during off-peak times. Even at reduced prices, these fares make a contribution towards the many trains, station staff, etc. needed to cope with the large volume of rush hour commuters but which are then underused for the rest of the day.

Fixed and variable costs combined make up **average costs** (AC). Included within this total cost is **normal profit**: this is the minimum amount of profit a firm needs to make in order to remain in business.

In fig. 8.5 the *AC* curve is initially higher than the *MC* curve. This is because the MC curve does not include fixed costs whereas the *AC* curve includes fixed costs in addition to variable costs. However, when the MC curve bisects the *AC* curve at its lowest point the *AC* curve will begin to rise. At this point the firm is making enough profit to stay in business but not so much that new firms are attracted into the industry as competitors.

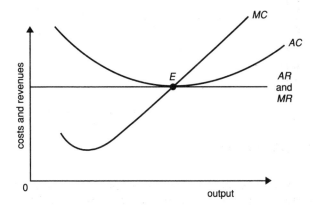

Fig. 8.5 The long run equilibrium position

Under conditions of perfect competition at point *E* the firm has achieved a position of equilibrium which can be maintained in the long term where:

$$MC = MR = AC = AR$$

However, in the short term it is possible for two other situations to apply:

- The firm may temporarily make abnormal profits which are higher than usual as shown in fig. 8.6. These are called **windfall profits** because the price is unexpectedly high. Factors such as the introduction of an innovative product or the adoption of new machinery which makes production more cost

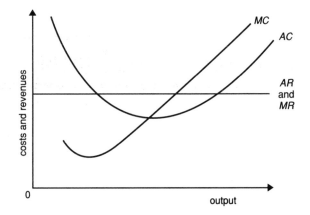

Fig. 8.6 Windfall profits, in the short run, where the price is unexpectedly high

effective can give the firm an initial sales advantage. But whatever the reasons for the higher than usual profits the advantage only lasts until competitors are attracted into the industry who erode away excess profits.
● The firm may temporarily make losses as shown in fig. 8.7. This occurs when average costs are at all times higher than average revenue. As the AC curve never cuts the AR curve it is obviously impossible for the firm to make a profit and although a loss can be sustained for a short time the firm would eventually be forced out of business.

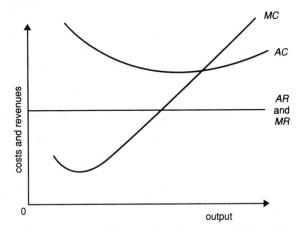

Fig. 8.7 Losses in the short run, where average costs are at all times higher than the average revenue

It can be seen, therefore, that there is a tendency for market conditions to gravitate towards the equilibrium position in the long run.

UNIT 9

Economic factors and price

9.1 Introduction

Prices are shaped by the broader economic environment outside the firm. Marketers need to be aware of these external economic factors when deciding what price they ought to charge for their products.

The structure of a market is influenced by the type of competition found, the interaction between supply and demand and the degree to which demand is elastic as it varies with price fluctuations.

In practice, these economic principles rarely apply to the real world as exactly as they are described in theory. Nevertheless, marketers should take into account the structure of the market in which they operate when making pricing decisions.

The dangers of setting prices which bear no relation to the market conditions of supply and demand are described by Robert Heller in his book *The Super-marketers*. He quotes the case of the tin industry, which in the early 1980s was trying artificially to support the price of tin by stockpiling it, as an example of what can happen when the market price is rigged:

'When the London tin market collapsed late in 1985, its members were shown in spectacular manner that the economists are right: price is the mechanism that allocates resources and creates the balance between supply and demand. Remove price, attempt to prevent economic forces from working through, and you build up pressure that, sooner or later, will result in the bursting of the dam – leaving someone owing $600 million on stockpiled tin that can't be sold, a market in utter confusion, and several producers wondering where their next peso or ringgit is coming from.'

During this period, demand was falling as aluminium began to be used more widely as an alternative to tin. Yet supply was being increased. As Heller points out, 'Why was production capacity being raised? Because of artificially high prices. Had the price been allowed to reflect fully the 25 per cent drop in tin consumption, nobody would have brought new capacity on stream.'

He concludes, 'First, an artificial price must mean, other things being equal, either an artificial demand or artificial profits. Either way one encourages artificial – or wrong – decisions. Second, the artificiality of the price prevents it from sending out signals. Instead of responding to the market, suppliers end up trying to make it respond to them. And that's the most slippery slope of all.'

9.2 Types of competition

The degree of competition found in a market is an influential factor in the pricing decision. Markets can be classified according to the type of competition which exists. At one end of the scale is a market of **perfect competition** where there are a multitude of sellers so that no one firm can influence prices, whilst at the other end of the scale is a **perfect monopoly** where a single supplier dominates the market and controls prices. Between these two hypothetical extremes lies the **imperfect market**. When there are a limited number of sellers the imperfect market is known as an **oligopoly** and when there are a large number of sellers producing similar but differentiated products, the imperfect market is said to have **monopolistic competition**.

9.3 Perfect market

(a) Perfect competition
For a state of perfect competition to exist, the following conditions would need to apply:

- A large number of buyers and sellers which means that no single firm can influence prices.
- Firms can enter or leave the market with ease as start-up costs are low.
- Firms sell identical products and no one product can command a higher price.
- Buyers and sellers have a perfect knowledge of the market which means that they can switch rapidly from one product to another when prices rise.

The markets for agricultural products such as wheat or cotton in countries like the USA appear at first glance to be examples of perfect markets. There are thousands of sellers and eventually millions of buyers selling an identical product. It is also easy for farmers to enter or leave the market by changing what they grow, and both farmers and buyers have a good knowledge of the market.

Yet even these markets do not have perfect competition. For instance, the number of sellers may be decreased by the formation of co-operatives and there may be a few large buyers who can negotiate huge discounts. As with other theoretical models based on a particular set of assumptions, the existence of distorting factors invariably serves to ensure that perfect competition is rarely found. Nevertheless, it is worth studying the characteristics of perfect competition as this represents the ideal working of a free market system.

Under conditions of perfect competition, a single firm cannot influence prices. A supplier which decides to raise prices would face no demand for its products. Equally, there would be no point in a supplier lowering prices as it can already sell whatever it produces at the market price. For this reason, the supplier is said to be a **price taker**. It cannot change the price and thus has to accept the market price which is offered.

(b) Perfect monopoly

The other extreme is a state of perfect monopoly which is where a market is controlled by a single supplier. A monopoly can exist even if this supplier does not account for all the production, providing it holds a dominant market position. In fact, a firm may be regarded as having a monopoly under the Fair Trading Act if it has a market share of more than 25 per cent. Examples of monopolies include Tate and Lyle in the sugar industry and the BOC group for industrial gases. Within the state sector are the nationalized industries such as British Rail and British Coal. However, the number of state monopolies has fallen in recent years with the privatization of British Telecom, British Gas, British Steel and the regional electricity boards.

The absence or limited nature of competition in a monopoly means that a single firm can influence prices. Even so, it will rarely have total control of a market. If any firm attempts to exploit its monopoly position by raising prices to an unacceptably high level the Government may step in and impose restrictions to curb the supplier's power. In addition, there is always the danger that consumers may switch to using alternative products – providing of course that substitutes are available.

9.4 Imperfect market

The imperfect market falls between the two hypothetical extremes of perfect competition and perfect monopoly. There are two types of imperfect markets:

(a) Oligopoly

This is where a market is dominated by a few sellers who, because of their large market shares, are able to influence prices to a certain extent. Oligopolies tend to be found in markets which are characteristically very capital intensive. In industries like steel, oil refining and airline services, start-up costs are high and the capital investment required to achieve huge economies of scale makes it difficult for smaller firms to break into the market. The fact that production is concentrated in the hands of a few suppliers rather than many suppliers is the reason why competition in oligopolistic markets is classed as imperfect.

The example most often quoted is of Unilever and Proctor and Gamble in the detergent industry. Within the car industry Ford, Austin Rover, Vauxhall and Peugeot Talbot account for most of the car production in Britain, and in the same way the main clearing banks, National Westminster, Midland, Barclays and Lloyds, handle most banking services.

Oligopolists avoid direct price competition, competing instead by differentiating their products or services on the basis of branding supported by heavy promotional budgets. This is the case with detergent brands, which despite having very similar basic ingredients, are each promoted as having quite different uses and advantages.

(b) Monopolistic competition

This is where a market has a large number of sellers offering a similar but differentiated product. Monopolistic competition is found in the markets for most consumer goods such as clothes, furniture, electrical goods and fast moving packaged goods (FMCGs).

Firms compete on the strength of the relative merits of their brands. These may be differentiated from other brands on the basis of such factors as quality, design or value for money and on the general image created by advertising.

The differences are often more apparent than real. Nevertheless, if a firm selling bottled mineral water, for instance, can convince consumers that their water tastes better than those of their competitors they can, in effect, gain a certain degree of monopoly power. The superior brand can often command a premium price into the bargain. It is this ability of some sellers to corner part of the market and set higher prices through the creation of successful products or brands that makes monopolistic competition imperfect.

9.5 Laws of supply and demand

Whatever the intensity of competition, i.e. whether there is just one, a few, or a large number of producers operating in a marketplace, pricing decisions are governed by the interaction of the forces of supply and demand. In essence, this is based on the principle that if the price of a good rises a consumer will buy less and if the price falls, he or she will buy more. This process can be seen most clearly in relation to **commodity products** such as wheat or barley and minerals such as tin, copper and aluminium.

However, it is worth remembering that the laws of supply and demand, along with other theoretical economic models, are based on the assumption of *ceteris paribus* (a Latin phrase meaning other things being equal). In the real world other factors do not, of course, remain constant. Government influence, competitors' activities and changes made in other elements of the marketing mix can all affect the pricing decision. Wise marketers will nevertheless take into account the general relationships between supply and demand and make their decision in the wider context of these forces operating in the marketplace.

9.6 The law of demand

Demand is a reflection of the quantities of goods bought in a given period of time by people who not only want to buy but can also afford to do so. This is an important distinction as although many people might wish to buy a Porsche, for example, the **effective demand** for a Porsche car is low because only a few people have the necessary income to fulfil that wish.

The law of demand states that, all other things being equal, when the price of a good goes down a greater quantity will be demanded. This is partly because existing buyers consume more and partly because new buyers enter the market who are able to afford the lower prices or who now think the product is worth buying.

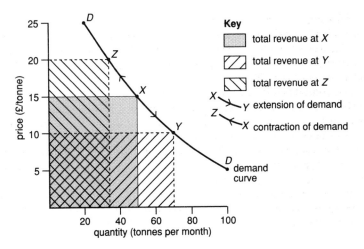

Fig. 9.1 Hypothetical demand curve for barley showing the inverse relationship between demand and price

The *inverse* relationship between demand and price is shown in fig. 9.1 with the hypothetical demand curve for barley (DD) sloping downwards from left to right. At point *X* when the price of barley is £15 per tonne, there will be a demand for 50 tonnes of barley a month. If the price falls to £10 per tonne, at point *Y*, there will be a demand for 70 tonnes. This is an *extension of demand*, whilst if the price rises to £20 a tonne, at point *Z*, there will be a *contraction of demand* to 34 tonnes.

These are examples of movements along the same demand curve. However, demand is also influenced by factors other than price, leading to a shift in the demand curve as shown in fig. 9.2. If more barley is bought, the demand curve

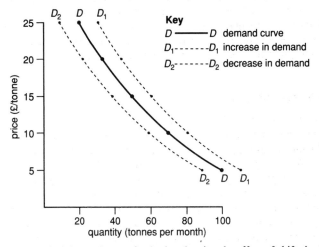

Fig. 9.2 Hypothetical demand curve for barley showing the effect of shifts in demand

will shift to the right ($D_1 D_1$). This *increase in demand* may occur when, for instance, buyers start to panic-buy following rumours of a bad harvest. If, on the other hand, less barley is bought the demand curve will shift to the left ($D_2 D_2$). A *decrease in demand* could be a result of buyers having stockpiled huge surpluses. Whatever the reasons, changing conditions will affect demand even though the price remains the same.

The total revenue gained at a given price is the price per unit multiplied by the quantity demanded. Thus at X in fig. 9.1, the total revenue is £750 (£15 per tonne × 50 tonnes). At the lower price of £10 per tonne at Y, revenue falls to £700 (£10 × 70 tonnes). This illustrates that a point is eventually reached beyond which revenue declines as price falls because the increased demand is simply not enough to offset lower prices.

(a) Exceptions to the law of demand
There are three situations which contradict the law of demand to create the opposite of what is expected. In other words – when price goes up, more not less is sold.

(i) Prestigious products   Certain expensive products such as Rolls Royce cars, Chanel dresses, Gucci handbags, Rolex watches and Cartier jewellery are sought after precisely because of their high price. In fact, a drop in prices would, if anything, cause demand to fall. With prestige products the price tag is a central part of the attraction. Since only a few people can afford them, the price ensures their exclusivity and association with a 'champagne lifestyle'. Once the necessary status symbol image has been created, price increases do not cause demand to fall. However, in the unlikely event of a substantial drop in prices, these goods would be within the reach of many more people, which would then increase demand.

(ii) Goods which are staple foods for poor families   In the nineteenth century, Robert Giffen noticed that the demand for goods which are staple foods for poor families such as bread or potatoes actually increased when prices rose. This was because workers, who at that time were paid just a few shillings a week, were having to spend most of their income on these staple foods just to survive. When the price of bread or potatoes dropped demand also dropped because families were then able to spend some of their income on meat or fish to vary their diet. But as soon as the price went up families once again had to spend all their income on bread and potatoes. After the failure of the 1884 Irish potato crop, demand for potatoes increased even though the price had gone up because poor families could not afford to eat anything else. In affluent western societies, this factor, which arises when a high proportion of household expenditure is devoted to one good, is unlikely to occur again, although it may be found in developing countries in relation to staple foods like maize or yams.

(iii) When further price increases are expected   Demand sometimes increases even though prices are rising because people think that they should buy before prices increase even further. The housing market, especially in the South East of England, provided a good example of this in the late 1980s when low interest rates fuelled a period of intense activity as people scrambled to buy before prices rose any further. The behaviour of speculators on the Stock Exchange every time share prices in a company start escalating is motivated by a similar desire not to 'miss the boat' and by the lure of quick profits. The demand for antiques and fine art, which have a rarity value because of their finite supply, has also increased tremendously despite continuous price rises because buyers have come to regard them as having an investment value. But perhaps the clearest example is provided by the 'hot money' investors who switch from currency to currency when interest rates (or prices) rise. In all these examples, the rise in prices is immediately followed by an increase in demand. It appears, therefore, that the price rises have stimulated demand. However, it is consumer expectations, not the high prices, which actually cause the increase in demand.

However, buyers do sometimes forget that there is a very real danger with speculative purchases, particularly those made when prices are soaring, of the 'bottom falling out of the market' as prices suddenly crash.

(b) Factors affecting changes in demand

(i) The level of income Income is usually linked to occupation. It affects the type of products bought in that an increase in income is likely to lead to an increase in demand for luxury non-essential products. The spending power dictated by a particular level of income is, of course, influenced by the cost of living. Thus **real income** is income related to the average price of goods and services. It determines what money will actually buy. Demand will increase only if real income is high in relation to prices.

(ii) The distribution of population Changes in population size will affect total demand. In addition, an increase in any one group in the population will result in a greater demand for whatever that group requires. For example, spectacles, false teeth and retirement homes in the case of the elderly, and toys, prams, disposable nappies and health clinics in the case of young children.

Regional densities of population can also cause variations with heavily populated regions of Britain such as the South East and West Midlands showing the highest demand for jobs, housing, goods and services.

Changes in occupational patterns have a far reaching impact. The increase in service industries, for instance, has led to a greater demand for office equipment and computers.

(iii) Tastes, habits, customs and fashions All these factors exert a powerful influence on demand. Vegetarians, slimmers and more recently 'green' consumers have all created their own patterns of demand for particular goods and services. In addition, demands are also created by those from particular religious backgrounds, such as the demand by Jewish people for kosher food. Changes in fashion affect demand to the point where clothes which have hardly been worn are discarded in favour of the 'look' for the next season. Here demand is kept at a high level by constant changes in minor fashion details.

(iv) Government influence   The main influence is through taxes. **Direct taxes** such as income tax affect income and **indirect taxes** such as value added tax (VAT) and excise duty affect prices. Higher taxes on cigarettes and alcohol, for instance, lead to a contraction of demand.

Demand can also be affected by the introduction of new laws. The increase in demand for seat belts when it was made compulsory to wear them is a good example. Similarly, government influence on interest rates, wage policies, regional grants and the ease or difficulty of obtaining credit can all increase or decrease demand.

(v) Seasonal factors and weather   Products which are only in demand at certain times of the year include Easter eggs, fireworks and Christmas trees. The cost of potted plants on Mother's Day or of red roses on Valentine's Day illustrates clearly the impact of demand on prices. Similarly, fuel consumption together with sales of anything from ice cream to umbrellas will tend to fluctuate greatly according to the weather.

(vi) Introduction of new or improved products   The increased demand for word processors has decreased demand for typewriters. The introduction of tights had a similar effect on the sale of stockings as did calculators on the sale of slide rules.

(vii) The impact of advertising   A successful advertising campaign can increase demand dramatically by increasing awareness of the brand and strengthening its image. A new campaign is often used to stress the advantages of the product in relation to those of competitors. It can also be used to give a tired product a new lease of life by creating a distinctive new image which helps to rejuvenate flagging sales.

(viii) The price of other goods   When goods are **substitutes** for each other as with beef and lamb, if the price of beef is increased then the demand for lamb will increase as more people switch to eating lamb.

When goods are sold together, for example petrol and cars, demand tends to be **complementary**, increasing or decreasing for both.

When goods require the use of others in the way that building a house requires bricks, tiles, wood and glass, demand tends to be **derived** with the demand for bricks being strongly influenced by the number of new houses under construction.

9.7 The law of supply

Whereas the law of demand is concerned with how much consumers will wish to buy at various prices, the law of supply deals with the other side of the coin, i.e. how much suppliers will wish to produce at various prices.

The law of supply states that, all other things being equal, when the price of a good rises a greater quantity will be produced. This is partly because existing suppliers find it worthwhile to increase production and partly because more suppliers enter the market. These new entrants tend to be the less efficient suppliers with higher costs who are able to cover their costs only when prices are high.

The oil industry in Britain is a case in point. With North Sea oil costing nearly five times more than Middle Eastern oil to extract, Britain is clearly a high-cost producer and it was only when world oil prices rocketed after 1973 that it became profitable to exploit the oil reserves. However, in this instance the oil would probably still have been extracted, albeit less profitably, in order to gain a strategic advantage in terms of reduced dependence on imports from a politically unstable region.

Unlike the inverse relationship between demand and price, in the case of the supply curve there is a *direct* relationship between supply and price. This means that as the price rises the quantity supplied also rises. This relationship is shown in fig. 9.3, with the supply curve sloping upwards from left to right. At point X when the price of barley is £15 per tonne, 50 tonnes are produced each month. When the price of barley rises to £20 per tonne the quantity produced is extended to 68 tonnes per month. Total revenue increases as the quantity supplied rises from X to Y.

In the same way as the effect on demand, changes in price also cause movements up or down the same supply curve leading to an extension or contraction of supply. An *extension of supply* occurs because existing farmers convert their land to growing barley and other farmers start growing barley who are only able to survive so long as prices are high. A *contraction of supply*,

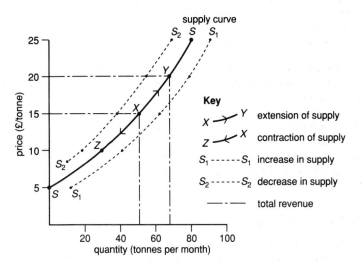

Fig. 9.3 Hypothetical supply curve for barley showing the effect of shifts in supply

on the other hand, takes place when prices are low and there are fewer farmers prepared to grow barley because it is more difficult to make a profit.

As with the demand curve, factors other than price can cause the entire supply curve to shift. A bumper harvest after a good summer, for instance, will cause the supply curve to move to the right due to an *increase in supply* ($S_1 S_1$), whereas a *decrease in supply*, perhaps due to the crop being ruined by a pest or disease, will cause the curve to shift leftwards ($S_2 S_2$).

Factors affecting changes in supply

(i) Changes in the price of raw materials   A rise in the price of any essential raw material or component will cause a drop in supply due to the increased costs of production and vice versa.

(ii) Natural and man-made influences on agriculture   The supply of agricultural products can be affected by such factors as the weather, pests and diseases, which can either destroy harvests or create bumper harvests influencing prices accordingly.

Man can increase supply by means of modern farming methods such as mechanization, irrigation and the use of fertilizers and insecticides, though supply can also decline as a result of problems such as soil erosion caused by careless farming practices.

(iii) Improvements in technology   The widespread introduction of automation, robotics and advanced manufacturing techniques within industry and the mechanization of farming has increased supply by improving cost efficiency and productivity and by enabling economies of scale to be made.

(iv) The regulation of supply   The supply of goods to the market may be restricted artificially in an effort to keep prices high. For example, the EEC controls the amount of butter that reaches the market by purchasing the surplus and storing it in warehouses or selling it cheaply to countries outside the EEC.

In years of bumper harvests the USA dumps wheat in the sea and ploughs cotton back into the ground thus avoiding the drop in prices which occurs whenever goods are in abundant supply.

The governments of many developed nations control the supply of foreign imports in order to protect their home industries. This is done by imposing **quotas** which limit the amount that is allowed into the country and through the levying of taxes or **tariffs** which are intended to raise the prices of imported goods to an uncompetitive level.

(v) The price of other goods   A rise in the price of wheat will encourage farmers to grow more wheat thus decreasing the supply of other crops such as barley.

Industries have less flexibility to change their particular products. Firms which manufacture a range of similar products can shift production between various lines to a certain extent. However, most firms would find it impossible to start making a completely different product.

9.8 The point of equilibrium

When demand and supply curves are brought together, the point at which they intersect in a market where perfect competition exists is the **equilibrium price**. At this point, which in the example shown in fig. 9.4 is achieved at a price of £15 per tonne, the quantity demanded by consumers, i.e. 50 tonnes, is equal to the quantity supplied by producers. The equilibrium point will of course move if the entire demand or supply curve shifts to the right or left.

At prices above the equilibrium price demand falls resulting in an excess supply of barley or a **glut**, whilst at prices below the equilibrium price demand rises creating an excess demand or **shortage**. Whenever a glut or shortage arises, suppliers soon adjust their prices. There is, therefore, a strong tendency for prices to gravitate from higher or lower levels towards the equilibrium price. This occurs because during a glut suppliers begin to lower their prices in order to stimulate demand and clear surplus stock. At the other end of the scale, when there is a shortage suppliers are able to take advantage of the excess demand to raise their prices. As a result, prices which are much higher or lower than the equilibrium price cannot be sustained for long.

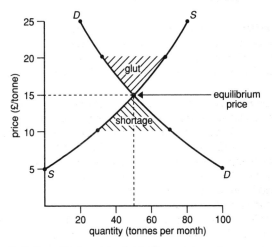

Fig. 9.4 Hypothetical equilibrium price for barley

Factors which distort the ideal equilibrium price

(i) Prices which are artificially supported This idealized view is, however, based on a simplified view of market conditions. In reality, there are many factors which distort the theoretical model and create **disequilibrium**. For example, the Common Agricultural Policy (CAP) of the EEC maintains the target price for a host of products such as butter, skimmed milk, wine and wheat far above the equilibrium price that would normally exist if free market forces were allowed to operate.

In order to subsidize farmers and stop them going out of business, the EEC sets a high **intervention price** and purchases the surplus produce which farmers cannot sell. These are stored in warehouses creating the infamous 'butter mountains' or 'wine lakes'. They are then sold off cheaply outside the EEC or even just ploughed into fields, the aim being to restrict supply and keep prices high. Clearly, this huge over-production of agricultural products is sustained purely because of the EEC's intervention in the market through supporting prices at an artificially high level.

In contrast, the post-war rent control legislation designed to ensure tenants in rented accommodation are not exploited has, as a result of inflation, created rents which are often fixed at a level well below the equilibrium price. The supply of accommodation has decreased as landlords have become reluctant to rent at low prices and as the people already in rented accommodation stay where they are. The rent controls introduced by the Government mean that the excess demand which would normally raise prices towards the equilibrium price has no impact because prices are maintained at an artificially low level. Artificial factors such as the CAP and rent control legislation interfere with the equilibrium price by not permitting free market forces to operate, though it would not, in any case, always remain static. Any increase or decrease in demand or supply will cause the equilibrium price to change.

(ii) Changes in demand   As shown in fig. 9.5, if demand increases the entire demand curve will shift to the right (DD to D_1D_1) and if it decreases, the demand curve will shift to the left (DD to D_2D_2). Assuming that the supply curve does not change this means that each demand curve now intersects the supply curve at different points along its length creating new equilibrium points. An increase in demand therefore results in a new equilibrium point (E_1), where the quantity demanded increases to Q_1 and the price rises to P_1. Conversely, a decrease in demand creates a new equilibrium point (E_2) where the quantity demanded decreases to Q_2 and the price falls to P_2.

(iii) Changes in supply   As shown in fig. 9.6, the same principles apply when the entire supply curve shifts to the right (SS to S_1S_1) due to an increase in supply or to the left (SS to S_2S_2) due to a decrease in supply. In this case it is the demand curve which remains static. An increase in supply results in a new equilibrium point (E_1), where the quantity supplied increases to Q_1 and the price falls to P_1. Conversely, a decrease in supply creates a new equilibrium point (E_2), where the quantity supplied decreases to Q_2 and the price increases to P_2.

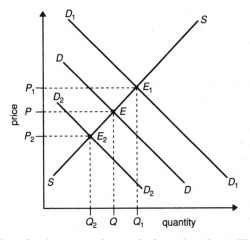

Fig. 9.5 The effect of an increase or decrease in demand on the equilibrium price

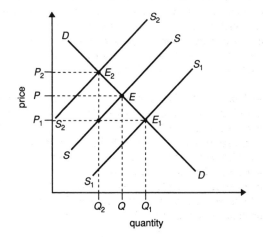

Fig. 9.6 The effect of an increase or decrease in supply on the equilibrium price

9.9 Elasticity of demand

Within the economy as a whole, the price mechanism influences the interaction between supply and demand to determine the general allocation of resources. On a smaller scale, however, firms tend to be more concerned with the crucial question of how much of their product they can sell at any particular price. They want to know what will happen to demand if they decide to raise or lower their prices. The degree to which the quantity sold will vary according to changes in the price charged is known as the **elasticity of demand**.

The extent to which demand changes in response to price fluctuations can be measured by the **coefficient of elasticity**. This is the percentage change in quantity demanded divided by the percentage change in price that actually caused the demand to change: e.g. if a 6 per cent increase in demand results from a 2 per cent drop in price the coefficient of elasticity has a value of 3.

Elasticity of demand varies with different goods and services. Two main groups are found at either end of the scale of price sensitivity.

(a) Elastic demand

Goods and services which exhibit elastic demand tend to be the 'luxuries' – non-essential durable consumer goods, e.g. cars, furniture, carpets and curtains, large electrical appliances, stereo equipment, etc., and non-essential services, e.g. life insurance, foreign holidays.

Demand for all these goods is very responsive to any change in price; i.e. demand stretches, hence the term elastic. A small percentage drop in price causes a correspondingly much larger percentage increase in demand. Goods in elastic demand have a coefficient of elasticity value greater than 1 because the percentage change in demand is higher than the percentage change in price. Personal computers are a good example. When Amstrad first introduced their personal computers at rock-bottom prices, thousands of new buyers entered the market who were previously unable to afford a personal computer. Demand for personal computers is therefore elastic as it increases significantly when prices are cut.

(b) Inelastic demand

Goods and services which exhibit inelastic demand tend to be the 'necessities' – essential and inexpensive staple goods, e.g. milk, bread, salt, flour, sugar, and essential public utilities, e.g. gas, electricity, telephone, public transport.

Demand for all these goods and services is not very responsive to a change in price. A small percentage drop in price (or even a small rise in price) causes very little change in demand. Goods in inelastic demand have a coefficient of elasticity value less than 1 because the percentage change in demand is lower than the percentage change in price.

Demand remains fairly constant for basic food items like milk and bread (though not for less essential items like coffee or chocolate where demand is more elastic). If the price of gas or electricity rises people will economize to a certain extent but as they still need to heat and light their homes consumption does not change very much. Demand for these essential utilities is therefore also inelastic. Not surprisingly, demand for cigarettes (which are addictive) has tended to be inelastic despite continual price rises.

(c) Impact of price changes on revenue

As shown in fig. 9.7, under conditions of elastic demand where the demand curve is fairly flat, when the price drops from *A* to *B*, a greater quantity is demanded and total revenue increases on balance.

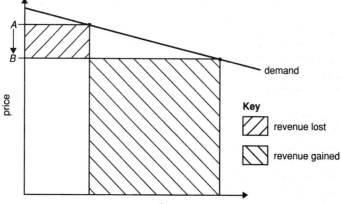

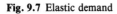

Fig. 9.7 Elastic demand

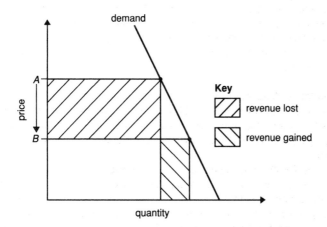

Fig. 9.8 Inelastic demand

In contrast, fig. 9.8 shows that under conditions of inelastic demand where the demand curve slopes steeply, even when there is a big drop in price total revenue decreases because the revenue gained due to the greater demand is much smaller than the revenue lost due to the price decrease.

If the percentage change in quantity demanded is exactly equal to the percentage change in price, which means that total revenue is unchanged, demand is said to be **unitary** with a coefficient value of 1.

Obviously, goods exhibiting elastic and inelastic demand respond very differently to price changes in terms of the quantities demanded and total revenue produced. It is essential, therefore, for firms to know which category their products or services fall into before making a decision to raise or lower prices.

The implications are clear. Firms selling goods or services with an inelastic demand have much more freedom to raise their prices, knowing that demand will change very little. By the same token this also means that lowering prices in order to increase demand would be ineffective as this would almost certainly lead to a drop in revenue. Conversely, firms whose goods or services exhibit an elastic demand cannot count on demand remaining much the same if prices are raised. However, they are in the position where even a small reduction in price can stimulate demand significantly.

9.10 Factors affecting elasticity of demand

(a) The price of other goods
The price of other related goods can often have an effect on the quantity demanded which is as great as a change in the price of the good itself. **Cross elasticity of demand** is the degree to which the amount demanded of one good varies according to changes in the price of another good. There are two situations when this can occur.

(i) **When substitute goods are available** If the price of coffee falls dramatically then many tea drinkers would switch to drinking coffee instead. Thus a fall in the price of coffee leads to a decrease in the demand for tea. This is an example of **positive cross elasticity** since a decrease in the price of coffee has brought about a decrease in the demand for tea.

Butter and margarine, Coke and lemonade and beefburgers and pizzas are a few examples of other close substitutes. Cross elasticity can also take place between completely different types of purchases. If, for example, the price of cinema tickets increased greatly then many young people might switch to other forms of entertainment leading to a rise in the demand for discos, bowling alleys, pop concerts, etc.

(ii) **When complementary goods exist** Where groups of goods are consumed together a price change in one good affects the quantity sold of the other. For instance, when the price of strawberries falls and more are sold the demand for cream also rises.

In the same way, when the price of personal computers decreased in the last decade there was a corresponding increase in sales of software programmes. This is an example of **negative cross elasticity** since a decrease in the price of computers has resulted in an increase in the demand for software. Other examples of complementary goods whose fortunes are linked in this way include cameras and film, fish and chips, shirts and ties and cars and petrol.

(b) Purchasing power and income
An individual's purchasing power is usually linked closely to income, although people with a relatively low income can, in fact, have a high purchasing power if their mortgage and other outgoings are low.

Income elasticity is the degree to which the quantity demanded of a product varies according to changes in the income of consumers. As purchasing power increases people can afford to buy new cars, furniture, computers, video and hi-fi equipment, large electrical appliances, foreign holidays and services such as life insurance.

Items such as cars for which there is a greater demand when income rises, are known as **normal goods**. They are said to have a **positive income elasticity** as an increase in consumers' income leads to an increase in demand. Conversely, items such as bread and potatoes are known as **inferior goods** because demand for them decreases as income rises. They have a **negative income elasticity** as an increase in income results in a decrease in demand. Goods such as salt where demand is not affected by changes in income are said to have a **zero income elasticity**.

When times are hard, as in periods of recession or high interest rates, and income is low, sales of non-essential luxury items suffer because people can postpone buying these goods until they have more money. Demand is therefore income-elastic. However, people cannot do without the basic necessities like food and groceries, heating and lighting, clothes and fares or petrol for travel to work, which makes demand for these essential items income-inelastic.

Nevertheless, it is worth remembering that the definition of what is considered essential or non-essential varies considerably between individuals. Many so-called luxury items such as colour TV sets have come to be regarded as essential. Cigarettes and alcohol actually show an inelastic pattern of demand.

(c) Importance of purchase within budget

For major purchases which represent a large part of a buyer's budget such as a car or furniture, price increases can cause a dramatic drop in the quantity demanded and vice versa. Demand for these items is therefore elastic. However, fluctuations in the price of inexpensive, everyday goods such as food, groceries, newspapers and stamps do not significantly affect the quantity sold. The cost of these minor purchases within the overall budget is so unimportant and the re-purchase done so automatically that a few extra pennies on the price of a loaf of bread, for instance, would probably not even be noticed. Hence demand for these kinds of goods is inelastic.

The role of promotion

People often equate promotion almost exclusively with advertising, which is hardly surprising given that advertising pervades every aspect of our lives – appearing not only on television, video, and posters and in newspapers and magazines, but also on every available surface from the sides of buses to hot-air balloons.

There is no doubt that advertising works. When Kelloggs decided to advertise its cornflakes on a million milk bottles, sales increased by 17 per cent. What is less commonly recognized, however, is the contribution made by other forms of promotion, i.e. personal selling (the work of sales representatives), sales promotions (money-off coupons, offers such as buy two get one free, etc.) and public relations (publicity, sponsorship, etc.).

Promotion performs an important function in the marketing mix in that it communicates to customers information on the other elements of the mix, i.e. the advantages of the product itself, details on the kind of place through which it is sold and details on the price. In the case of consumer durables, many of which are essentially parity products (see page 83), promotion has become the main method of differentiating a product or service. For example, advertising is often used to create a distinctive image, personality and market positioning for brands which may be virtually identical products.

10.1 The aims of promotion

(a) Persuade
One of the most important aims of promotion is to persuade consumers to act, i.e. to go out and buy the product. It may also be used to encourage consumers to adopt a particular attitude towards a product or to improve the image of the company as a whole.

(b) Inform
Promotion conveys factual information on the product such as the name and price, details on where it is available, as well as pointing out the technical

features it offers and any other significant benefits. This is particularly important for newly launched products.

(c) Remind
Promotion may be used to remind consumers that an old-established product is still available, thus prompting repurchase.

(d) Reinforce
Promotion is often used to reinforce consumer satisfaction with a purchase by emphasizing that they have made a wise choice, thus increasing the likelihood of them repeating the same purchase decision.

The overall aim of promotion, or persuasive communication as it is sometimes called, is to encourage the buyer to proceed smoothly through the various stages of the decision-making process. The changes in behaviour leading up to the point where consumers actually make a purchase decision are summarized in the well-known AIDA model of buyer behaviour.

As shown in fig.10.1, there is a hierarchy of effects as buyers move through each stage. Initially, buyers are unaware of a product or service. The challenge for marketers is to capture the Attention of consumers in some way so that they become aware of the existence of the product or service. The promotional strategy should make enough impact for the consumer to become Interested, which then creates a Desire to purchase, leading ultimately to the Action of making a purchase.

The AIDA model is particularly appropriate to purchase decisions involving expensive items that are infrequently bought, e.g. high-involvement goods such as cars, washing machines or foreign holidays. However, it is less applicable to purchase decisions involving cheap items that are bought regularly or on

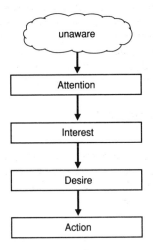

Fig. 10.1 The AIDA model of buyer behaviour

impulse, e.g. low-involvement goods such as bread, newspapers or soft drinks. Where low-involvement items are concerned, people are unlikely to proceed through the early stages of knowledge, interest and desire. Instead, they tend to purchase such items automatically without stopping to consider what they are buying. Once a particular brand has been bought it will continue to be bought out of habit. Evidence suggests that low-involvement items are often first bought in response to an advertisement that has been seen.

10.2 Factors influencing the promotional strategy

The various elements of the promotional strategy need to be blended together in order to achieve the desired marketing objective. If the campaign is to be effective, the advertising, sales promotions, public relations and personal selling need to form a co-ordinated whole so that they do not communicate conflicting messages. Before deciding on the best combination of promotional elements, marketers need to take into account the following factors:

(a) Stage reached in the product life cycle
Different promotional techniques may be used at different stages of the life cycle. When a product is first launched onto the market, advertising is used to make consumers aware of the product and its benefits. Similarly, sales promotions such as coupons and free samples are often used to stimulate trial usage and encourage repeat purchases. During the growth stage, when competing products have usually entered the market, sales promotions can be crucial in determining whether one product is bought in preference to very similar rival offerings. Once a product has reached the mature stage, advertising is often used to stimulate demand, whilst sales promotions can help a firm to maintain its market share, by making the firm's product more attractive than competing brands.

When sales begin to decline, the firm may decide to withdraw the product, and all forms of advertising are then reduced to a minimum in order to avoid wastage. Alternatively, the firm may decide to support the product; in which case it may invest in a new advertising campaign, introduce a variety of sales promotions and so on.

(b) The nature of the product
The promotional strategies for companies marketing consumer durables tend to consist mainly of advertising and sales promotion. However, the strategies for companies marketing industrial products and services and specialized consumer services rely more on personal selling, although advertisements may occasionally be used to target industrial buyers through trade magazines.

(c) Demand mechanisms
When marketers aim their strategies at customers and end-users, they are said to be adopting a **pull strategy**. This means that advertising and sales promotions

are used to stimulate demand, which then 'pulls' the product through the distribution channel from manufacturer to customer. Pull strategies are commonly used by companies selling fast-moving consumer goods.

Alternatively, marketers can encourage demand amongst retailers and wholesalers with the use of sales-promotion and personal-selling methods. This is known as a **push strategy**, because demand is created by the intermediaries who then promote the product to customers and consumers.

(d) The promotion budget
The type of promotional method chosen is also influenced by the size of budget available. Though effective in reaching a large audience, advertising on television may prove too expensive for all but the largest companies. Certain products and services do not in any case need to be promoted to a mass-market audience. In fact, marketers can achieve better results, especially for products and services targeted at a particular niche market, by advertising in specialist magazines and newspapers or by using direct mail.

Similarly, for products aimed at industrial markets, visits made by sales representatives to the key personnel involved in the decision-making process are likely to prove more cost-effective than the use of methods such as advertising and sales promotions which are designed to reach a general audience.

10.3 The communication process

All forms of promotion aim to communicate a particular message from the organization. Given that effective promotion depends on effective communication, it is obviously essential to understand how the communication process works before designing a promotion strategy. As shown in fig. 10.2 (overleaf), the communication process starts when a person or firm (i.e. the source) decides to send a message through a particular channel (i.e. the media) in order to reach a specified audience (i.e. the receiver). If the communications process is to be successful, the sender must encode the message in such a way that the audience can interpret or decode the message correctly.

(a) The source
The communication starts when a person or firm wishes to send a message. The impact of that message hinges directly on factors such as the trustworthiness and credibility of the sender. Product claims made by firms with a strong brand portfolio and/or good corporate image tend to be received favourably by the audience. Technical competence can also be influential, which is why advertisements often quote 'expert' testimonials. Consumers are more likely to accept messages from people with whom they can identify, hence the success of commercials portraying 'real-life' situations and 'ordinary' families. Nevertheless, people are also influenced by those they like or admire, which explains why celebrities are still widely used to endorse products.

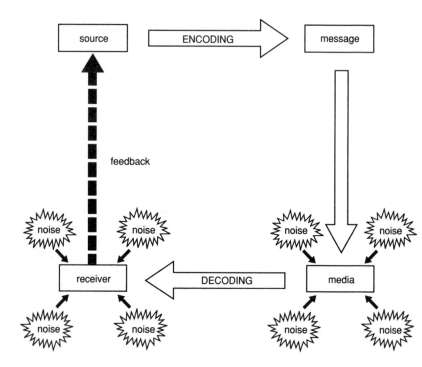

Fig. 10.2 The communication process

(b) Encoding

The message must be delivered in a form that is clear and understandable by the audience. In his book *Marketing*, Peter Bennett describes what happened when Lever Brothers first introduced Lemon Light dishwashing detergent. Several hundred thousand free samples of Lemon Light were sent to consumers: 'The initial package design prominently featured a bright, juicy-looking lemon to convey the idea of freshness and cleanliness. But some consumers took the message literally and sprinkled Lemon Light onto their salads and other foods. The marketers thought they had encoded the message "lemon-scented", but some receivers apparently read that message as "lemon-flavoured". Lever Brothers was forced to redesign its package and include a warning against eating Lemon Light.' Clearly, then, the encoding must make use of words, pictures and symbols that can be easily understood by the majority of the target audience.

(c) The message

The nature of the message itself is influenced by the marketing objectives that have been identified in the overall promotion strategy. The objective might be to increase sales, alter consumer perceptions of a brand, reinforce a previous purchase decision and so on. The impact of the message is increased when the promotional campaign concentrates on one key benefit. The most memorable campaigns are invariably those that emphasize a feature or attribute of the product where it has a particular strength relative to the competition.

(d) The media

The message can be transmitted via a number of different communication channels, including well-known forms such as television, radio, newspapers and magazines, direct mail, personal selling and posters as well as carrier bags, restaurant menus and hot-air balloons. We are exposed to promotional messages even when riding in a taxi, standing in a queue at the post office or visiting the doctor's surgery.

The choice of medium depends on the nature of the product itself (e.g. expensive products tend to be advertised in glossy magazines), the message that needs to be conveyed (e.g. direct mail may be used to inform existing owners that a new model of a particular car is being launched) and the objectives of the promotional campaign (e.g. door-to-door distribution of free samples may be used to encourage trial usage of a new product). The eventual choice may also be influenced by factors such as the size of audience that needs to be reached and the time scales involved. This is quite apart from cost and budget considerations. For example, television, which is arguably the most effective medium for transmitting messages to a wide audience, is extremely expensive.

(e) Decoding

Decoding involves translating or interpreting the message in order to understand its meaning. This sounds very straightforward. In reality, however, consumers do not always pick out the correct message that the source intended them to receive. Evidence suggests that consumers perceive information selectively, picking up and remembering some cues and ignoring others.

(f) The receiver

The way in which the target audience accepts and responds to a particular promotional message is influenced by the attitudes, values and beliefs that are held. These are in turn influenced by factors like their cultural background, level of education, income, occupation, personality and so on.

The effectiveness of the communication process is reduced if the receiver fails to understand the message or interprets it incorrectly. This is why much effort goes into ensuring that the promotional message is appropriate to the ability level of a majority audience. This has led to charges of advertisers catering for the 'lowest common denominator'.

(g) Feedback

Communication is a two-way process. Marketing research can be used to monitor the effectiveness of the promotional message. Sales representatives can provide valuable direct feedback to their managers on areas that need improvement. Feedback from the receivers enables the sender of the message to modify the communication process where necessary, for example by changing the media used, targeting a different audience and so on. In some cases the problem is not that the message has been misunderstood, but that it is ineffective, i.e. it has not stimulated the desired consumer response.

(h) Noise

The communication process rarely proceeds smoothly through the stages described. Messages may be interrupted or distorted by a variety of outside factors. For example, people watching commercials on television may be interrupted by the telephone ringing, other members of the family talking to them, or they may simply decide to get up and go out of the room to make a cup of tea. People reading an advertisement in a magazine may have their attention distracted by an interesting article on the facing page. All these factors act as 'noise', which interferes with the accurate reception or understanding of a message. Ironically, it is the marketers themselves who are responsible for creating much of the problem. As consumers are bombarded with more and more promotional messages, 'noise' stems increasingly from the sheer volume of competing messages. It is hardly surprising, then, that consumers absorb only a fraction of the messages to which they are exposed each day. As ever, the challenge for marketers is to ensure that *their* message is the one that makes an impact and is acted upon.

10.4 The advertising process

(a) Set objectives

The first step in the advertising process is to set objectives for the campaign that are realistic and achievable. Ideally, the objectives which are identified should be stated in terms that are specific and quantifiable, i.e. capable of measurement. This allows marketing planners to evaluate whether the objectives have actually been achieved. Most importantly, planners need to ensure that the campaign is *capable* of achieving the desired result.

A classic example of advertising expenditure being wasted is provided by Malcolm McDonald in his book, *The Marketing Plan*: 'A machine-tool company could not understand why, after an expensive advertising campaign in Germany in which they emphasized the extremely high quality and reliability of their products, they made little headway in the market. Subsequent market research showed that their customers already believed this company had the best product. What they were concerned about, and why they were not buying, was their dissatisfaction about delivery and customer service.'

Objectives fall into two broad categories:

(i) Sales objectives   One of the most common objectives of advertising is to move customers (both existing and potential) nearer to the point of making a purchase decision. **Direct-action advertisements** aim to prompt consumers into taking immediate action, whereas **delayed-action advertisements** are designed to influence buying behaviour in the long term by shaping underlying preferences and attitudes.

The kind of objective that is adopted varies according to the stage reached in the life cycle of the product or brand, with the emphasis shifting from initiating sales amongst new users in the introductory stage to increasing sales amongst existing users in the growth phase and finally to stemming a decline in sales during the final stage.

When a product is first launched, **informative advertising** is often used to tell consumers that the product is available and to publicize its benefits. As sales start to grow and competitors are attracted into the market, **competitive advertising** may be used to defend market share by encouraging consumers to buy a particular product or brand in preference to the others on offer. Once the product has reached the mature stage, **reminder advertising** may be used to encourage habitual re-buying by keeping the product in the forefront of consumers' minds.

(ii) Non sales objectives These objectives are not aimed directly at increasing sales. Advertising is often used to foster favourable attitudes towards a product and also to alter particular beliefs and attitudes that are held, i.e. that a product is unreliable, poor quality, too expensive and so on. Advertising is invaluable for changing the **market positioning** of a product (see the Lucozade case study on pages 83–4).

Alternatively, advertising may be used to make consumers aware of the existence of a product. This has important spin-off benefits. Increasing consumer awareness makes the job of the sales force easier, because distributors and retailers are more willing to stock items that they know have advertising support. In the case of commercial and industrial products, organizational buyers are more likely to place orders and meet sales representatives from companies whose products they have seen advertised.

(b) Decide budgets

The next step is to decide on an advertising budget which is appropriate to the objectives that have been set. This is not an easy task – planners need ultimately to find a balance between spending too much and spending too little. There are a number of techniques that can be adopted.

(i) Percentage of sales This is the most widely used method, where the budget set is based on a given percentage of the sales forecast figure for the coming year. In the case of heavily advertised FMCGs (fast-moving consumer goods), the figure could be as high as 10 per cent of sales revenue. Industrial products on the other hand, which do not generally need to reach a mass-market audience, tend to devote a much lower proportion of their revenue to advertising – typically around 1–2 per cent of sales revenue.

The main advantage of this method is that it tends to reinforce existing sales patterns, since advertising is increased for products whose sales are growing and decreased for those which are declining. It therefore promotes potential winners whilst starving the weaker products of investment – investment which could arguably enable the stragglers to improve their performance in the long term.

However, the main weakness of this approach stems from the fact that sales forecasts, being projections of the figures achieved in previous years, may be set at a level which is unduly optimistic or pessimistic. Advertising budgets based on such figures may in turn be set at a level which is too high or too low for present market conditions.

There are, in any case, times when the size of the advertising budget bears no relation to sales revenue – when management decide to invest funds in reviving a declining product, for example.

(ii) Competitive parity   This is where firms spend the same amount of money on advertising as their major rivals, in order to maintain their share of the market. Products which are essentially very similar, like the different brands of washing powder, can lose market share very rapidly if they are not advertised to the same extent as their neighbours on the supermarket shelf. The main disadvantage of this method is that it is a defensive strategy and as such could result in the company failing to exploit new market opportunities.

(iii) All-available funds   As the term implies, this approach involves firms spending as much as they can afford on the advertising budget, based on the assumption that it is impossible to spend too much on advertising. It is a common strategy for newly launched products. When Alberto Culver introduced its VO5 shampoo in the 1960s, it spent over 60 per cent of its turnover on a television campaign in the first year of the launch.

As a method of setting advertising budgets, it is better than the competitive parity approach, because it takes into account the amount that companies have available to spend rather than stating the amount that they ought to allocate. This is an important consideration, particularly for small companies and for those whose products are aimed at specialized niche markets.

(iv) Objective and task   This is the most logical method and it overcomes many of the weaknesses inherent in the approaches previously described. It grew out of a study carried out in 1961 called **Defining Advertising Goals for Measured Advertising Results**, or **DAGMAR** for short. The study found that the reason why so many companies were having difficulties in evaluating the effectiveness of their advertising budgets was because they had not established beforehand what they wanted the advertising to achieve. In other words, the budget should be influenced by the objectives that are set. If the **objective** is to increase sales by 5 per cent over the coming year, the size of the budget should reflect the cost of all the **tasks** needed to accomplish that particular objective.

Objectives are usually devised around two fundamental concepts: **coverage**, which is the percentage of the target group that will see the advertisement at least once during the campaign, and **frequency**, which is the number of times, on average, that the advertisement is seen by each person in the target group.

(c) Create campaign

The next step, the creative campaign, is best demonstrated by the following case study, the Levi's 501 campaign.

> **Case study** *Levi's 501s* **The campaign that revived a faded market** The scene is a typical laundromat in the American Midwest of the late 1950s – the kind of place where nothing much ever happens – until, that is, a handsome young man walks in. To the strains of Marvin Gaye's 'I Heard It Through The Grapevine', he proceeds to strip off his clothes down to a pair of boxer shorts, puts them into the machine and then calmly sits down with the other customers while they are washed. This advertisement, 'Launderette', was the first in a campaign developed by advertising agency Bartle Bogle Hegarty (BBH) to accompany the European relaunch of the Levi's 501 range of jeans. It is a campaign that has received widespread critical acclaim and won awards by the dozen, both in the UK and internationally. Most importantly, the campaign succeeded in its key objective of boosting sales.
>
> From the outset, 'Launderette' set the pace by creating a level of demand which left rivals and observers gasping. In the UK alone, sales increased by a staggering 800 per cent within the first year. Consumer reaction was unprecedented. Shops were inundated with people asking to try on the jeans that 'the bloke in the launderette wears'. Levi's sold three months stock of 501s in just three weeks.
>
> This was a far cry from the situation that existed prior to the introduction of the advertising campaign. In 1984, Levi Strauss was suffering from a serious downturn in demand. Sales in the European jeans market had slumped from 250 million pairs in 1981 to 150 million pairs in 1985. During the sixties and seventies, jeans were a symbol of youthful rebellion. However, today's parents are the same people who as kids defied their parents by wearing denim. This was the root of the problem. The 16 to 24 year olds who constitute the main target group, accounting for well over half of all jeans sold, had begun to associate jeans with something Mum and Dad wore as a hangover from their teenage days.
>
> In addition, the company was feeling the effects of ill-advised forays into other markets. Unfortunately, the decision to diversify the product base, which had resulted in products ranging from

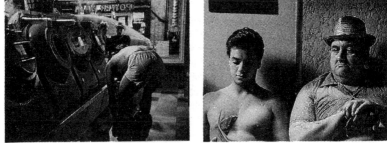

Fig. 10.3   Stills from Levi Strauss's TV commercial 'Launderette'

socks to flannel shirts, had begun to dilute the Levi's brand name to the point where it was in danger of looking cheap. Overheads mounted with the ever-widening product lines, and traditional standards of quality were eroded with the drive towards short-term fashion volume. All the major brands made similar mistakes in this period.

By 1984, the situation facing the company was serious as it emerged from a shattering year of restructuring in which dozens of factories were closed worldwide and thousands of jobs lost. At this point, Levi Strauss decided to abandon the **diversification strategy** and go back to selling jeans. It was a bold move – calculated to bring about a reversal in the company's fortunes.

Central to this 'back to basics' strategy was the relaunch of their original five-pocket western jean. The main challenge facing Bartle Bogle Hegerty in designing this advertising campaign was to lower the age profile of Levi consumers which had crept upwards in line with the brand's worsening image. In short, the objective of the campaign was to persuade a whole new generation of young people that 501s were *the* definitive jean.

Before developing the **creative strategy**, the agency carried out market research which uncovered some interesting trends. America in the 1980s, the America of Reagan and cruise missiles, was seen in a negative light. Yet there was a fascination with a mythical America of the past – the America that had produced James Dean and Elvis Presley, the '57 Chevrolet, and Sam Cooke. It was an emotionally charged mix, but it confirmed the fifties look was 'in'. Related to this was the growing desire for clothes and objects with a genuine heritage – Ray Ban, Bass Weejuns and Zippo to name but a few.

According to Tim Lindsay, the account director in charge of the Levi Strauss account at BBH, 'The **creative brief** was to persuade the 15 to 20 year old males who represent the core of the jeans market that 501s were the right look and the only label: the right look because "anti-fit" was the way jeans were being worn by those in the know; the only label, because only Levi's 501s had laid genuine claim to the heady jeans heritage that was rooted in the fifties.' As the campaign was to be shown throughout Europe, the advertisements also had to be clear without the use of speech.

Having decided on the strategy, the next step was to put it into practice. As part of the **creative execution**, three scripts were prepared in rough form and then tested in **group discussions**. Results confirmed that the fifties nostalgia theme was an effective motivator. The research also highlighted the importance of pop classics in creating the right mood. BBH eventually presented two of the scripts to Levi Strauss and were given an immediate go-ahead.

'Launderette' and 'Bath' went on air in December 1985, followed soon after by 'Parting' and 'Entrance'. Within the next few years other presentations were developed – 'Cochrane', 'Refrigerator' and 'Pick up', all of which reinforced the nostalgia theme.

The results were stunning. Levi's market share increased from 13 per cent to 18 per cent. In fact, the campaign transformed the entire jeans market. Over the years, Levi's have cemented their position as market leaders, gaining a 20 per cent share of a market worth £1 billion by 1990.

Most importantly, the campaign succeeded in its original objective of adjusting the brand's consumer profile back to the core of the market, thus returning the company to profitability. There were other spin-off benefits. The 'golden oldies' which formed the soundtracks all sold well when they were re-released. According to trade sources, 'Launderette' created a new fashion with over 2 million pairs of boxer shorts being sold in 1986!

(d) Select media

Media planners need to allocate their budgets between several different media in order to ensure that the advertisement reaches a significant proportion of the target audience, i.e. that it attains the right **coverage** and is seen the required number of times, thus achieving the right **frequency**. Media planners need to balance a variety of considerations in selecting the best combination of media to achieve their objectives.

(i) **Coverage**   Planners need to take into account the degree of coverage offered by the different media. Figures are calculated on the basis of the number of people who have an **opportunity to see** (OTS) an advertisement. This can range from an OTS of over 90 per cent for television to an OTS of less than 5 per cent for cinema.

(ii) **Frequency**   Evidence suggests that for a particular advertising campaign to be effective people must be exposed to the message several times before it really sinks in. Media planners therefore try to ensure that the target audience has several opportunities to see an advertisement during the course of the campaign. Inevitably, however, a compromise has to be drawn between achieving maximum coverage and maximum frequency. If planners wish to spread their budgets across several different media in order to reach the majority of the target audience, they may not be able to advertise frequently enough in expensive media like television.

(iii) **Cost-effectiveness**   In choosing between different media, planners use the **CPT index**, which is the estimated cost of reaching 1000 people in the target audience. For example, the CPT of advertising on a particular TV programme is calculated by dividing the cost of a 30-second commercial slot on that programme by the number of viewers.

(iv) Type of product Television is generally acknowledged to be the most effective medium for products geared to a mass-market audience. However, it would be a waste of resources to use TV for products targeted at specific groups of consumers. For example, it is better to advertise products aimed at niche markets in special-interest magazines like those on gardening, photography or computers. These magazines also offer an opportunity to provide the long technical explanations required.

(v) Type of message Media like television, radio, cinema and posters are best for campaigns with short, simple messages. Newspapers and magazines are more appropriate for messages that need detailed explanation.

(vi) Budget constraints Firms marketing consumer goods aimed at mass-market audiences find it more economic to use a medium like television because the cost can be offset against the large number of units produced. Firms with a small advertising budget would find advertising in local newspapers and radio stations a more effective use of their resources.

Table 10.1 Types of advertising media

Medium	Advantages	Disadvantages
TELEVISION	● Wide coverage, as almost all homes now own a television set.	● Air time is expensive to buy, especially during peak viewing times like early evening and also during popular programmes that draw large audiences.
	● Very persuasive medium. The impact of the message is greater than in print media because TV advertisements can make use of colour, sound and movement as well as a host of visual techniques.	
		● Production cost of advertising is very high.
	● Rapid build-up of coverage. An advertisement can reach several million people at once. The most effective medium for reaching a mass-market audience.	● Large amount of air time generally needs to be bought in order to ensure that the target audience has been exposed to a particular advertisement for the required number of times.
	● Accurate and reliable data on the size and composition of viewing audiences is available for the different independent television companies in the country. This enables advertisers to target specific geo-demographic segments.	● Message has to be short and uncomplicated in order to grab and hold the attention of viewers.
		● Difficult to reach ABC1 market segments who tend to watch, on average, fewer hours of television than other groups.

Table 10.1 Continued

Medium	Advantages	Disadvantages
NATIONAL NEWSPAPERS	• High level of coverage. Effective in reaching large audiences, especially those with high circulations. • Rapid build-up of coverage. • Advertisers can target specific socio-economic groups, e.g. the 'qualities' cater for a different readership from the tabloids. • Specialized audiences can be targeted even more precisely by advertising on particular days, e.g. teachers and lecturers read the *Guardian's* Education section on Tuesdays. • Newspaper advertising campaigns are simple to design and set up. • Advertisements can have a topical content as there is no long lead time for copy. • Advertisements placed in colour supplements have a greater impact, partly because of the glossier presentation and partly because the supplements tend to be kept for longer and read more thoroughly.	• Advertising space is expensive, especially in newspapers with high circulation rates. • Advertisements in black-and-white print have a reduced impact due to the limitations of printing and 'flat' presentation. • Daily newspapers have a short lifespan and are soon discarded. • Few people read a newspaper from cover to cover, which means that they are likely to miss seeing a proportion of the advertisements. • Difficult to demonstrate the exact nature of the product and its benefits.
LOCAL NEWSPAPERS	• Good coverage within a defined local catchment area. Free papers achieve 'blanket' distribution to homes in an area. • Quick and simple to insert advertisements.	• Impact of message is reduced by the limitations of printing and 'flat' presentation. • Local newspapers are soon discarded.

Table 10.1 Continued

Medium	Advantages	Disadvantages
	● Effective method for industries and retailers whose products and services are targeted at a local market. ● Advertising space is much cheaper than in national newspapers.	● Readers are likely to miss a proportion of the advertisements. ● Many free newspapers are thrown away without being read at all.
MAGAZINES	● Magazines are generally aimed at a specific market segment with defined socio-economic characteristics or particular hobbies and interests. ● Advertisements can convey long and complex messages, especially in the specialist magazines and technical journals. ● Good coverage, especially for magazines with high circulation rates. ● Impact of the message is increased by use of colour, glossy presentation and layout. This is particularly important for advertising expensive cars, perfumes, etc. ● Magazines have a long lifespan and are often passed on to other people. Some may be kept indefinitely as a source of reference. Magazines may therefore be read by a wider audience than the circulation figures would suggest.	● Advertising space is very expensive, especially in the 'glossies' like *Vogue, House and Garden* and *Country Life*. ● Long lead time, of three months or more, for inserting copy. This means that the advertising cannot be given a topical slant. ● Advertisers experience considerable competition from rival advertisers. ● Magazines have a long and complicated lifespan, which makes it difficult to evaluate the effectiveness of a campaign. ● Sales take place over a period of time which results in a slow build-up of coverage.
RADIO	● Rapid build-up of coverage.	● Coverage limited to a restricted geographical area.

Table 10.1 Continued

Medium	Advantages	Disadvantages
	● Inexpensive form of advertising, especially on small local radio stations, though prime-time spots on stations like Capital Radio are more expensive.	● Advertising message must be short and uncomplicated.
	● Local stations generally cater for a mixed audience, though special interest programmes allow more precise targeting.	● Impact of message limited by fact that listeners may not be fully concentrating, i.e. they have the radio on as background music.
	● Quick and easy to book air time, which allows advertisers to incorporate topical material.	● Difficult to obtain accurate data on audience composition.
		● Difficult to explain what the product is like when it cannot be seen.
CINEMA	● Impact of advertising message is increased because cinema allows the use of colour, movement and sound. The product or service can be demonstrated in use.	● Cinema audiences continue to decline.
	● Recall levels for cinema advertisements are higher than for those on television.	● Poor overall coverage, though effective for targeting the youth market.
	● Useful medium for advertisers who want to target a local audience.	● Most cinema-goers do not visit the cinema regularly, which means there is a slow build-up of coverage as the target audience is gradually exposed to a particular advertisement.
	● Effective medium for targeting young people who constitute the majority in cinema audiences.	● Expensive to produce cinema advertisements.
	● Advertisers are in a strong position because they can direct their messages at a captive audience which cannot be distracted by competing messages.	● Expensive to produce duplicate films for distribution to hundreds of cinemas in a national campaign.

Table 10.1 Continued

Medium	Advantages	Disadvantages
OUTDOOR POSTERS AND TRANSPORT MEDIA	● Effective medium when used to reinforce a message that is communicated by a press or TV campaign.	● Though posters may be seen frequently, their impact is reduced by the fact that people may stop noticing them after a while.
	● Relatively cheap form of advertising, though poster sites are often bought in packages of 500–1000.	● Advertising message has to be brief as the amount of information conveyed is limited to what can be absorbed in a short space of time, e.g. a few seconds in the case of drivers passing a poster.
	● Wide variety of locations which makes it possible for advertisers to achieve a high coverage.	
	● There may be little competition from other messages where the audience is captive, e.g. at a bus stop.	● Slow build-up of coverage. Production costs, especially for large posters, are very high.
	● Advertising message is often seen frequently.	● Best sites can be monopolized by some advertisers for months on end.
		● Difficult to obtain accurate data on size and composition of audience.

(e) Evaluate campaign

Once the media have been chosen, the next step is to evaluate the effectiveness of the advertising. This can be done at two stages: **pre-testing** takes place before the commercials have been run, whilst **post-testing** is carried out after the commercials have appeared.

(i) Pre-testing   This enables advertisers to assess whether the creative execution adopted is likely to be successful in meeting the objectives of the campaign. The advertisements are tested on a sample of consumers in order to establish whether they are capable of generating interest, increasing awareness, improving attitudes and so on. Pre-testing can also be useful in identifying the most effective presentation when marketers need to decide between a number of alternative ideas for an advertisement. Clearly, then, the main advantage of pre-testing is that it can help to filter out advertisements that elicit a weak or negative response from the test group.

In fact, even advertisements that are basically sound can benefit from this close scrutiny, which highlights modifications that need to be made before the campaign is run. By allowing advertisements to be fine tuned, preferably when the idea is still at the story-board stage, pre-testing prevents expensive reworking later on.

(ii) Post-testing   This enables advertisers to assess whether the creative execution has been successful in producing the desired consumer response. Most importantly, it can determine whether the campaign has had the required impact on sales or market share. **Recall tests,** which ask respondents to state what they remember about an advertisement, provide an indication of the strength of the message based on the principle that if consumers are able to remember some details, without being prompted, then the advertisement must have hit home to some extent. However, the fact that consumers can recall parts of an advertisement does not mean that they found it persuasive. To be effective, an advertisement must stimulate a purchase decision or some other change in attitude or behaviour.

In view of these limitations, advertisers tend to rely more heavily on tests which involve in-depth interviews with consumers, carried out at regular intervals during the course of the advertising campaign. By measuring changing trends in the attitudes of the target audience towards a product or brand, these **tracking studies** provide a more realistic analysis of the impact of a campaign.

Where firms wish to evaluate the effectiveness of a campaign before incurring the expense of a national launch, they will first introduce the product into a small **test area** – often a TV region which is representative of the country as a whole. If the campaign fares well in this region, it is expanded nationwide. If it flops, then at least the damage is restricted to one area and the company has avoided a large-scale disaster.

> **Case study**   *Yellow Pages*   **'Not just for the nasty things in life'**
> When advertising agency Abbott Mead Vickers first pitched for the *Yellow Pages* account in 1983, its preliminary research revealed some interesting findings. People used *Yellow Pages* only when they had a problem such as a leaky pipe and needed to find a plumber. As a result, they associated *Yellow Pages* almost exclusively with these kinds of situations and so did not think of using it again until the next problem arose. The new campaign developed by Abbott Mead Vickers was designed to break this vicious circle. The objective of the advertising was to encourage people to view *Yellow Pages* in a more positive light so that they would then think of using it for many different purposes.
> This is the common theme underlying the **creative execution** of the campaign. Each *Yellow Pages* advertisement that is developed is a brief portrayal in the 'slice of life' genre, conveying the key message, 'Good old *Yellow Pages*. We don't just help with the

nasty things in life, like a blocked drain, we're there for the nice things, too.'

As with any new campaign, several possible ideas were considered. In fact, the agency presented three scripts initially: 'J.R. Hartley', 'Pony' and 'Hungarian Band'. When these were subsequently tested by **group discussions,** the 'J.R. Hartley' script emerged virtually unscathed from the research. However, the other two ideas were not well received. In the 'Pony' script, which involved a little girl being given a pony as a surprise birthday present, the humour was seen as being too 'up-market' and the pony itself was thought to be an unrealistic present in terms of appealing to a majority audience.

The 'Hungarian Band' script was confusing because it contained too many examples. Worse still, it did not communicate the central message clearly enough, although one scene, which showed a young boy admiring his new bicycle, was universally liked. The agency decided to substitute this for the pony in the other script, as a more 'down to earth' example of a present. At the same time, the whole story was reworked so that it took place in an ordinary northern family – a setting which was more appropriate to a mass-market audience. In developing a successful advertising campaign, the elimination of some ideas and modification of others illustrates clearly the importance of **pre-testing** advertisements at an early stage of their development.

Fig. 10.4 Stills from *Yellow Pages'* TV commercial 'Party Party'

Changing times, fashions and lifestyles render many campaigns obsolete within a short time, but the campaign for *Yellow Pages* continues to have an enduring appeal amongst consumers. A variety of commercials incorporating the theme of 'Not just for the nasty things in life' have been developed, including 'J.R. Hartley', 'Bike', 'Party Party', 'Gardener' and 'Hat'.

The central aim of the advertising strategy was to encourage consumers to consult *Yellow Pages* for the 'nice' classifications. Most importantly, it has succeeded in creating an environment where usage rates have dramatically increased. When the campaign was launched in 1983, *Yellow Pages* was used 53 million times per month. By 1989, this figure had increased to 85 million.

10.5 Sales promotions

(a) The role of sales promotions

Why should a company like Coca-Cola choose to spend £18 million on engineering a new kids' craze? At first sight, this might seem more than a little rash. Yet when we learn that over 4 million yo-yos bearing the Coca-Cola brand name were sold in the space of a few short months during 1989, the decision starts to make sense. In fact, the yo-yos were bought by 85 per cent of all children in the 8 to 15 year old target group. Clearly, then, the aptly-named 'Spinner' project, which required children to submit several proofs of purchase in order to obtain a yo-yo, succeeded in its objective of increasing sales during a particular period of time. It was, therefore, an example of an effective **sales promotion**.

Sales promotions involve a whole host of techniques ranging from fairly simple methods, such as reduced price packs and the distribution of coupons or samples, to the use of more complex methods, such as charity promotions, competitions and free-gift offers. Marketers are limited only by their imaginations in dreaming up original and exciting promotions. Nevertheless, despite the range of techniques adopted, all promotions exist to serve one purpose – to provide an incentive for consumers to buy.

Whereas advertising aims to increase awareness or build favourable attitudes towards a brand, sales promotions are calculated to increase the actual purchases made by new or existing buyers. Promotions are designed to boost short-term sales performance, rather than to foster long-term sales growth. By implication, therefore, promotions can revive a flagging sales curve temporarily, but they cannot be expected to arrest long-term decline caused by a deep-rooted problem such as a product which is poor quality, wrongly priced, or targeted at the wrong market segment. Promotions operate on two levels: those that offer an **immediate** incentive to purchase, like price reductions and bonus pack offers (Table 10.2), and those that offer a **delayed** incentive, for instance where consumers have to send off for a free offer or wait for the results of a competition to be announced (Table 10.3).

Table 10.2 Sales promotions offering an immediate incentive to purchase

Type of promotion	Advantages	Disadvantages
REDUCED PRICE PROMOTIONS Price reduction marked on pack, e.g. 20p off.	● Popular with consumers because packs represent good value. ● Quick and easy to implement. ● Reliable impact in terms of increasing sales volume.	● Expensive for manufacturers. ● If price cuts are matched by competitors, can escalate into a price war. ● Additional sales are likely to be from regular users of the brand who have merely brought forward their purchases. ● Requires specially printed packaging.
BONUS PACK OFFERS Pack contains additional quantity of product at no extra cost.	● Popular with consumers because packs represent good value. ● Popular with manufacturers because it is cheaper to give away more product than to reduce the selling price. ● May encourage consumer to buy larger pack in future. ● Quick and easy to set in operation.	● Expensive for manufacturers to produce the larger, non-standard packaging. ● Additional sales are likely to be from regular users of the brand. ● Storage and transport costs are greater for the larger packs. ● Requires specially printed packaging.
HOME SAMPLING Free sample of product (which is often newly launched) is distributed to selected areas by hand or post.	● Most effective method of encouraging consumers to try a new or improved product. ● Stimulates wider trade distribution – retailers are forced to stock new product when consumers who have tried the free sample ask for that brand by name.	● Most expensive type of promotion for manufacturer. ● Expensive to produce small, trial-sized sample packs. ● Economic only for brands aimed at large mass-market audiences. ● Some wastage is inevitable, e.g. samples thrown away.

Table 10.2 Continued

Type of promotion	Advantages	Disadvantages
	● Can be targeted at areas with the required geo-demographic characteristics based on classifications like ACORN.	
MULTI-PACK OFFERS The 'buy two get one free' type of offer.	● Effective in encouraging repeat purchases amongst regular users of the product. ● Quick and easy to set in operation. ● Effective for brands aimed at specialized markets.	● Unlikely to attract new users to the brand. ● Easily copied by the competition.
BANDED OFFERS One product is banded together with a free sample of another (often related) product from the same or a different manufacturer, e.g. bottle of shampoo with a free bottle of conditioner.	● Inexpensive method for manufacturers of distributing samples. ● Stimulates trial usage amongst the right target group, i.e. people who buy a particular brand of shampoo are more likely to buy the conditioner in the range.	● Less easy to target a particular geo-demographic segment than the home sampling method. ● Uneconomic for brands purchased frequently, as each consumer may receive several free samples. ● Small, trial-sized samples require special packaging.
PREMIUM OFFERS Free gift is provided with every purchase, e.g. free glasses with petrol, plastic toys in packets of breakfast cereals.	● Effective in encouraging trial usage amongst new users. ● The best gifts can increase sales significantly. ● Where a set of gifts can be collected, consumer interest can be sustained over a very long period.	● Use of the most desirable items may erode a manufacturer's profit margin too much, which is why most free gifts have little intrinsic value. However, this also means they have a limited appeal for consumers.

Table 10.2 Continued

Type of promotion	Advantages	Disadvantages
COUPON OFFERS 'Money-off' coupons are distributed to selected areas by hand or mailed. Coupons can also be placed in newspapers, magazines, etc. Coupon usually redeemed at point of sale, e.g. supermarket checkout.	● Next best method (after distribution of free samples) of encouraging trial usage for new and improved products. ● Where the home distribution of coupons is carried out, the promotion can be targeted at areas with the required geo-demographic characteristics based on classifications like ACORN. Can also be targeted at specific market segments by insertion in the appropriate newspapers or magazines.	● Home distribution of coupons is expensive for manufacturers. Placing of coupons in newspapers and magazines is less expensive. ● Redemption rates are low because consumers have to make an effort to redeem the coupons. ● Misredemption rate (where consumers redeem a coupon against the wrong brand) is often very high. ● Unpopular with retailers because of the administrative difficulties of handling coupons.

Table 10.3 Sales promotions offering a delayed incentive to purchase

Type of promotion	Advantages	Disadvantages
SEND-AWAY PREMIUMS Consumers collect a certain number of packet tops, labels, tokens and so on as proofs of purchase and are sent a free gift by the manufacturer. **SELF-LIQUIDATING PREMIUMS** Consumer sends both a nominal sum of money and the	● Effective in encouraging repeat purchases amongst regular users, though attractive gifts may also encourage new users. ● Not easily copied by the competition, especially if distinctive gifts are offered. ● Little expense (or risk) for the manufacturer as gifts are bought in bulk and therefore cost very little.	● Likely to appeal mainly to existing users of the brand. ● Response rate is lowered when basic gifts are offered with a limited consumer appeal. ● Difficult to gauge the level of consumer response. If it is lower than expected, manufacturers are left with unwanted stocks. If it is higher than expected, manufacturers risk

Table 10.3 Continued

Type of promotion	Advantages	Disadvantages
required number of proofs of purchase in order to obtain the free gift.	● In the case of self-liquidating premiums, the gift pays for itself. ● Consumers may make the extra purchases but not bother to claim their gift.	losing consumer goodwill if they run out of stock. ● Requires specially printed packaging.

COMPETITIONS

Skill Contests With tiebreakeres, e.g. 'Place these features in order of importance, and say why you think brand X is better . . .'	● Quick to set in operation. ● Cheap to set up and administer.	● Generates little consumer interest. ● Often has no impact on sales.
Sweepstakes Where consumers enter a prize draw, e.g. 'Win a trip to EuroDisney.'	● Quick to set in operation. ● Cheap to set up and administer. ● Generates more entries than skill contests.	● Illegal for manufacturers to require proof of purchase from consumer. This means consumers can enter the draw without making a purchase.
Games e.g. Rub-off cards, Bingo, Spot the Ball, etc.	● Consumer interest can be sustained longer than with most sales promotions. ● Well-designed games can increase sales substantially. ● Difficult for competitors to copy. ● Effective in attracting new users. ● Most effective with products purchased frequently, e.g. petrol, newspapers, groceries.	● Needs to be designed professionally, e.g. to avoid printing too many winning cards. ● Expensive to design and administer scheme.

Table 10.3 Continued

Type of promotion	Advantages	Disadvantages
REFUND OFFERS Consumers are offered a refund for a specific number of proofs of purchase.	● Popular with consumers because a cash-back offer. ● Quick and easy to set up and administer. ● Useful for encouraging repeat purchases amongst existing users.	● Easily copied by competitors. ● Likely to appeal mainly to existing users of the brand. ● Appropriate only to products purchased frequently.
TRADING STAMPS Consumers collect stamps with each purchase which can then be used to obtain gifts from a catalogue, e.g. Green Shield Stamps, Texaco Star tokens, etc. Alternatively, the stamps can be cashed in for a discount against a purchase or a lump sum, e.g. Co-op Dividend stamps.	● Can be effective in attracting new users, especially if the gifts or dividend rates are worthwhile. ● Best schemes can generate considerable consumer interest and increase sales significantly. ● Scheme easy for retailers to administer.	● Additional sales are likely to be from regular users of the brands. ● Gift catalogue system expensive for manufacturer to administer.
CHARITY PROMOTIONS The sponsoring company sends a specified amount to the chosen charity for a particular number of proofs of purchase.	● Best schemes can generate considerable consumer interest and increase sales substantially. ● Response rate is increased when groups like schools, youth clubs, scout groups and so on get involved in collecting tokens. ● Often a spin-off benefit for companies which come to be seen in a more caring light.	● Appropriate only to brands aimed at a mass-market audience. ● May be difficult to find a major charity that a large number of people would wish to support. ● Requires considerable investment of management time in setting up scheme. ● Expensive to administer. ● Likely to require support of other promotional elements, e.g. advertising campaign, sales force, etc.

(b) The benefits of sales promotions

Sales promotions have several benefits. They can be used to:

- encourage consumers to try out a newly launched product or brand;
- entice new users to try out a product which is already available;
- provide consumers with a reason for buying a particular product in preference to the competing brands on offer;
- encourage existing users to purchase a particular product more frequently and/or in greater quantities;
- counteract the effects of seasonal demand by stimulating off-season purchases.

10.6 Personal selling

(a) The importance of personal selling

Personal selling is an important part of the promotional mix. It offers a number of advantages over the other elements, the majority of which stem from the fact that personal selling allows face-to-face contact between buyer and seller. Buyers have the opportunity to ask questions and raise queries. Salespeople, in turn, can adjust their sales messages to suit the needs of particular buyers and can respond immediately to any objections that are raised. Personal selling is used whenever two-way communication is important. This is why companies marketing industrial products and services, which tend to be targeted at a handful of organizational buyers rather than a mass-market audience, devote most of their promotional budget to personal selling.

The stereotyped image of the fast-talking, door-to-door salesman with a glib line in sales patter is an outdated caricature. In reality, it is now widely recognized that professional salespeople occupy a key position in the marketing team and perform a variety of important roles.

(b) The roles performed by salespeople

The many roles performed by salespeople include:

- seek out and acquire new customers;
- make suitable sales approaches to customers;
- deliver sales presentations of the right standard;
- secure orders by matching product benefits to the customer's needs and requirements;
- sell the required range and quality of products;
- achieve the best possible sales quotas in terms of profitability as well as sales volume;
- build good long-term relationships with customers;
- resolve problems and complaints that may arise;
- liaise with buyers to provide after-sales support, e.g. training courses
- recommend changes where necessary, e.g. to the product specification
- organize the frequency of sales visits and travelling time in order to minimize costs.

The above list emphasizes the advantages offered by personal selling over other impersonal methods of communication. However, the demanding nature of the job means that salespeople need to possess a special set of skills in order to succeed. It is debatable whether there is any truth in the old adage that 'good salesmen are born not made'. Training can certainly improve performance, although the 'naturals' are often distinguished by their innate abilities – persuasiveness, outgoing personality and so on.

(c) The skills and attributes required by salespeople

The skills and attributes required by salespeople include:

- a detailed knowledge of the product or service being sold;
- a detailed knowledge of the customer's needs and requirements;
- an attractive personality that enables them to get on with people;
- the ability to persuade a buyer into making a purchase decision in favour of their product or service;
- the ability to work independently, use their own initiative and motivate themselves in the absence of direct supervision, i.e. salespeople need to be self-starters;
- a good sense of timing that enables them to judge when it is right to give the customer a small push in order to finalize or close a sale.

10.7 Setting objectives for the sales force

All firms set objectives that the sales force are expected to reach. Ideally, the goals set should be challenging yet attainable, which is why sales managers usually try to involve their staff in the eventual decision. Unrealistic targets, imposed from on high, merely lead to resentment and serve to demotivate the sales force. However, the fact remains that sales representatives may have a vested interest in setting low **sales quotas**, particularly if bonus payments are made when quotas are exceeded. In order to arrive at an unbiased figure, managers will therefore take into account information from a variety of sources, such as marketing research surveys and government economic reports. Objectives are generally concerned with the following measures:

(i) Sales volume Salespeople are often expected to achieve a particular volume of sales within a given period of time. Firms that concentrate on sales-volume objectives are said to focus on the **top line**.

(ii) Profit As the cost of maintaining a sales force in the field continues to rise, companies are increasingly evaluating the performance of their representatives in relation to profit objectives. Firms emphasizing profitability are said to focus on the **bottom line**.

(iii) Market share Goals are often set which require the sales force to increase the firm's market share by a given percentage within their own particular sales territory.

(iv) Customer service   In order to improve standards of customer service, sales representatives may be asked to meet objectives like reducing the number of customer complaints by a given percentage or increasing the number of visits to important customers.

(v) Market information   The sales force normally functions as the 'eyes and ears' of the company in the marketplace. Being close to the customer enables them to provide valuable feedback on matters like the needs and requirements of consumers, changing market conditions and competitor activity. Most importantly, the sales force is in an ideal position, because of their regular face-to-face contact with customers, to assess consumer reaction to a newly launched product. Long before the results of marketing research studies become available, the sales force can pin-point improvements and modifications that may be necessary.

10.8 Organization of the sales force

The sales force can be organized by geographical area, type of product or type of customer. A company generally structures its sales force on the basis of one factor, although the larger corporations may use a combination of all three methods.

(a) Geographical region

This is where the sales force is divided by geographical region, with the greatest concentration of salespeople occurring in the areas of highest population density, i.e. the major conurbations and industrial regions, as these constitute the largest markets.

Firms whose products are geared to specific industries usually locate near their customers. For example, firms supplying components for the automobile industry tend to be clustered in areas like the West Midlands.

(b) Type of customer

This is where the sales force is divided up by type of customer. It is a system that is particularly appropriate for firms whose products or services are used by many different groups of customers. As salepeople deal exclusively with a particular type of customer, they can gain a better understanding of the needs and requirements of that customer group. For example, a large computer manufacturer might have separate sales divisions that specialize in systems geared to the differing needs and requirements of banks, insurance companies, hospitals and travel agencies.

(c) Type of product
This is where the sales force is divided up according to the type of product or service sold. It is a common system amongst firms with a diverse range of products aimed at several different markets. As salespeople concentrate on selling a particular type of product, they can acquire the necessary specialist knowledge and technical expertise to deal with buyers in that industry.

10.9 The selling process

Figure 10.5 shows that the selling process can be divided into six stages:

(a) Prospecting for buyers
The first step in the process is to identify **prospects**, i.e. potential buyers. One method, often used by firms selling double glazing, is to knock on the doors of all the houses in a street that do not have replacement windows. This is known as **cold calling**. It is a very hit-and-miss method and wasteful of time and resources, which is why firms generally prefer to use more systematic methods of identifying prospects. Preliminary research can help to locate potential buyers. Trade directories, computer databases, specialist journals and magazines can all generate useful **leads** that are worth pursuing. Leads may also come through business contacts, friends and family and of course recommendations from existing satisfied customers. Advertisements placed in suitable newspapers, magazines and journals can often produce a good crop of enquiries.

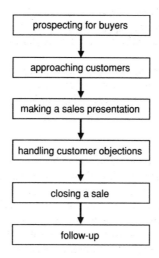

Fig. 10.5 The selling process

Preliminary enquiries are usually vetted before a sales visit is made, as requests for information do not necessarily lead to a sale. Sales representatives will therefore **qualify** an enquiry, perhaps by telephoning first, in order to evaluate whether the prospect is likely to be a serious buyer. At the same time, they also need to establish whether the buyer can afford to pay for the product. In the case of organizational buyers, they need to establish whether the buyer is actually in a position either to authorize the purchase or to make a strong recommendation.

(b) Approaching customers

Once the prospect has been qualified, the salesperson will usually try to arrange an appointment to visit. If the prospect is reluctant to agree, the saleperson may need to embark on a preliminary **sales pitch**, explaining some of the product benefits, mentioning any special offers and discounts, etc. Once the visit has been arranged, the salesperson will try and find out as much as possible about the prospect's needs and requirements. A check may also be made on the prospect's financial status.

(c) Making a sales presentation

The first few minutes are often spent in getting to know the customer in order to build the relationship. In the process, the salesperson will be trying to discover what kind of problems the buyer is trying to solve, so that the **sales presentation** can be tailored to emphasize how this particular product matches the customer's needs and requirements better than competing products. A good sales presentation is determined not only by an articulate speech and impressive visual materials, but also by the intangible aspects of personal communication – tone of voice, facial expression and body language, for example.

When delivering the presentation, the salesperson will follow the AIDA approach, beginning with an opening statement to grab the buyer's **attention**. An example might be: 'I will now show you how this computerized accounting system can reduce your costs by 25 per cent.' This is followed by a description of the particular product or service which is designed to generate **interest**. By stressing the likely benefits in terms of the savings to be made in staffing levels, administration costs, storage requirements or whatever, the salesperson can stimulate the buyer's **desire** to purchase the product. The buyer should then be prepared to take the **action** of making a purchase.

(d) Handling customer objections

However, the deal will not go ahead unless the objections raised by the buyer have been handled satisfactorily. These may relate to any number of factors: the product specification, delivery times or maintenance contracts. Objections need not present a great problem. In fact, experienced salespeople use objections as an opportunity to emphasize the existing benefits of the product. An objection like 'Why do you offer an annual maintenance contract rather than a six-monthly contract?' might be countered by the answer: 'The reliability of our products is such that most of our customers do not want a six-monthly contract.'

Though it sounds contradictory, many objections are in reality **buying signals**, which show that the buyer is actually interested. For instance, the buyer who says, 'I don't like that style/colour/design', may in fact be trying to find out what other options are available. A good salesperson will view an objection as a chance to provide more information and persuade the buyer into action.

(e) Closing the sale
Once the salesperson has moved the buyer to the point where he or she is ready to sign a purchase agreement, this is known as **closing the sale**. One strategy that is often used to close a deal is the **assumptive close**. It involves asking the buyer questions like:

- 'Where would you like the machine installed?'
- 'Would you prefer the large model or the small model?'
- 'We can arrange the delivery for the end of April – is this going to be soon enough for you?'

In other words, by assuming that the order has already been placed, the salesperson makes it harder for the buyer to make a direct refusal. Firms selling double glazing or life insurance have become notorious for using another tactic which involves forcing consumers into making a decision there and then with variations on the theme of 'You need to make your mind up today because the sale/special discount/free fitting offer only lasts until the end of the week.'

(f) Follow-up
The sales process does not end with a successful close. Even once the order has been secured, negotiations may continue concerning the amount of discount and credit that is to be allowed. Financial arrangements will need to be agreed and delivery dates finalized. A training programme for company employees may need to be designed. The salesperson is responsible for ensuring that all these arrangements are organized efficiently. Experienced salespeople will stay in close contact with the new buyer even after the equipment or service has been installed. This provides valuable feedback on improvements that need to be made. More importantly, it fosters a good relationship with the client which may well result in further sales in the future.

The right place

11.1 Distribution – the invisible element of the marketing mix?

Distribution is the process of getting goods from producers to domestic consumers and organizational buyers, which essentially means ensuring that products and services are available where and when they are required. Until the 1960s and 1970s the value of distribution or place as a marketing tool was not appreciated fully by marketers. Unlike the other elements of the marketing mix, i.e. product, price and promotion, which have always been recognized as key factors, place has often been relegated to a position of secondary importance.

However, marketers can no longer afford to disregard the role played by distribution in the marketing mix. Cameron, Rushton and Carson in their book *Marketing* describe what happened when a leading manufacturer of electrical appliances launched a particularly compact travel iron. 'The product was right, the launch timing and promotion were right and the price was right. But there was still a problem: it was almost impossible to buy one because the shops just didn't have them to sell. Something had gone awry with the distribution planning to such an extent that most shops ended up receiving their launch stocks weeks late. Soon afterwards another manufacturer came out with an almost identical product. It is this version that is now stocked by most of the high street multiples and which most people buy. The high street retailers stock it because deliveries have always been reliable, and the consumers buy it because it is the one most readily available. Through not having place properly sorted out, the original manufacturer has lost both the marketing initiative and a lot of money.'

This example illustrates the vital role played by distribution within the marketing mix. As far as consumer products are concerned, the Institute of Logistics and Distribution Management estimates that 34 per cent of sales turnover is accounted for by distribution costs. Every time we buy a packet of crisps, a T-shirt or a magazine we do not pause to think about how the goods have arrived in the shops for us to buy. Yet behind the scenes firms have been deciding which channels of distribution they should use, considering whether it would be worthwhile for them to use wholesalers as middlemen and selecting the most appropriate system of physical distribution.

11.2 Channels of distribution

Channels of distribution are made up of a series of organizations through which goods and services pass from the producer to the end-user. The chain or path between producer and end-user can include a number of *intermediaries* or middlemen such as agents, wholesalers and retailers. All marketers are concerned to establish the most efficient and cost-effective way of moving their product to the consumer.

The number of levels found in a channel of distribution can vary greatly as shown in fig. 11.1. When no middlemen are involved the channel is very short and is known as a **zero-level channel**. This occurs when the producer sells directly to the end-user – a process known as **direct marketing**. All the signs suggest that direct marketing, particularly of shopping from mail-order catalogues, is increasing in importance. Direct marketing is also a potentially more cost-effective way of reaching particular types of consumers than general widespread distribution.

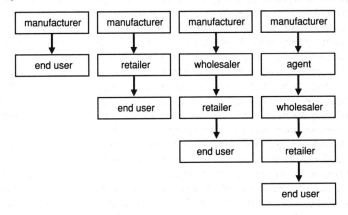

Fig. 11.1 Distribution channels

In a recent article in *Campaign* magazine Robert Dwek described how some firms were using direct marketing as a way of narrowing the field of potential customers to those who are most likely to buy. 'When Ford US found itself unable to shift a particular model, it jettisoned the brand advertising in favour of four-page press inserts – incorporating reply forms and telephone numbers – and 60 second direct response TV advertisements. This generated 30 000 leads and 3000 immediate sales. Pharmaceuticals giant Warner Lambert set up a free information service providing details on the pollen count during the summer months. It used the database generated by this to help market its allergy remedy Benadryl, gaining substantial market share in the process.'

Shorter distribution channels are also used when the product is fragile and handling must be minimized, as with frozen foods, or where the product is bulky, like furniture.

The selling of Avon cosmetics, double glazing and encyclopaedias to consumers in their homes are all examples of the first channel. The second channel, where manufacturers sell to retailers, is common amongst department stores and larger retailers. Smaller retailers, such as independent grocery shops, who cannot buy in bulk from manufacturers may have to buy from wholesalers as in the third channel. The use of agents as in the fourth channel is typical of the sale of holidays and insurance.

Many consumer products pass through distribution channels involving as many as three different levels. Manufacturers of fast moving consumer goods generally need long channels of distribution with many levels of intermediaries such as agents, wholesalers and retailers, in order to build up a supply network enabling them to reach many millions of consumers, including people buying from local corner shops as well as from large supermarkets. A manufacturer of crisps could not hope to sell directly to every person who buys a packet of crisps! For the same reason, they also tend to have very wide channels of distribution, where each level in the channel is made up of many members. A manufacturer of breakfast cereals, for instance, will sell to literally hundreds of wholesalers and many thousands of retailers.

In contrast, industrial products are generally sold direct to the end-user or through short one-level channels. This is largely because manufacturers sell to a few industrial buyers who buy in large amounts. They also tend to buy technically-complex machinery and products which require skilled installation and training for users. These factors explain why manufacturers prefer to sell direct to their industrial customers by means of personal selling methods, rather than through wholesalers and retailers.

However, if manufacturers decide at any stage to target consumer markets instead a shift in **channel strategy** will obviously be needed. Peter Bennett in his book *Marketing* makes this point in relation to IBM: 'Until the introduction of its personal computer in 1981, IBM had sold various computer and office products only through its sales force directly to organizational buyers. Management realized, however, that a new (for IBM) market segment – small businesses and individuals – could not be reached effectively by personal sales representatives. Before its first personal computer rolled off the assembly line, the company made a strategic decision to seek distribution through retail chains like Sears, specialist computer stores and new retail outlets of its own. This strategy worked. Helped in no small part by its widely recognized name, IBM sold 150 000 micro-computers in the first year of sales. In two short years, IBM was the segment leader with a 26 per cent market share, passing major rivals Apple and Tandy Corporation.'

The concept of channels of distribution is applicable to services as well as consumer and industrial products. Businesses such as hairdressers, dry-cleaners and banks sell their services direct to the end-user. Firms like film-processing laboratories operate through retailers. Airlines, hotels and ferry companies sell through travel agencies who act as agents for their services. In the same way, most insurance companies sell their policies through insurance brokers.

Once a suitable channel of distribution has been chosen, it is important that producers are flexible enough to respond to changing market conditions. This may involve them switching to a completely different channel. In his book *Offensive Marketing*, Hugh Davidson cites Avon as an example of a company which was slow to move away from the direct-marketing techniques which had brought it success in the 1960s and early 1970s:

'The basis of Avon's success was the greater security women felt about buying cosmetics in the privacy of their home, the availability of large numbers of part-time saleswomen and the ability to contact people at home. All these factors have now changed. Women have greater self-confidence in choosing cosmetics, and methods of retail selling have improved. The much wider range of employment opportunities has made the role of "Avon Lady" relatively less attractive. Finally, women spend less time at home during the day, as an increasing number have paid jobs.'

From its peak of $140 in 1973, Avon's share price plummeted to $18 by June 1985 – reflecting the company's continued reliance on direct selling techniques which were no longer appropriate to current market conditions.

11.3 Selection of channel members

Before deciding on the type of channel that is to be used to distribute a particular product or service, marketers should first ensure that the chosen channel will be suitable in terms of cost, efficiency, reliability, etc. Inevitably, there will need to be some kind of trade-off between these objectives. For instance, it may not be possible to design an efficient distribution channel which is also cheap.

Producers need to consider many factors when deciding which wholesalers and retailers should be used to distribute a particular product.

(a) Type of product or service
Frequently purchased convenience goods which are easily substituted and have a low unit cost such as newspapers, bars of chocolate and cans of soft drink need to be widely available otherwise sales are lost. For example, Coca-Cola and Pepsi-Cola are on sale everywhere – in supermarkets, grocery shops, newsagents, restaurants, pubs, clubs and vending machines.

In contrast, expensive, infrequently purchased speciality goods such as cars, furniture, computers and home appliances do not need to be so widely available as consumers are usually prepared to spend more time shopping around for them. Products such as these are available through a limited number of retailers who can provide a trained, knowledgeable sales force and the degree of after-sales service required.

Expensive, complicated products which require expert installation are usually sold direct to the consumer. This is also the case with most industrial products.

(b) Image and nature of the product or service
The image of the retail outlet must match that of the product or service. This is why Chanel perfume, Rolex watches and Gucci handbags are sold in the top department stores and not in discount retailers.

(c) Perishability of the product
Products requiring special conditions, e.g. frozen food, can only be sold through wholesalers and retailers with the appropriate storage equipment.

(d) Stage reached in product life cycle
Consumers will usually go out of their way to find an innovative product which has just been launched. However, as the product reaches maturity it will have to be widely available if sales are to be maintained.

(e) Location of customers
Short distribution channels are possible when customers are concentrated in one geographical area. Longer distribution channels are necessary for products which need to be distributed nationally or internationally.

(f) Distribution strategies adopted by competitors
Firms providing a particular product or service will generally tend to use the same channels. All manufacturers of watches, for instance, will sell to department stores and high-street jewellery shops. Swatch, the Swiss manufacturer of inexpensive, 'fun' watches, have instead chosen to sell to a wide variety of retail outlets including discount stores. Adopting this alternative distribution strategy has given Swatch a significant competitive edge.

11.4 Distribution strategies

Having selected the number and types of channel members that are to be used in the distribution process, taking into account the factors previously outlined, the marketer then needs to decide on a distribution strategy which is appropriate to the chosen target market. There are three options:

(a) Intensive distribution
This is a strategy used for inexpensive, frequently purchased convenience goods and services, which need to be widely available and accessible to as many buyers as possible, since customers are not prepared to shop around for such goods. Sales are lost unless they are available in practically every distribution outlet. Examples include most fast-moving consumer goods such as biscuits, soft drinks, bread, milk, etc., some services, e.g. banks, post offices, dry-cleaners, etc., and certain industrial parts and supplies, e.g. lubricating oil, screws and nails, etc.

(b) Exclusive distribution

At the other end of the scale, this is a strategy used for expensive, infrequently purchased speciality goods and services, which need to be available and accessible to a few buyers only. Prestige products are available in a limited range of exclusive, up-market outlets which are chosen to reflect and enhance the image of such products. Buyers are prepared to spend time and effort getting to these outlets. In fact, the difficulty of obtaining these goods is often a significant part of their attraction. Examples include expensive perfume, jewellery and designer clothes which tend to be sold through the top department stores as well as expensive cars and yachts which tend to be sold only through specialist dealers.

(c) Selective distribution

This is a strategy used for goods which are fairly expensive and purchased infrequently, but which are not prestige products. Goods and services are available and accessible to a variety of buyers, though the producer will sell only through reputable outlets. Outlets are selected on the basis of factors such as whether they can hold the right amount of stock, provide the right kind of trained and knowledgeable sales staff and so on. Examples include mid-priced domestic appliances, electrical goods, jewellery, clothes, furniture and cars.

> **Case study** *Filofax* **in Japan   The impact of an appropriate distribution strategy**   A few years ago the so-called 'personal organizer' was rapidly climbing the wave of western fashion. A small British firm called Filofax suddenly found that its old-established product (a glorified loose-leaf diary with a collection of printed sheets for various notes, facts and guides) looked fresh and new, and was selling like hot cakes in Britain and America. In Japan, on the other hand, it was not clear whether this one-product firm would gain any sales at all.
>
> Yet by 1987 Japan had become Filofax's fastest-growing export market, bigger even than America. This was thanks to a firm called Apex Incorporated which, three years earlier, had become Filofax's exclusive distributor in Japan. Filofax's retail sales there have risen from Y10 m in 1984 to Y300 m in 1985 and to Y800 m in 1987.
>
> What Apex did for Filofax was to ensure that its product was distributed properly. In Japan, the benefit of having an exclusive distributor is that it has a strong incentive to promote your product. Apex immediately found 300 outlets, 60 of them in Tokyo, for Filofax binders and loose-leaf sheets. It also started spending judiciously on magazine advertisements showing Dianne Keaton and Steven Spielberg using their Filofaxes.
>
> As sales began to rise, competitors piled in. Quicker and more skilful than those in Britain, Japanese rivals offered imitations that were actually better than the original and one-third of the price. There are now more than 30 makers of imitation Filofaxes,

at least a dozen books telling you how to use them, and two magazines devoted to the lifestyle of Filofax or look-alike users.

In response, it would have been tempting for Filofax to cut prices. That, thought Apex, would annoy people who had already coughed up Y36 000 for a Filofax, and it would devalue the product's snob value in future. Fortunately, the rising yen after 1985 meant that the cost of their imported Filofaxes fell steadily. So they put that extra profit margin to three good uses:

- Apex spent Y1200 on a smart box for each Filofax, to distinguish it from cheaper imitations. In Japan a top-class product needs top-class packaging. Apex's staff also began to open each paper refill as it arrived in Japan, repacking it in a more expensive plastic bag bearing the Filofax name.
- The firm sent out fancy display cases for Filofax products to 50 shops, costing Y1 m a piece. That boosted sales in the smartest outlets, such as Seibu's department stores in Tokyo.
- It added accessories to the product. Rather than just supplying a leather binder, Apex began to send out boxed Filofaxes already complete with five refill packs and 100 different sample note sheets. It has instituted a gold-card club which sends out sales information to its members.

The idea of all this was to turn Filofax from a mere piece of stationery into as much of a 'lifestyle' good as a Louis Vuitton bag or a pair of Christian Dior spectacles. This has been highly successful. Filofax is now at the top of the market, charging half as much again as its chief competitor, Bindex. In volume terms, Bindex is the bestseller. In value terms, though, Filofax is definitely top dog.

Source: Adapted from *Organized but not personally,*
The Economist, 12 November 1988.

11.5 Channel power

Traditionally, channels of distribution have been composed of members who are independently owned and run. As a result, members at each level have tended to focus on their own goals without considering the effect that their actions are likely to have on other channel members. When there is no co-operation or integration between different members conflicts of interest are common as each member tries to improve their own sales and profit margins by negotiating the best possible terms.

For example, if manufacturers decide to discount their products very heavily retailers' profit margins can be eroded to the point where they are forced out of business – not to mention the ever-present danger of creating a vicious price-cutting war. In fact, this is exactly what happened in the early 1980s when Japanese manufacturers of low-cost photocopiers such as Canon, Sharp,

Minolta and Ricoh attempted to wrest market share from Xerox, the industry leader. The round of price-cutting which followed eroded retailers' profit margins by more than 25 per cent, a drop which some of the weaker dealers could not survive.

It is important to remember, however, that the balance of power in a particular channel of distribution can change at any time. As James Myers points out in his book *Marketing*, 'At one time Mattel was the leading toy manufacturer in the United States. Because its toys were in such demand, it had the power to force many of its less desirable toy lines upon retailers, who had to accept these lines in order to get the fast-moving items such as Barbie Dolls.

'One day the worm turned. In a volatile business like toys, every manufacturer will have off-years, when even their best new items turn sour in the marketplace. When this finally happened to Mattel, retailers struck back with a vengeance. They not only refused to take any items they did not want, but they also bought minimal amounts of even the faster-moving ones. And many toy retailers – even some of the largest – refused to buy any more Mattel toys from that time on.

'The effects upon Mattel were dramatic. These bad dealer reactions were a major factor in producing losses of approximately $25 to $30 million for two years in a row. At that time, Mattel was considered to be near to bankruptcy. Since then the company has improved its dealer relations greatly, but it still did not get some of its retailers back for many years.'

The lesson is clear. The most powerful member in a particular channel of distribution needs to maintain good relationships with other members as there are no guarantees that they will always occupy the same position of strength.

Changes in the balance of power can also occur on a much wider scale. The widespread shift in the balance of power between manufacturers and retailers in post-war years is a case in point. Whereas channels of distribution have been traditionally dominated by manufacturers, it is the retailers (especially within the grocery industry) who are now able to wield most power.

Given that a small number of retailing chains (Sainsbury's, Tesco, Safeway, etc.) now account for the vast majority of grocery sales, it is essential that manufacturers maintain good relationships with these retailers. The fact is unless a new grocery product is stocked by the major supermarket chains it is unlikely to succeed as it will not reach a wide enough market.

The buying power of the major supermarket chains enables them virtually to dictate their own terms to manufacturers, particularly with 'own label' products, influencing everything from delivery times and quantities right through to the product specification, packaging and even the price. Hugh Davidson points out in his book *Offensive Marketing*, 'The division between manufacturers and retailers is becoming blurred. Retailers like Marks and Spencer, Habitat and MFI specify, brand and market their own products using manufacturers as sub-contractors.'

In the final analysis, the smooth operation of any distribution channel hinges on the degree of co-operation which exists between channel members. It is essential, therefore, for firms to establish good inter-relationships with channel members. This fosters the team-work spirit essential for an integrated distribution system to operate successfully.

11.6 Vertical integration of channel members

There has been a marked increase in the use of integrated channels or **vertical marketing systems** in recent years, as firms have attempted to control and organize channels of distribution more effectively in order to reduce the likelihood of conflict developing. Vertical integration occurs when members at different levels in a channel of distribution work together in order to ensure the smooth operation of the channel. Vertically integrated channels may be owned by one organization like the manufacturer or the retailer. Alternatively, the integration may stem from one powerful member who is able to exert an influence on the other channel members even though those members are independently owned.

In a **corporate system**, the channel leader (often the manufacturer) owns all the other members of the channel such as wholesalers and retailers. In this system the potential for conflict is reduced as the channel leader controls the operation of the system.

In a **contractual system**, channel members are independently owned but co-operation is achieved by the legal agreements which exist between the channel members and the parent company. The potential for conflict is minimized because of the legal contracts which exist.

In an **administered system**, channel members may be influenced by one large and powerful member. Some of the large retail chains can, by virtue of their sheer buying power, dictate their own terms to suppliers. For instance, Marks and Spencer lays down its own rigorous standards of hygiene for the factories of manufacturers supplying them with food.

The direction of ownership and control in a particular channel of distribution may be forward or backward. If a manufacturer decides to buy a wholesaler or the chain or retail stores through which its goods are sold, this is known as **forward integration**. Alternatively, if retailers acquire control over the manufacturing firms who produce goods for them, this is known as **backward integration**.

11.7 The role of wholesalers

Channels of distribution often include wholesalers who act as intermediaries or middlemen, buying products from manufacturers in the large quantities they find economical to sell and then dividing them into the much smaller quantities that are practical for retailers to buy. This process is known as **breaking bulk**. Wholesalers do not normally sell directly to consumers.

Many people mistakenly believe that the selling price of a product is increased when wholesalers are used because the mark up they take as their profit adds onto the cost of the product. Yet although this may be the case with certain products, wholesalers are in fact very widely used, particularly in consumer markets where manufacturers may otherwise need to deal with many thousands of retailers, because they generally reduce costs. Wholesalers can prove useful to both manufacturers and retailers for a number of reasons.

11.8 The advantages of using wholesalers

(a) Fewer transactions

One of the main advantages of using wholesalers is that they cut down the number of transactions needed between manufacturers and retailers and hence the cost of maintaining these lines of distribution. Thus, if each of the four manufacturers in a particular market had to sell directly to ten retailers, forty transactions would be needed, as illustrated in fig. 11.2. In other words each manufacturer would need to make ten separate delivery trips, ten calls by sales representatives, etc.

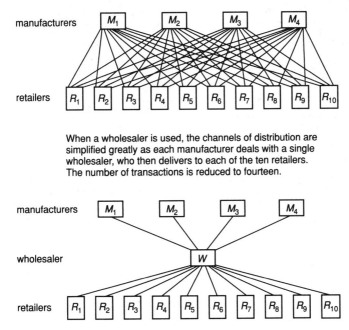

When a wholesaler is used, the channels of distribution are simplified greatly as each manufacturer deals with a single wholesaler, who then delivers to each of the ten retailers. The number of transactions is reduced to fourteen.

Fig. 11.2 The impact of using wholesalers

In this hypothetical example there are only four manufacturers and ten retailers. In reality, the markets for many consumer goods may be made up of hundreds of manufacturers and several thousand retailers. It is easy to see how it would be prohibitively expensive for manufacturers to deal directly with retailers in every part of the country. By the same token, firms who export the majority of their production would find it almost impossible to deal directly with retailers all over the world – an important consideration for manufacturers as global marketing becomes progressively widespread.

(b) Lower transport costs

Wholesalers divide the products they have bought in bulk from manufacturers into smaller quantities for selling on to retailers. Transport costs are lowered for manufacturers as they need only deliver to a few wholesalers in a limited number of geographical locations. Wholesalers then have the responsibility of supplying a large number of retailers in the surrounding area. Manufacturers would not find it economical to make the regular van deliveries of small quantities that retailers require, particularly if this involved delivering to stores which are spread over a wide area.

(c) Less warehouse storage

Wholesalers provide warehouse storage space for goods bought in bulk from manufacturers. Manufacturers and retailers both benefit because they do not have capital tied up in stock-piled goods. The reduction in warehouse facilities releases space which can then be used for other purposes, such as increasing production capacity or increasing the available floor area for displaying sales merchandise.

(d) Lower administration costs

Administration costs are reduced when manufacturers deal with a few wholesalers as opposed to a large number of retail customers. All the paperwork associated with each sales transaction such as order notes, delivery slips, invoices and statements would be multiplied several thousand times over if manufacturers had to supply retail customers directly. This is quite apart from all the extra sales representatives, drivers and clerical staff that would be needed.

(e) Improved cash flow

Wholesalers generally pay manufacturers as soon as the products have been received. The fact that manufacturers get paid more quickly than if they were supplying retailers directly greatly improves their cash flow situation. It also avoids the problems of slow payment and non-payment that would arise if they were dealing with a large number of small customers. In addition, wholesalers usually offer their customers credit facilities – a period of three or four months, in which to pay for the goods. Retailers thus also benefit from an improved cash flow.

(f) After sales service

Wholesalers usually offer an after-sales service for products which have been sold through retailers. It is often more convenient for retailers to send faulty products such as small electrical appliances to local wholesalers for repair, rather than to send them back to manufacturers. This is also a cost-effective arrangement for manufacturers.

(g) Sales and promotional back-up

Wholesalers generally employ sales representatives to call on local customers and tend also to promote products in their own catalogues and sales literature. Manufacturers will often subsidize the cost of these activities, recognizing that they form a valuable local extension to their own national marketing efforts.

(h) Advice on local market

Wholesalers tend to have a better knowledge of local market conditions than manufacturers. They understand local purchasing patterns and the special needs and requirements of their customers. They are also aware of the strengths and weaknesses of major competitors.

Most importantly, they know which product lines are selling well and why. Wholesalers are therefore in a good position to advise manufacturers on the kinds of products they should be concentrating on making. They can also advise retailers on which product lines to buy, what price to charge, etc. It is particularly important for firms targeting overseas markets to export their products through wholesalers in those countries, as they are likely to have a more detailed knowledge of local market conditions.

11.9 The importance of good logistics

Logistics management involves managing the physical movement of products from the supply of raw materials and components through the processes of production, warehousing and distribution until the goods finally reach the customers. This overall process can be divided into two separate aspects: **physical supply** involving the purchase, storage and movement of raw materials and components required during the manufacturing process and **physical distribution** dealing with the storage and distribution of finished products after the manufacturing process has ended.

Physical distribution therefore involves getting the finished product to the customer or end-user. It is this aspect of logistics management which has always been of concern to marketers. It concerns such issues as how often deliveries should be made in order to maintain an agreed level of customer service, what mode of transport is most appropriate for the particular product and whether it is best for firms to operate their own warehouses and fleet of delivery vehicles or to sub-contract all aspects of distribution to a specialist firm.

An increasing number of firms now recognize that it pays to organize both aspects of logistics as a continuous process, based on the principle that a decision taken in one part of the chain will inevitably have a direct impact further along the line. Traditionally, logistics has been managed as a series of separate steps, with the purchasing, production, marketing and distribution departments only taking responsibility for the flow of materials and products in their specific part of the chain. A lack of overall co-ordination means that problems such as bottlenecks and excessive stock-piles, which can increase costs and cause unnecessary delays, are not spotted easily.

In contrast, firms such as Nissan illustrate the benefits of adopting an integrated approach towards logistics. According to Dr Martin Christopher in a recent article in *Director* magazine, 'Car industry experts suggest that each car made by Nissan's new Tyneside plant will be produced for about £600 less than it would cost a British manufacturer to make. This cost advantage is not just due to more effective use of labour, but dramatically superior logistics. Nissan manages the total material flow from component source to the final car as a single entity. Throughput times, transport and distribution are greatly reduced.'

This kind of streamlined **physical distribution management** (PDM) involves the co-ordination of the entire logistics process from the supply of raw materials to the distribution of finished products. It includes the following tasks:

- purchasing;
- materials handling;
- stock control;
- warehousing and storage;
- packaging;
- order processing;
- transportation;
- customer service;
- after-sales support.

Many firms, particularly the large retail chains, now operate **distribution centres**, in order to minimize both storage and transportation costs. Instead of having many small warehouses scattered around the country, firms set up a few very large warehouses, located near the major population centres they are designed to serve. The bulk warehouse facilities are large enough to justify the expense of installing highly-automated, computerized systems for handling stock. Suppliers can ship goods directly to these distribution centres which then redistribute them in smaller quantities to meet orders from individual stores.

As Dr Martin Christopher points out, 'Good logistics is seen by retail group Sainsbury's, for example, as an important element in the company's outstanding recent growth. Like its direct competitors, the company retails a growing range of perishable foodstuffs that are subject to stringent "sell by" provisions. Distribution is governed by strict central controls. A national network of over 22 distribution centres undertakes over 1000 deliveries to individual stores every day, meeting 75 000 separate orders for a range of over 10 000 different products.

'Computerized systems have been installed in 284 Sainsbury's stores, providing immediate information for ordering, stock control and space allocation. Better control over distribution now means that the company can reduce deliveries to many stores from over 60 a day to less than 12.'

Distribution is now regarded as an area of such importance that firms are increasingly sub-contracting their physical distribution to specialist firms such as Exel Logistics, Federal Express, Securicor Express, Lynx, United Parcels Service and the Royal Mail's own Parcelforce division.

Companies such as Exel Logistics (which controls two of the seven Tesco distribution centres in the UK) use sophisticated computer modelling systems which can be updated daily to take account of traffic black spots. The system can devise delivery schedules which plan the best routes for drivers as well as organize stock in the warehouse.

However, it goes without saying that if distribution firms are to operate efficiently, further improvements need to be made to the **transport infrastructure**, i.e. roads, railways, airports and ports. Most importantly, ways need to be found of encouraging private motorists to use roads less, especially in congested urban areas.

In the future, growth looks set to continue with Britain's entry into the Single Market, particularly as distribution firms have since July 1990 been allowed to operate within other member states. This should help to fill some of the lorries which were previously forced to return home empty after cross-border journeys.

11.10 Balancing the twin objectives of cost and customer service

In any physical distribution system there is a direct conflict between the two major objectives of maintaining the highest possible standard of customer service at the lowest possible cost. In general usage the term customer service includes anything connected with treating customers well and providing a good after-sales service. However, in the context of physical distribution the term has a more specific meaning relating to the number of sales orders which can be met by goods taken directly from stock, i.e. *product availability*, or the number of days in which a given percentage of orders can be fulfilled, i.e. *order cycle time*. For instance, a company may set itself a physical distribution objective of delivering 90 per cent of all orders within three days of them being placed, which represents what it regards as a reasonable level of customer service.

To provide a better level of customer service the company may need to transport goods by road, or perhaps even by air, in order to ensure faster delivery. This works out far more expensive than using rail or sea transport. In order to fulfil customer orders more quickly the company may also need to store large amounts of stock in warehouses around the country which obviously leads to a sharp increase in storage costs. At very high levels of customer service (i.e. 95 per cent), the increase in inventory costs may be such that it is not worth improving the service much more (i.e. to 97 per cent), particularly as customers may not be able to notice any significant improvement in the service offered.

In any case, decisions concerning the level of customer service need to be made in the context of general market conditions. Is the company the only supplier of the product? Do competitors make close substitutes? What level of customer service do competitors offer? Is the product vital to consumers?

Given that providing a high level of customer service inevitably entails very high costs, some kind of trade-off between the two objectives is usually necessary. Companies therefore provide a level of service which they know will satisfy the majority of their customers, but which is at the same time cost-effective.

Central to this argument is the notion that better standards of customer service are prohibitively expensive to achieve. However, it is also worth remembering that improving the level of customer service can increase sales dramatically, to the point where they offset the higher distribution costs. Companies can gain a significant competitive edge by using levels of customer service as a means of differentiating their products or services from those of their competitors. It is all the more surprising, therefore, that physical distribution is an area of the marketing mix which has, until recently, remained largely untapped by marketers.

However, the rewards can be high for those firms who do successfully differentiate themselves in this way. Marks and Spencer's recent diversification into the sale of furniture is a prime example. The company's response to the perennial problems of long delivery times and broken appointments has been to offer a guaranteed delivery date of two weeks or less together with a firm delivery appointment within a two-hour period. Marks and Spencer is able to offer this level of customer service because it sells a range of standard products which are distributed from a small number of delivery points. Deliveries are sub-contracted out to Pickfords, the removals firm, under a joint-venture agreement.

11.11 Setting high standards of customer service

Suppliers need to ensure that their physical distribution systems are:

(i) Fast   Once they have made a decision to buy and have placed an order customers want their goods to be delivered as quickly as possible. Similarly, wholesalers and retailers want goods to be delivered quickly in order to replace the items which have been sold.

(ii) Reliable   If deliveries arrive late, there is the possibility that retailers and wholesalers may lose business through items being out of stock. Whilst this is not a cost directly incurred by the firm, it does nevertheless represent an **opportunity cost**, i.e. an opportunity to earn revenue which has been lost. In the case of industrial buyers, late deliveries of raw materials and components can cause production delays with workers and machines standing idle. More seriously, if production falls too far behind schedule manufacturers run the risk of those contracts being cancelled.

Deliveries which arrive earlier than expected can cause almost as many problems. For one thing, there may not be enough storage space in the warehouse. Early delivery also results in far too much capital being tied up in stock or **inventory**.

The fact is firms do not necessarily require the fastest distribution service – what they want is a service they can count on. If wholesalers and retailers know that an order will be delivered without fail in seven days, they can then organize their stock levels accordingly. This is why firms generally prefer to deal with suppliers who provide reliable on-time deliveries.

(iii) Safe There is not much point in providing a fast or reliable delivery if the goods arrive damaged. It is important, therefore, for suppliers to ensure that products are properly packaged and are handled and transported carefully. If goods do prove to be defective on arrival, customers need to feel confident that they will be promptly replaced.

(iv) Accurate Suppliers need to ensure that deliveries are accurate in terms of the amount and types of goods that have been ordered. If deliveries are inaccurate or incomplete retailers and wholesalers may lose sales as a result of items being out of stock, whilst industrial buyers may face production delays and cancelled contracts.

The need to maintain a high standard of customer service has become even more essential, particularly for firms supplying organizational markets, as **just-in-time** (JIT) methods of stock control have become more widely adopted. The JIT system of inventory management is based on the principle that materials and components are delivered only when needed, the main advantage being that the cost of storage is reduced as large amounts of stock do not have to be held. In addition, the freed warehouse space can be used, in the case of retailers, to increase the available floor area for sales and in the case of manufacturers to release more space for production. Though as might be expected, the smooth operation of the system is dependent on reliable on-time deliveries at regular intervals, accurately fulfilled orders, and defect-free goods.

11.12 Choosing the most appropriate form of transport

Since the actual physical distribution of goods from A to B accounts for the largest proportion of distribution costs, suppliers will obviously need to establish the most cost-effective method of getting their products to customers. Figure 11.3, which compares the relative advantages and disadvantages of each major form of transport, shows that marketers need first to reconcile the conflicting considerations of cost and speed, as the fastest forms of transport are invariably also the most expensive.

Firms that export their products abroad will obviously require complicated distribution channels with goods being loaded and unloaded between several modes of transport. However, the widespread use of **containers** in recent years has streamlined this transfer of goods considerably. The use of standard-sized containers enables them to be lifted on and off lorries, freight trains and container ships with mechanical handling equipment, which works out much quicker and cheaper than the manual methods previously used.

In the final analysis, the form of transport which is adopted will depend on

Forms of transport	Advantages	Disadvantages	Types of products carried
Rail	• cheap on a mile-for-mile basis • cheaper than road over long distances • faster than road over long distances	• not a door-to-door service. Restricted to location of railway stations • products need to be loaded on and off lorries or ships at either end of the journey • inflexible service, deliveries are restricted to set time-tables	• bulky, heavy goods of low unit cost, e.g. coal, oil, steel, iron-ore, minerals, heavy machinery, chemicals, etc.
Road	• door-to-door service. Goods can be delivered directly • flexible service. Goods can be transported at any time of the day or night • convenient service. Goods do not need to be loaded on and off other forms of transport	• expensive for large bulk shipments of goods • dearer than rail over long distances • slower than rail over long distances • delays can occur due to traffic jams, diversions, etc.	• products which are not too bulky or heavy, e.g. machinery, equipment, farm produce, petrol, cars, packaged goods, etc.
Air	• the fastest form of transport	• very expensive on a mile-for-mile basis • not a door-to-door service as there are few airports • goods need to be loaded on and off lorries or trains at either end of the journey • inflexible service. Deliveries are restricted to set time-tables • delays can occur due to extreme weather conditions	• small, light, high-value goods, e.g. jewellery, cameras, small components, computer chips, etc. Also perishable goods like tomatoes, strawberries and exotic fruit
Sea	• very cheap on a mile-for-mile basis	• the slowest form of transport • not a door-to-door service as there are few ports • goods need to be loaded on and off lorries or trains at either end of the journey • inflexible service Deliveries are restricted to set time-tables • delays can occur due to extreme weather conditions	• bulky, heavy non-perishable goods of low-unit cost, e.g. coal, iron-ore, oil, wheat, timber, cotton-bales, etc. Also high-value goods such as cars and machinery which are not economical to export by air

Fig. 11.3 Comparison of the major forms of transport

the type of product, i.e. whether it is heavy and bulky and therefore expensive to transport, and also on whether the product is valuable enough to warrant the cost of fast transport methods.

Road tends to be the most popular form of transport as it is the most flexible method, offering a door-to-door service without the restrictions of rail transport. Rail is, however, cheaper for bulky goods. It can also compete with road over long journeys where the door-to-door factor becomes less critical. Air is used for light, expensive and perishable goods. Sea is used for bulky commodities like oil which are transported over long distances.

Glossary

Glossary

Adoption The process whereby a newly-launched product is bought by households, industrial consumers and commercial organizations.

Ansoff matrix Framework for classifying the strategies adopted by a firm in relation to the two key areas of products and markets.

Augmented product Products which offer superior features such as good after-sales service, in comparison to the basic core product.

Balanced product portfolio Portfolio consisting of a range of products all of which are at different stages in their life cycles, thus avoiding the danger of having 'all your eggs in one basket'.

Biogenic needs Needs which are inborn, e.g. the need for food and water.

Blind tests **Marketing research** technique which compares consumer reaction to competing products. The labels are hidden so that consumers are not influenced by their perception of the products.

Boston matrix Matrix which enables firms to classify their products on the basis of two key variables: relative market share and market growth.

Bottom-down forecasting Projected sales figures prepared by the sales force.

Brand A name, symbol, image and identity that imbues a product or service with an individual personality which then serves to differentiate it from rival brands.

Break-even point The lowest point at which a firm can operate without losing money, where the sales revenue received exactly covers the total costs incurred.

Breaking bulk Wholesalers act as 'middlemen', buying products from manufacturers in the large quantities they find economical to sell and then dividing them into the much smaller quantities that are practical for retailers to buy.

Buyers' market   Occurs when supply exceeds demand. Buyers have the power to dictate their own terms.

Cannibalization   Occurs when newly-launched products steal sales away from the leading **brand**.

Cash cows   Products that generate large amounts of cash. They hold a high **relative market share** within a mature market.

Cluster sample   Sample drawn from a small number of accessible areas or clusters, which researchers consider to be representative of the market being investigated.

Cognitive dissonance   Consumers experience doubts about the wisdom of their choice after they have made an important purchase.

Competitive advertising   Encourages consumers to buy a particular product or brand in preference to the others on offer.

Complementary products   Products which are consumed together, e.g. computers and software, A change in the price of one product affects demand for the other product.

Concept testing   Detailed drawings or scale models are produced in order to test consumer reaction to a potential new product.

Consumer panels   A form of continuous research which involves groups of consumers recording their purchase or viewing habits in a diary.

Continuous innovation   Modifications of existing products which are easily accepted by consumers because they do not require any changes in behaviour.

Contribution costing   When times are hard a firm may accept an order which does not cover all its costs providing that the job covers any **variable costs** like wages and raw materials and makes a contribution towards **fixed costs**.

Convenience samples   Samples made up of people selected at the convenience of the researcher, e.g. from a shopping arcade.

Copycat products   Rival firms introduce their own versions soon after the launch of a new product.

Cost-plus pricing   Firms add a percentage **mark-up** onto their variable costs in order to cover overhead costs and provide a profit margin.

Creative execution   The process whereby the advertising agency creates the scripts that are to be used in an advertising campaign.

Creative strategy   The process whereby the advertising agency identifies the key message that is to be communicated by the advertising.

Cross-elasticity of demand Degree to which the amount demanded of one product varies according to changes in the price of another product.

Customers People who make the purchase decisions but are not necessarily the eventual consumers.

Decision making unit (DMU) Groups of people who make purchasing decisions, e.g. the family in the case of consumer markets, and formal committees in the case of organizational markets.

Demographics The influence of factors such as age, sex and socio-economic group on consumer behaviour.

Derived demand Demand which is influenced by the demand for other products.

Desk research The process of collecting existing data from internal and external sources. Desk research provides background information and is therefore a useful starting point in any investigation.

Differentiation Products which are often virtually identical are promoted on the basis of a particular advantage or strength. This distinguishes them from rival products and enables them to be aimed at a specific market segment.

Diffusion The process whereby a newly-launched product comes to be accepted by whole sections of society over a period of time.

Direct competition Firms experience competition from others providing the same or similar products and services.

Direct mail A form of promotion which involves sales literature being sent through the post to the people on a mailing list. Often known as 'junk mail'.

Discontinuous innovations Innovative products which are very different to existing products and are less easily accepted because they require a complete change of behaviour.

Discretionary income Amount of personal income remaining after paying for necessities such as mortgage, food, clothes, fares, etc.

Disequilibrium Prices set far above or below the level that would otherwise exist if free market forces were allowed to operate.

Disposable income Amount of personal income remaining after deductions such as tax, national insurance and occupational pension schemes have been made.

Distribution channels Series of firms and organizations through which goods and services pass on their way from the producer to the end user. The number of levels can vary greatly.

Dogs   Ailing products which have little future and are a drain on a company's resources. They will gradually be phased out or sold off.

Early adopters   Consumers who are willing to try a new product before it has gained widespread acceptance.

Early majority   Consumers who will only try a new product once it has become socially acceptable.

Effective demand   Level of demand which reflects the ability of consumers to pay for the items they want to purchase.

Elastic demand   Demand for goods like furniture and services like air travel is very responsive to changes in price.

End consumers   People who consume the products but do not actually make the purchases, e.g. children.

Equilibrium price   Achieved when the quantity demanded by consumers is equal to the quantity supplied by producers.

Expected product   Products with features which have, over a period of time, come to be expected as standard.

Experience curve   A graph demonstrating that costs tend to decrease as firms gain more experience in producing that product.

Experimental research   **Marketing research** method which aims to discover the influence of one factor on another, e.g. the impact of a change in price.

Exponential smoothing   Statistical technique used in sales forecasting which provides an indication of future trends because it gives more weight to recent changes in the pattern of sales.

Extension strategies   Strategies used to prolong and rejuvenate a product whose sales are declining.

Family life cycle   The stages which people pass through during the course of their lives, e.g. newly-married couples, solitary survivors, etc.

Fast-moving consumer goods (FMCGs)   Goods which are sold in huge quantities and are aimed at a mass-market audience. They include most of the products found on supermarket shelves.

Field research   Process of collecting data first-hand from consumers, often by conducting surveys in the field. Essential for obtaining information that is specific to a company's requirements.

Fixed costs   Costs which do not immediately change with variations in the level of output, e.g. land, buildings and machinery. These costs have to be borne even if the firm is operating at less than full production capacity.

Forecasting techniques Techniques which aim to predict the level of sales that is likely to be achieved in a particular market, under a given set of conditions.

Fragmentation Occurs when crowded markets become subdivided ever more finely. Eventually, it becomes uneconomic for firms to cater for such small segments.

Gatekeepers People who control the flow of information from outside to members of the **DMU** and also to prospective suppliers.

Generic products Basic unbranded products which are often simply packaged and cheaper than their branded counterparts.

Gross national product (GNP) The total market value of all the goods and services produced within the economy, together with the country's overseas earnings for any given year.

Group discussions Small groups of 6–8 people of similar backgrounds and interests brought together to discuss a particular product.

High-involvement decisions Buying decisions involving a detailed and systematic evaluation of available products and suppliers. Typical of expensive, infrequently purchased items, e.g. cars, houses.

Income elasticity The degree to which the quantity demanded of a product varies according to changes in the income of consumers.

Indirect competition Firms experience competition from those in other industries who offer alternative items that may be bought in place of their goods.

Inelastic demand Demand for essential goods like milk and bread and essential services like gas and electricity is not very responsive to changes in price.

Informative advertising Used to tell consumers that the product is available and to publicize its benefits. Commonly adopted with newly-launched products.

Intermediaries The organizations such as agents, **wholesalers** and retailers through which goods and services pass along the channel of distribution from manufacturer to end-user. Often known as 'middlemen'.

Judgement samples Samples selected on the basis of the researcher's knowledge and judgement.

Just-in-time (JIT) Method of stock control which involves raw materials and components being delivered only when required, thus reducing the amount of warehousing space needed and the amount of capital tied up in stock.

Laggards　Individuals and organizations who resist a newly-launched product and may never accept it.

Late majority　Individuals and organizations who will adopt a newly-launched product only after overwhelming evidence from others encourages them to overcome their reservations.

Latent needs　Needs which are unconscious until exploited by an innovative new product.

Lead time　Period of time needed to develop and launch a product onto the market.

Line extension　'New' product which is merely a modification of the parent product. Often used to extend the life cycle of a flagging product.

Low-involvement decisions　Buying decisions involving little conscious thought. Typical of inexpensive, frequently purchased items, e.g. newspapers, soft drinks.

Marginal analysis　Analysis of the effect on a firm's costs and revenue of producing each additional unit.

Mark up　Method of pricing which involves firms adding a given percentage onto their costs in order to provide a profit.

Market positioning　The platform occupied by a product or service in the market relative to those of competitors.

Market research　The investigation of specific markets.

Market segmentation　The process of dividing up the overall market in order to identify groups of buyers who share similar needs and have certain characteristics in common.

Marketing effort　Includes all marketing activities, i.e. assessing customer needs, identifying target groups and conducting **market research**, together with the development of the product and its pricing, promotion and distribution.

Marketing mix　Marketers co-ordinate the four key elements of product, price, promotion and place, i.e. the four Ps, in order to bring about the desired consumer response.

Marketing orientation　Firms concentrate on producing what the market wants.

Marketing plan　Involves assessing the existing situation, setting goals and deciding on the strategies needed to implement those objectives.

Marketing research　Involves the investigation of every aspect of the marketing process covering consumers' attitudes as well as their reactions to the product itself and the way it is priced, promoted and distributed.

Mass market products   Products designed to appeal to the majority of the population.

Material culture   All the tangible things people like to buy, use and do.

Media   Communication channels which can be used to convey advertising messages, e.g. television, radio, newspapers, cinema.

Monopolistic competition   Occurs when there are a large number of sellers producing similar but differentiated products.

Moving averages   A statistical technique used in sales forecasting which provides an indication of underlying trends because it averages out seasonal variations in the pattern of sales.

Need competition   Firms experience competition from other needs that consumers may wish to fulfil.

Niche marketing   Firms concentrate on selling to a small specialized market segment or niche.

Noise   Factors that interrupt or interfere with the accurate reception of advertising messages by consumers.

Non-material culture   Shared rules and guidelines which influence what is generally regarded as acceptable or unacceptable behaviour in society.

Observational research   Trained observers or hidden cameras are used to watch consumer behaviour.

Oligopoly   Occurs when there are a limited number of sellers who dominate the market and control prices.

Opportunity cost   The loss of potential revenue which may be regarded as a cost even though it has not been directly incurred by the firm.

Organizational markets   Includes manufacturing and service industries as well as wholesalers and retailers, government organizations and non-profit-making organizations.

Overheads   Costs associated with the general administration of the firm which cannot be directly attributed to any particular product.

Pareto rule   An observed phenomenon that 20 per cent of a firm's customers account for 80 per cent of its sales.

Parity products   Products which are virtually identical to each other apart from variations in the way they are packaged, priced and promoted.

Penetration pricing   Firms set low prices for newly-launched products in order to capture mass markets quickly.

Perceived risk   Degree of risk associated with an important purchase linked to the fear of making the wrong decision.

Perfect monopoly A single supplier dominates the market and is therefore able to control prices.

Physical distribution management The co-ordination of the entire logistics process from the supply of raw materials to the distribution of finished products.

Predatory pricing Firms set very low prices, even to the point of making a loss for a limited period, in order to undercut their competitors and drive them out of business.

Premium price differential The extra amount charged for the **augmented product** in comparison to the basic core product.

Price-cutting war When a firm cuts its prices and competitors retaliate by lowering their prices even more, creating a relentless downward spiral of prices.

Price discrimination The same product or service is sold to different groups of consumers at different prices.

Primary data Data collected first-hand from consumers by survey, observation and experiment.

Production orientation Firms concentrate on producing what they want to make.

Product life cycle The stages which a product passes through in its life from introduction through growth and maturity to decline.

Projective techniques Form of **marketing research** which involves respondents being asked to project their image or opinion of a product onto another object or situation.

Prospects Potential customers as regarded by the sales force.

Psychogenic needs Needs which are acquired or learned through the process of **socialization**, e.g. the need for status.

Pull strategy Advertising and sales promotions are used to stimulate demand which then pulls the product through the **distribution channel**.

Push strategy Demand is created by the **intermediaries** who then promote the product to customers.

Qualitative research Research involving detailed interviews or discussions with small groups of people. It is designed to clarify the problem that needs to be investigated and is therefore exploratory in nature.

Quantitative research Research based on a statistically valid sample of a target market. It is designed to provide the data that managers need in order to make commercial decisions and is therefore confirmatory in nature.

Question marks Newly-launched products whose future is uncertain because they are a drain on the company's resources.

Questionnaires Common tool for collecting data in market research studies.

Quotas Limits set by governments which restrict the amount of specified imported goods that are allowed into the country.

Quota samples Samples composed of a given number of people with a certain characteristic in terms of age, sex, socio-economic group, etc.

Real income Income related to the average price of goods and services, i.e. spending power is related to the cost of living.

Recall tests Tests which require respondents to describe, from memory, whatever they can remember about an advertisement.

Recycled product life cycle Products are given a new lease of life when an increase in sales lifts a flagging sales curve. This can be done by creating a new advertising campaign, introducing a new **line extension**, opening up new markets, etc.

Reference groups Groups which people look to for guidance on how to behave, e.g. family, friends, school, employer, etc.

Relative market share The market share held by a firm relative to its largest competitor.

Reminder advertising Designed to keep the product in the forefront of consumers' minds.

Re-positioning Occurs when a product occupies a new platform within the market and is therefore targeted at a new segment of buyers.

Retail audits Continuous research which measures the performance of products sold through supermarkets.

Return on investment (ROI) Firms aim to achieve a specified level of income as return on investment.

Roll out The national launch of a product in stages as it proceeds from region to region across the country.

Sales promotions Promotional tactics which are designed to achieve a short-term increase in sales, e.g. money-off coupons, etc.

Secondary data Data previously collected from internal sources such as sales reports or from external sources such as government publications.

Sellers' market Occurs when demand exceeds supply. Suppliers therefore have the power to dictate their own terms.

Simple random sample The process whereby each individual has an equal and known chance of being selected to form part of a sample.

Skimming Firms set high prices initially for newly-launched products.

Social class groups Groups of people who differ from each other in terms of income, level of education and lifestyle.

Socialization   The process whereby cultural traditions are transmitted from generation to generation as children learn the physical, intellectual and social skills which they need to function as members of society.

Stars   Products found in growth markets. They hold a high market share relative to competitors.

Stratified random sample   The process of dividing the total population into strata or groups on the basis of factors such as age or income. The sample selected must mirror the total population in some important respect.

Substitute products   Products which are alternatives for each other, e.g. tea and coffee. A fall in the price of one product leads to a decrease in demand for the other.

SWOT analysis   Framework for taking stock of the existing situation. Firms analyse their internal strengths and weaknesses, as well as the external opportunities and threats presented by the wider environment.

Systematic random sample   The process whereby researchers select every *n*th name from a list, having started with a randomly chosen number.

Target markets   Firms concentrate their **marketing effort** on the **market segments** which have been identified as containing the most potential buyers for their products or services.

Tariffs   Taxes levied by governments on specified imported goods which are designed to make the price of these goods uncompetitive relative to home-produced goods.

Test markets   Firms often use a small town or small ITV region for testing a new product before committing themselves to the expense of a national launch.

Top down forecasting   Sales forecasts prepared by a variety of experts and a firm's own senior management.

Total costs   The sum of **fixed costs** and **variable costs** at a given level of production.

Tracking studies   Studies which monitor the impact of an advertisement at intervals during the campaign.

Umbrella pricing   Firms set high prices creating a price umbrella under which competitors charging lower prices can flourish.

Unique selling proposition (USP)   A product or service occupies a unique position in the marketplace by virtue of its better design, performance, reliability and so on. This advantage enables it to stand out from the competition.

Universe   The total population which is potentially capable of being surveyed during a **marketing research** study.

Value engineering The process of weeding out new products which are impractical or uneconomic to produce by looking into the availability of raw materials and components and probable manufacturing costs.

Variable costs Costs which vary according to the level of output, e.g. labour, raw materials and fuel.

Vertical marketing systems Members at different levels in a channel of distribution work together under the ownership or influence of a powerful manufacturer or retailer.

Wholesalers Act as **intermediaries** buying products from manufacturers in bulk and then selling them on to retailers in smaller quantities.

Index

Page numbers in *italics* refer to definitions given in the Glossary.